Understanding Comparative Politics

2nd Edition

Understanding Comparative Politics: A Framework for Analysis presents a concise and accessible overview of some of the most important theoretical contributions to the field of comparative politics, from the discipline's earliest days up until today. In this second edition, new chapters analyze some of the latest approaches to comparative politics that have become popular over the last decade or so, and also present a more detailed analysis of Kamrava's own theoretical synthesis. After surveying the main contributions of existing approaches to comparative politics, the book provides an alternative, multi-disciplinary framework for comparative analysis, and then applies this framework to the comparative study of states, revolutions and state collapse, and democratization movements.

This is a book of great value to both intermediate and advanced students of comparative politics, as well as to scholars specializing in the field.

Dr. Mehran Kamrava is Director of the Centre for International Regional Studies, Georgetown University School of Foreign Service in Qatar. His specialties include political development, comparative politics, and Middle Eastern Studies.

Understanding Comparative Politics

A framework for analysis
2nd Edition

Mehran Kamrava

Routledge
Taylor & Francis Group

LONDON AND NEW YORK

First published 1996, 2008
by Routledge
2 Park Square, Milton Park, Abingdon, Oxon OX14 4RN

Simultaneously published in the USA and Canada
by Routledge
270 Madison Avenue, New York, NY 10016

Routledge is an imprint of the Taylor & Francis Group, an informa business

© 2008 Mehran Kamrava

Typeset in Times New Roman MT by
Taylor & Francis Books
Printed and bound in Great Britain by
Antony Rowe, Chippenham, Wiltshire

British Library Cataloguing in Publication Data
A catalogue record for this book is available from the British Library

Library of Congress Cataloging in Publication Data
Kamrava, Mehran, 1964-
Understanding comparative politics : a framework for analysis / Mehran
Kamrava. – 2nd ed.
    p. cm.
Includes bibliographical references and index.
[etc.]
    1. Comparative government. I. Title.
    JF51.K27 2008
    320.3–dc22
                        2007021703

ISBN13: 978-0-415-77304-1 (hbk)
ISBN13: 978-0-415-77305-8 (pbk)
ISBN13: 978-0-203-93622-1 (ebk)

For Melisa, Dilara, and Kendra

Contents

Tables

Preface

Sixteen years separate the second edition of *Understanding Comparative Politics* from the book's first edition. In the interim period, significant theoretical and empirical advances have been made to the study of comparative politics. Space and time limitations have not allowed me to examine these newer contributions in as great a detail as I would have liked. Nevertheless, I have presented summaries of some of the main approaches that are currently prevalent in comparative politics throughout the book. My main purpose in this second edition has been to add greater depth to the theoretical framework that was initially presented in the first edition. In doing so, I have replaced three of the chapters from the first edition with new ones here, two of which apply the analytical framework to the two phenomena of revolutions and democratic transitions. Earlier drafts of these three chapters have appeared in some of my previous publications, and their inclusion here is meant to add to the depth of the analytical framework presented.

Over the years, I have benefited from the comments and suggestions of many colleagues and students, and I am especially thankful to my students for having made teaching graduate and undergraduate courses on comparative politics so rewarding.

As always, my wife Melisa has been a source of constant support and sustenance. I am thankful to her for giving me the time and the opportunity to work on this book, always with a radiant smile and much understanding. At a time when our young daughters demanded great attention, she patiently made puzzles with Dilara again and again and made sure Kendra didn't climb over the family dog, all so that I could sit behind the computer undisturbed. I am thankful to her for making it possible for me to write this book, and to our beautiful daughters for adding so much joy to our lives in the process. It is to the three of them that I dedicate this book.

1 Introduction

> Political science in the mid-twentieth century is a discipline in search of its identity. Through the efforts to solve its identity crisis it has begun to show evidence of emerging as an autonomous and independent discipline with a systematic theoretical structure of its own. The factor that has contributed most to this end has been the reception and integration of methods of science into the discipline.[1]

Thus began the discussion of the discipline of "political science" in the 1968 edition of the *International Encyclopedia of the Social Sciences*. Indeed, the discipline within which this book falls has been one in search of an identity, defining and redefining its very core, its analytical agendas, and the concepts and methodology with which it has sought to prove its points. The sub-field with which the book is specifically concerned, that of comparative politics, has undergone even wider oscillations in its search for an adequate paradigm, an overall conceptual and theoretical framework based on a certain methodological approach. But there has also been a growing realization by a number of comparitivists that, because of its very nature, comparative politics does not need achieve *a* paradigm, nor can it really do so: the best the discipline can do is to build testable explanatory theory. It is within this vein that the present book is written. The book presents a modified framework for comparative political analysis; but its approach is not radically new, nor does it pretend to be. What the book does is to draw on existing explanations and approaches in order to give theoretical cohesion and to explicitly spell out an approach that the logic of the recent literature on comparative politics implies.

Comparative politics has undergone significant theoretical and paradigmatic changes in recent decades. Particularly since the 1980s, a new generation of scholars have revamped and rejuvenated the study of the subject. The discipline, or at least specific paradigms within it, have been brought "back in". Yet interest in society, which dominated the field in the 1960s and the 1970s, has not completely subsided, and there is still reference to it in relation to the state, even if only implicitly and as an auxiliary. It is the interrelationship between state and society that the present work seeks to examine. Thus, the reader may soon note a deliberate measure of continuity in the arguments presented here and those put forward in some of the previous publications on the subject. Although analytically different in its arguments and emphases from the current "mainstream" genre of literature on comparative politics, the present study is a logical outgrowth of the scholarly works of the past decade or so. The arguments contained in the following chapters form the implicit underpinning of many recent thematic as well as case-study comparative examinations. The aim here is not necessarily to lay out a new paradigm to comparative politics but rather to give more explicit direction to a newly emerging analytical framework that seeks to examine politics within different national, political, social, and cultural settings.

In the following chapters, the book calls attention to the inseparability of "state" and "society", and more importantly to their mutual interaction, as the very essence of comparative politics. In its theoretical odyssey from the start to the present, comparative politics has been marked by shifting emphases on one or other of these two domains of analysis. But politics is made up of a complex web of political as well as social forces and events. Put differently, politics takes place within the state, and within society, and also *between* state and society. Only the so-called systems approach, by now largely discredited, has sought to examine the entire systemic context within which states and societies operate. The contribution of this approach lies in its detailed attention to the links that bind state and society. Nevertheless, the approach's insistence on the fusion of state and society minimizes, and at times even discards, the quite separate roles that states and societies may play in shaping the political arena. The framework outlined here, on the other hand, highlights the separateness of state and society, both analytically and in reality, but maintains that the two remain in constant interaction. It is this interaction, the book argues, itself a product of characteristics and forces within state and society, that forms the very essence of politics.

Politics is the process and the context within which state-society interactions are formulated and take place. Therefore, it is a naturally changeable and diversified phenomenon. Its character and nature—its determining dynamics, its norms and values, its limitations and boundaries, and its overall direction—all vary according not just to the existing social and political institutions within a polity but also according to unique historical events, prevailing international circumstances, and the types and extent of available economic resources at the disposal of both state and social actors. States and societies relate to one another in a unique and particular way, one that represents the "national politics" of a given country. Yet, despite this uniqueness, there are broad similarities to be found among various types of political systems. While the exact nature and manner of interaction between states and societies may vary among different nations, enough parallels in *patterns* of state-society relations and in the functions of state and social institutions exist to enable the comparativist to classify various nations into different political categories. In other words, it is possible to find certain societies and certain states whose interactive relations are shaped by more or less similar dynamics and follow basically similar patterns. Cross-national and comparative analysis must thus concentrate on three specific levels: the similarities that underlie certain states, the similarities that underlie certain societies, and the similarities that underlie the relationships between the two.

The book is divided into four parts. Part I examines the various paradigms in comparative politics. Despite the rich and in-depth contribution that each of these paradigms has made to the study of the discipline, chapter 2, which presents an overview of some of the main approaches to the study of comparative politics over the last century or so, argues that each framework fails to consider one or other of the central aspects of analysis. Part II concentrates on an alternative framework of analysis, entailing discussions on state and social institutions in chapters 3, 4, and 5. Chapter 3 lays out the main arguments of an alternative framework for comparative analysis, the details of which are further discussed in chapters 4 and 5. This analytical framework is then applied in subsequent chapters to the study of states and two of the most dramatic events that can happen to them. Chapters 6 and 7, both in Part III, examine the underlying characteristics of democratic and non-democratic states respectively. Both chapters draw attention to the different ways in which varieties of democratic and non-democratic states interact with society. Chapters 8 and 9, in Part IV of the book, take the analysis of state-society interactions one step further, examining processes whereby states are, respectively, overthrown through revolutions or are forced to democratize through processes of democratization. The book's main arguments and thesis are summed up in chapter 10.

Part I

Approaches to comparative analysis

2 Theories of comparative politics

A brief overview

Despite having been a subject of intellectual curiosity for centuries, comparative politics did not begin to attract serious scholarly attention until the closing years of the nineteenth century. It was only then that a growing number of scholars began studying and comparing politics on a cross-national basis. Most of these early comparativists were English speaking, and a majority American. Not surprisingly, their early writings did not extend far beyond comparative examinations of American and European politics. Over the years and decades since, the schools of thought and the approaches employed by these and other comparativists, as well as the areas of their focus, have undergone a number of substantive changes. The scope, direction, and focus of comparative politics has been—and continues to be—influenced by a variety of diverse and disparate phenomena, a development not unlike that experienced by most other disciplines. Variables such as the evolving international system, the growth of the modern nation-state and its far-reaching social and political ramifications, diplomatic alliances and hostilities, prevailing prejudices and preferences, and ideological predispositions and biases have all contributed to the ways in which comparativists interpret politics and develop methodological approaches to the subject. In more ways than comparativists like to admit, the study of comparative politics has been captive to perspectives of its principal scholarly interpreters, as well as, at times, the changing beats of history. That shifts in the major theoretical and methodological approaches to comparative politics happen to correspond loosely with changing historical eras is more than simply coincidental. In fact, such changes in the study of comparative politics have in most instances been, even if indirectly, a result of evolving historical, national, or international circumstances. It is with this understanding that the different approaches to comparative politics need to be examined. Some of these key theoretical and methodological changes to the study of comparative politics form the focus of the present chapter.

As we shall see throughout this book, the concept of "state" has always been pivotal to the general study of political science and that of comparative politics in particular. In the present century, concern with the state has passed far beyond debate over its mere definition. An overwhelming number of scholars, both past and present, have come to view the state as the locus of political power and thus as the primary area where analytical focus needs to be concentrated. In fact, up until the "behavioral revolution" of the late 1950s and 1960s, the study of the state virtually dominated the field of comparative politics. The emphasis on the state was somewhat over-shadowed in the 1960s and the early 1970s, and, instead, concepts and approaches such as "systems analysis" gained increasing popularity. But the retreat of the state was short-lived and its utility to comparative analysis was rediscovered by a new generation of scholars in the late 1970s and the 1980s. Since then, *neo*-statist analyses of various kinds have once again become dominant. Essentially, the discipline had come full circle. Within a few decades, it had discovered, abandoned, and rediscovered the centrality of the state to comparative politics.

The State

Until the twentieth century, political science existed largely in the shadows of the disciplines of history and philosophy. But the growing complexity of politics, coupled with a concurrent rise in the domestic and international functions of the state in the mid- to late 1800s, attracted a number of scholars to the systemic and scientific study of politics, which many at the time called "the science of the state".[1] Thus, from the very beginning, the study of politics and that of the state were considered to be intricately connected. Political science, and comparative politics with it, became of particular interest to scholars in Europe (especially in Britain) and in the United States, where separate historical developments had begun pushing politics into the forefront of intellectual curiosity. In Britain, by the end of the nineteenth century, the British state was gradually changing from a liberal into a liberal-democratic one. The coming of age of the American political system, having withstood the ravages of the Civil War of the 1860s and having become increasingly more complex in the process, similarly attracted the attention of a growing number of scholars in the United States and elsewhere.

Formal-legalism

In both Britain and the United States, prevailing political and constitutional circumstances prompted scholars to concentrate on the legal and institutional facets of politics, thus popularizing an approach that has since come to be known as formal-legalism.[2] In the United States, in fact, the establishment of the American Political Science Association in 1903 was a direct result of efforts by interested academics to study "comparative legislation".[3] "Political institutions", declared one of the Association's first presidents, "by which I mean constitutions and forms of government, representative assemblies, national and local, and such like matters, are the principal subjects with which our science deals."[4] These state institutions and other "structural forms" became the primary focus of students of the emerging discipline of political science.[5]

The early pioneers of formal-legalism viewed the state as a natural and universal phenomenon. "Of all ... social institutions, the state has been one of the most universal and the most powerful", wrote Raymond Gettell, a noted political scientist at the time.[6] Similarly, W.W. Willoughby, a contemporary of Gettell, argued that "the state is an almost universal phenomenon", adding:

> Everywhere, and in all times, we find men, as soon as their social life begins submitting to the control of a public authority exercising its powers through an organization termed Government.[7]

Considerable attention was paid to the origin and nature of the state and to the sources of rational justification for its authority.[8] Texts such as James Dealey's *The Development of the State* and Willoughby's *An Examination of the Nature of the State* dominated the field.[9] The state was seen as neither artificial nor deliberate, owing its origins instead to "certain essential human attributes".[10] Its development was viewed as part of civilization's natural evolutionary progress,[11] its spheres of influence multiple, and its functions numerous.[12] The state was seen as an integral part of the human equation, its importance, particularly in the context of global politics immediately before and after World War I, amplified by its growing domestic and international assertiveness and the increasing complexity and differentiation of its structures.[13] Even the "non-political agencies" that regulate social order, such as social customs and human interest, were seen as somehow inextricably bound with such overtly political factors as the rule of law and political authority.[14]

Some of the other prominent characteristics of this "traditional", state-centered approach to the discipline included a strong emphasis on description as opposed to analysis, a prevailing parochialism in terms of the variety of cases studied, a general sense of conservatism, and, frequently, a lack of detailed attention to theory.[15] To a large extent, the fact that most of the early comparativists were European or American resulted in their focus on the political institutions of their respective countries at the expense of the rest of the globe. German scholars, inspired by the writings of Max Weber, focused on (and glorified) the role of the state and its increasingly professional and influential bureaucracy.[16] Both American and British scholars, meanwhile, of whom the Englishman James Bryce was a prime example, were interested in the dynamics and the mechanisms through which democracy operated both in the United States and in Britain.[17] From the 1930s, the scope of the comparativists grew to include such countries as France, Germany, and the Soviet Union, but the essentially parochial and ethnocentric nature of the discipline remained unchanged. For the legal-formalists, most non-Western governments appeared to lack formal and legal governmental structures and therefore contained little that could be studied anyway.[18]

Much of the early scholarly production of the time was also descriptive, presenting accounts of different types of political arrangements and their distinguishing features. States were seen as either "pluralistic" or "monistic", and their organizations were described in terms of their "juristic and political processes".[19] What mattered was whether a particular government was constitutional, non-constitutional, democratic, or undemocratic.[20] Comparative analyses seldom extended beyond comparing the distinguishing features of republican versus monarchical governments. In most comparative publications, nevertheless, comparisons were rare and emphasis was instead placed on examining one state in itself as opposed to comparing it with others. This descriptive nature of early comparative politics in turn robbed it of a strong theoretical basis and an ability to formulate and develop testable generalizations relating to political processes.[21] Concentration on existing political institutions also brought in a measure of conservatism that tended to stress the permanent and the unchanging features of political systems. Existing political institutions were seen as having attained their highest forms, leaving little room for future changes and transformations.[22]

Realism

The formal-legal or "statist" approach remained prevalent until well after World War II. The focus and emphasis of the approach was, however, slightly altered in the 1930s. Whereas in the 1910s and 1920s comparative politics had concerned itself with historical and institutional description, coupled with a good deal of pontificating—"a nation of missionaries", in the words of one scholar[23]—the post-World War I era was marked by a sobering realism and by greater attention to detail. The idealism that characterized earlier writings was rudely shattered by the War, the Great Depression, and the rise of totalitarianism in Europe. The emphasis of comparative politics thus turned towards the examination of more concrete phenomena and towards inductive empiricism.[24] The discipline became both more "scientific" and more "comparative". Systemic, cross-country analyses and comparisons became more prevalent, even if for the most part still elementary in character.[25] Description and data collection were seen as only one facet of the three-dimensional nature of the "comparative method"; discussions of "causality" and "ethical evaluation" were deemed to be equally essential.[26] The "territorial" state, unevolved and not very sophisticated in its conduct and its administration, was said to have collapsed and been replaced by an entirely new type of state.[27] This was a state whose primary concern was with geopolitics and with space—political, international, and economic space.[28] This new state, itself the product of a changing global context, required new forms of analysis. Especially immediately before and for a long time after World War II, the new state was operating within an environment that contained such previous unknowns as the atom bomb, the Cold War, NATO, and national liberation movements, to name a few.[29] These were all new variables and phenomena that comparative politics now needed to take into account. Any approach to comparative politics, it was now assumed, no matter how thorough and theoretically sound, could no longer afford to focus on the state alone and ignore the many other dimensions of politics.

The Political System

It was partly as a result of this very realization and partly as a direct consequence of the social upheavals of the 1960s that an alternative, non-statist approach to comparative politics took hold in the 1960s and 1970s. Moreover, the post-World War II era awakened political scientists to the limitations of their parochial and ethnocentric approaches and the inescapable need to examine the non-Western polities of Latin America, Asia, and Africa. Such widely prevalent phenomena of the 1960s as "modernization", "liberation", "political development", and others could not be adequately explained or conceptualized through the prevailing methods of comparison. The growing importance of the Third World in international politics only accentuated the need for alternative frameworks.[30] The ensuing search for alternatives was most fruitful, leading not only to a proliferation of scholarly works on the subject but indeed to the coming of age of comparative politics as a securely established field of intellectual inquiry.[31] What resulted was a "behavioral revolution" within comparative politics, in turn resulting in the development of an approach far richer in its theoretical underpinnings and its methodological applications.

The new approach had three broad characteristics. Most notably, it focused on dynamic and ongoing *processes* and called for the rediscovery of the impact of policy decisions on such processes. It also drew itself closer to other social sciences, sociology and social psychology in particular, in order to account for the various multi-dimensional phenomena linked to politics. Lastly, it embodied and in turn led to what one scholar has called "a theoretical reorientation of the whole field".[32] Overall, the focus shifted away from the state and on to society. No longer was mere notice of state institutions and their legal obligations sufficient; the "political system" as a whole needed to be considered, its processes, its policies, and its environments—in other words, its "functions" as well as its "structures"—all needed to be taken into account.

Systems approach

Much of the groundwork for this new approach to comparative analysis was laid by Ervin Laszlo and David Easton, both of whom were largely responsible for popularizing the concept of "system" and what subsequently came to be known as the "systems approach". Inspired mostly by the natural and biological sciences, Laszlo argued that the animate universe can be seen as one unending array of systems and subsystems, each of which is itself made up of smaller systems and is, in turn, part of a larger one. "A systems science can look at a cell or an atom as a system", he wrote, "or it can look at the organ, the organism, the family, the community, the nation, the economy, and the ecology as systems, and it can view even the biosphere as such. A system in one perspective is a subsystem in another."[33] Although writing (in 1972) a few years later than Easton, Laszlo wanted to set forth a general theory based on a systems philosophy.[34]

For his part, Easton was more specific in his utilization of the systems approach and applied it to political life. He maintained that (i) a political system distinguishable from the environment in which it exists and is open to influences from it; (ii) its internal structures and processes are determined by the nature of its interaction with its surrounding environment; and (iii) its ability to persist is dependent upon the flow and availability of feedback from the environment back to decision-makers and to other political actors.[35] Thus, what is important is the degree and nature of social interactions between individuals and groups.[36] Political structures and their exact characteristics are only of secondary importance. There are, Easton argued, "certain basic political activities and processes characteristic of all political systems even though the structural forms through which they manifest themselves may and do vary considerably in each place and each age".[37] It is the "processual nature" of political interactions that must form the focus of analysis. Successive scholars, impressed by Easton's arguments, later fused the terms "structure" and "function" into this line of analysis.[38]

Structural functionalism

Perhaps the most comprehensive and paradigmatic formulation of the systems approach was developed by the late Gabriel Almond and his frequent scholarly collaborator, G. Bingham Powell, Jr., who built on the general premises laid down by Laszlo and Easton. They argued that all political systems exist in both a domestic and an international "environment". Environment in this sense is taken to mean the domestic civil society or the international arena, which is itself made up of other political systems. The system receives "inputs" of demands and supports from these environments, converts them, and returns them to the environment through its "outputs".[39] Inputs and outputs are transactions between the system and its environment; the conversion process is internal to the political system.[40] The input functions through which a system interacts with its environment include political socialization and recruitment, interest articulation, interest aggregation, and political communication, while the

Table 2.1 Input-output functions according to Gabriel Almond

Input functions	Output functions
political socialization	rule-making
political recruitment	rule application
interest articulation	rule adjudication
interest aggregation	
political communication	

output functions are made up of rule-making, rule application, and rule adjudication.[41] Inputs may be initiated by elements within the domestic society, by the political elites, or by the international environment. Outputs, meanwhile, can be extractive (in terms of, for example, taxes or personal services), regulative (influencing forms of behavior and participation), distributive (bestowing goods, services, opportunities, and the like), or symbolic (affirmation of values; displays of political symbols, etc.).[42] See Table 2.1.

Inputs, outputs, and the life of a political system in general, cannot be fully understood without an adequate appreciation of the nature and role of the prevailing "political culture". Almond originally defined political culture as a "particular pattern of orientations to political action".[43] He (and Powell) later refined this definition in order to tie it more closely to political development. "The political culture", they claimed, "affects the conduct of individuals in their political roles, the content of their political demands, and their responses to laws … [It] shapes the actions of individuals performing political roles throughout the political system."[44]

Within this framework, there are four characteristics that all political systems have in common and on which they can thus be compared:

1 All political systems, including the simplest ones, have political structures. They may thus be compared to one another according to the degree and form of structural specialization.
2 The same functions are performed in all political systems, though these functions may be performed by different kinds of structures and with different frequencies. Systems may be compared on the basis of their functions, the frequency of such functions, and the kinds of structures performing them.
3 All political structures, no matter how specialized and regardless of whether found in primitive or modern societies, are multifunctional. Political systems may be compared according to the specificity of function of structure.
4 All political systems are "mixed" in a cultural sense. There are no all-modern or all-primitive societies based on their respective degrees of rationality or traditionality. Comparison can be made by focusing on the dominance of one aspect over another.[45]

The question that structural functionalists ask is explicit and direct: in each political system, what structures perform what functions?[46]

Within this vein, the systems approach sought to develop a systemic theory through which the discrepancies between the developed and the developing countries could be explained. Throughout the 1960s and 1970s, dubbed by the United Nations as "the decades of development", political development, or lack thereof, became the prime concern of a growing number of structural functionalists, and a number of influential publications on the subject soon followed.[47] Consistent with its basic tenets, structural functionalism pointed to the comparative lack of structural differentiation and the paucity of functional complexity on the part of some states vis-à-vis others. "Political development", "modernization", order and stability— these and the many other phenomena associated with the "new states"— were all analyzed and examined within the theoretical framework proposed by structural functionalism.

Here, again, the essence of the inquiry pointed towards processes and policies: the developing countries, by virtue of "developing", are engaged in the process of modernization. The process of modernization is at once revolutionary, complex, global, lengthy, homogenizing, phased, irreversible, progressive, and systemic.[48] Modernization means mass mobilization; mass mobilization means increased political participation; and increased participation is the key element to political development.[49] If a political system is "developed"—i.e. if it is characterized by sufficient degrees of institutionalization and an ability to foster and thrive on political participation—then it can survive. Otherwise it crumbles and falls.[50] Political development is the institutionalization of political organizations and procedures.[51] A political system that can "maintain stability and cope responsibly with *social conflict*" is considered to be developed.[52] But, according to this perspective (or paradigm, as its proponents view it), political development is not merely "political"; it entails a series of other, related changes—or "crises"—that can have fundamental ramifications for the social system in general and for individual members of the community in particular. In his seminal work on the subject, Leonard Binder isolated five specific changes or crises: the crisis of identity, the crisis of legitimacy, the crisis of participation, the crisis of distribution, and the crisis of penetration.[53]

A critical appraisal

Despite the considerable intellectual excitement that Eastonian systems theory and Almond's structural functionalism generated in the 1960s and 1970s, a number of deficiencies within the dominant paradigm sent the comparativists of the 1980s in search of yet other alternatives. A number of substantive objections were raised against the structural-functionalist approach. To begin with, there were a number of significant ambiguities and shortcomings within the theoretical underpinnings of structural functionalism itself. With time and more critical examinations, the once popular approach came under increasingly critical scrutiny. Specifically, the structural-functionalist school was criticized on the grounds of its inherent conservative bias, its conceptual obfuscation, flaws in its internal logic—particularly the tautological nature of its central premise—and its limited applicability.[54] The approach's assumption of constant and regularized interaction between a political system and its environment overlooks (or at best minimizes) the possibility of change and ignores the potential for societal or political conflict. In short, the approach assumes the maintenance of the status quo under most if not all circumstances.[55]

The preoccupation of Almond and Powell with confusing jargon and their tendency to present rather simple phenomena in complicated ways also hinder an adequate understanding of their structural-functionalist perspective. But, more importantly, the resort to jargon prompted a number of observers to question the approach on substantive grounds: "old story in new terminology", "reformulation of old topics", "otiose and confusing", to quote from a few critics.[56] One observer went so far as to argue that "what Almond has to say could have been said without using this systems approach and it would have been said more clearly".[57]

Lastly, the structural-functionalist approach suffered from a not too subtle ethnocentrism. The paradigm's concern with a structurally differentiated and secular political system, with regular interaction between the political system and its environment, and with a "processual flow" of input and output make it far more readily applicable to the democratic systems of the West than to authoritarian and dictatorial ones. Cases in which socially originated political inputs were non-existent or minimal, as in most non-democracies, were often left out of structural functionalism or, if they were discussed, their political characteristics were reinterpreted in order to fit the analysis. In examining developing countries, interestingly, Almond and his collaborators chose to focus on political inputs rather than on the operations of the system as a whole.[58] In another similar study on political culture, only the democratic systems of Britain, West Germany, Italy, the United States, and Mexico were examined.[59]

Besides these internal shortcomings, structural functionalism began confronting challenges from another emerging—or, rather, re-emerging—perspective in the late 1970s and the 1980s. In the intervening decades, new global and political realities prompted comparativists to shift their focus of analysis once again. The societal and psychological focus of the behavioral revolution had been spawned by an intellectual curiosity associated with such developments as the mass-mobilizing effects of fascism and the psychologically unsettling upheavals of the 1960s.[60] But did this approach adequately conceptualize and explain politics? For many, structural functionalism shed useful light on the importance of, and the interplay between, previously overlooked dynamics. But it also overlooked one central force: the state. In systems terminology, nobody looked inside the "little black box" on which inputs, outputs, and feedbacks operated.[61]

It was within this context that the analytical utility of the state was once again discovered. The dissatisfaction with theoretical premises of the systems approach was reinforced by its incongruence with a number of international political and economic developments taking place around the world, especially in the 1970s and the early 1980s. Scholars began taking a second look at the state and its significance as a focus of study. In the developing world as well as in the West, it was increasingly thought, the nature of politics could be better conceptualized by refocusing attention on the state. Especially in the developing world, the state was seen as the prime engine and force responsible for development in the political, social, cultural, and economic arenas. Except in cases of revolution and other extraordinary political circumstances, the flow of influence from state to society was seen as far stronger than that from society to state. The growth of the "welfare state" in some Western European countries and the omnipotence of the state in the former communist bloc also called for a reorientation of analytical energies. The expansion of governmental intervention in societal affairs after World War II, even in the advanced democracies, coupled with the growing distinction between what is considered "public" and what is "private", necessitated the re-evaluation of the role of the state.[62] Especially in centralized, command economies, the role of the state could not be considered as being on equal terms with that of other parts of "the system".[63] Moreover, the manner in which international politics had evolved, particularly within the context of the Cold War, called for increasing attention to be paid to the dynamics and the ramifications of inter-state relations.[64] Even after the end of the Cold War in the late 1980s, the Balkanization of numerous countries is bound to ensure the relative supremacy of the role and nature of the state in determining the political character of the emerging new countries. The "neo-statist" era was thus ushered in and there were calls for "bringing the state back in".

Bringing the State Back In

From the early 1980s until the present day, a number of significant works have been published as a direct result of the movement aimed at refocusing attention on the state as the primary tool of comparative analysis. Earlier, an increasing number of authors had emphasized the role of the state either in specific case studies (especially in relation to the countries of Latin America), or in relationship to other domestic or international phenomena.[65] One of the most influential of these publications was a book under the title of *Bringing the State Back In,* published in 1985, which dealt specifically with the importance of the state as the focus of analytical inquiry.[66] The book grew from research done by members of the newly established Research Planning Committee on States and Social Structures of the Social Science Research Council (SSRC). The Committee, founded in 1983, was designed to "foster sustained collaborations among scholars from several disciplines who share growing interests in states as actors and as institutional structures".[67]

Broadly, there are two distinguishable groups of scholars who have in the last two decades or so called for the need to refocus attention on the state. On one side are those who point to the state's authority as the determining factor in political life. What is important for them is the nature and composition of the state, its actors, its functions, and its ability to withstand challenges from within and from the outside. Preference is given to examining the "institutional structures" of the political system, particularly those from which power and influence flow, namely the state.[68] Theda Skocpol and Eric Nordlinger are two of the more notable "neo-statist" scholars.[69] On the other side are scholars with decidedly more pronounced ideological inclinations. These are the "radical" critics of the structural-functionalist approach and its conservative underpinnings. The alternative they propose points to the dependent relationship between the developing world and the capitalist West, one which, they maintain, is most apparent in the relationship between the "centre" and the "peripheral" *states*. Immanuel Wallerstein and Fernando Cardoso (who later became the president of Brazil) are just two examples of many proponents of the dependency theory. These and other dependency theorists have been around since the 1960s, but the general rediscovery of the state in the 1980s recast a more favorable light on their earlier writings.[70]

Dependency theorists are not usually credited with putting emphasis on the role and nature of the state. Instead, they are noted for their virulent ideological debate with modernizationists.[71] This is not without some justification, as some of the notable dependency theorists do indeed minimize—or altogether overlook—the importance of the state and politics in general in favor of economics.[72] Nevertheless, some *dependentistas* have paid careful attention to the state as the crucial institution through which a lopsided and unequal relationship between a "hegemonic core" and a "dependent periphery" is maintained.[73] One of the most notable architects of the approach is Immanuel Wallerstein.[74] Wallerstein views an examination of the state to be key to understanding the various institutions of society such as classes, ethnic and national groups, and households. These institutions are "defined by the state, through the state, in relation to the state, and in turn create the state, shape the state, and transform the state."[75] He also maintains that there exists a single "interstate" or global "capitalist world-economy" system.[76] This system originally developed in sixteenth-century Europe and remains intact to this day. Within this capitalist world-system, "the state is an institution whose existence is defined by its relation to other 'states'".[77] This relationship with other states, a relationship which like all other capitalist relations is motivated by profit incentives, determines the powers of states, their authority, and the extent of their sovereignty. At all historical junctures, according to Wallerstein, there has been a "power hierarchy" of states, but at no time has the hegemony of the powerful states been totally unchallenged.[78]

Wallerstein's arguments notwithstanding, the central concern of the dependency approach remains the economy rather than the state. In fact, it is only recently that some proponents of the dependency theory have begun modifying their strict reliance on the economy alone.[79] The state, its functions and its changing nature, has also attracted the attention of some who are not avowed dependency theorists but whose intellectual curiosity was ignited by the approach and in whose writings its traces can still be found.[80] Avowed neo-statists, on the other hand, have argued their point more forcefully, if not necessarily more convincingly. They have also called for increased attention to the roles and functions of the state in relation to other societal or environmental (to use systems theory jargon) forces. To enhance the credibility of their approach, the neo-statists have frequently attempted to link it closely with the "mainstream" of political inquiry.[81] Nordlinger, for example, maintained that concern with "institutional explanations, problems of rule, control and order, a polity's disjunctures, stresses, and struggles over allocational and procedural issues, and the past as it patterns the institutional present" have been longstanding preoccupations of political scientists.[82]

Unlike structural functionalists, state-centered theorists do not see the political system as an entwined organism, and they draw analytical distinctions between the state and society. Emphasizing the importance of the state, they start with the assumption that most if not all policies are imposed on society from above. Within this context, they see the state not as weak and under the influence of various social groups and classes, but rather as autonomous from pressures emanating from below.[83] In cases when the interests of the state and of society happen to differ, state actors have several capacities and opportunities that enable them to "forestall the emergence of preferences that diverge from the state's".[84] The state can be defined as a collection of individuals who make public policy through bureaucratic and other governmental agencies and in turn derive their authority from them.[85] These "public officials" invariably "translate their own preferences into authoritative actions", regardless of society's preferences, through

1 their capacity to be autonomous from society and an ability to reinforce societal convergence, deference, and indifference;
2 bringing about a shift in societal preferences so as to align them with their own preferences;
3 freeing themselves from societal constraints; and
4 relying on the inherent powers of the state.[86]

Nordlinger later argued that this does not necessarily mean that the state regularly has a greater impact on society than society has on the state. "Without in any way minimizing the importance of societal actors and variables," he wrote, "the state can advantageously be accorded analytical priority."[87]

Skocpol, who was one of the main figures behind SSRC's Research Planning Committee on States and Social Structures, has similarly called for increased attention to the role and significance of the state. States, she argues, are an integral and highly significant part of domestic and international political equations. For Skocpol, an examination of states must consider both the domestic environment over which they govern as well as the international context within which they operate.[88] She claims that states not only maintain and manipulate the domestic social and political order but also must maneuver for survival and advantage in relation to other states.[89] In their domestic and international pursuits, states must grapple with two intertwined variables: the extent of their "autonomy", and their "capacities". A state has autonomy when it can "formulate and pursue goals that are not simply reflective of the demands or interests of social groups, classes, or society".[90] The extent of this autonomy is not constant and may vary over time, depending on such factors as the nature of official strategies and policies and "the structural potentials" for pursuing autonomous action that a state may have at a given time.[91] The ability to reach these autonomous goals is dependent on a state's "capacity". Simply put, state capacity refers to an ability "to implement strategies and policies".[92] Such enforcing abilities may vary according to a state's sovereign integrity, the effectiveness of its administrative and military control, the loyalty and skill of its officials, and the amount and nature of the resources at its disposal.[93]

Skocpol also points to an important additional element. She maintains that states are significant because their structures, activities, and strategies have not only *intended* domestic and international consequences but *unintended* ones as well. "States matter not simply because of the goal-oriented activities of state officials", she argues.

> They matter because their organizational configurations, along with their overall patterns of activity, affect political culture, encourage some kinds of groups formation and collective political action (but not others), and make possible the raising of certain political issues (but not others).[94]

The investigator needs to look "more microscopically at the ways in which the structures and activities of states unintentionally influence the formation of groups and the political capacities, ideas, and demands of various sectors of society".[95]

The arguments of other neo-statists are not very different from those of Nordlinger and Skocpol. Most call for a reversal of the psychological reductionism which they consider to be inherent to systems theory.[96] Instead, they argue, the state needs to be taken seriously as "a powerful, authoritative ensemble of institutions that enjoy an autonomy to advance state interests sometimes against the interests of weighty groups in society and economy".[97] Far from being an integral part of a larger whole, states by themselves perform a number of crucial functions. They have their own objectives and interests, as well as the capacity to put such objectives and interests into effect.[98] They regulate, enforce, and define what is in the interests of the community and the individual, and distinguish between those interests that are legitimate and those that are not.[99] In the advanced capitalist countries of the West and in other countries with "strong" states, states often have considerable powers to regulate, penetrate, and organize society. Their functions range from generating income by imposing taxes to mustering popular support in order to reorient social order. Not all states, however, can be autonomous or sufficiently strong to survive or to function effectively, with their ability to formulate and implement goals and policies varying according to circumstances.[100]

The neo-statists are not, of course, without their critics. Almond and others have especially questioned the neo-statist approach on several significant conceptual and analytical points.[101] Almond challenged the assertion that systems theory and structural functionalism are reductionist of the state and governmental institutions. He claims that his approach merely "recognized the processual character of politics" and examined institutions "in terms of what they actually did".[102] State-centrist theorists, on the other hand, Almond argued, employed concepts that are "loosely defined". Except for Nordlinger, whose definition of state Almond sees as too narrow and specific, neo-statists are accused of not adequately defining many of the concepts which they frequently use. State, society, "strong and weak states", or "strong and weak societies"—all common in the neo-statist parlance—are said to be hardly defined or conceptualized.[103] "So many dimensions are conflated here", Almond said of the neo-statist school, "that they cannot expect this approach to research to be taken seriously."[104] Another observer argued that "the statists hit on a good idea ... but they went too far with it".[105] Since the statist approach deals with such abstract concepts as "state" and "society", the question of where the boundary of one ends and the other begins is never fully answered. Thus, the concept of "state" as a unitary, solitary reality, and as a measurable force is poorly defined.[106] Some have in fact gone so far as to maintain that neo-statism is "neither a theory nor a coherent critique of one. It is simply an argument that the organization of political life makes a difference".[107]

Conclusion

Since the early 1900s, comparative politics has undergone significant changes in its focus, methodology, and arguments. It has changed from being a descriptive science, focusing almost solely on institutions and organizations, into an evolved and complex series of approaches explaining the inner workings of society and later the state. Within the span of a century or so, comparative politics has discovered the centrality of the state, then society, and then the state again. Nevertheless, to maintain that the discipline has come full circle is less than completely accurate, for in the process it has drawn itself closer to and has retained some of the insights offered by psychology, sociology, international relations, and history.

The debate concerning the superiority of one approach over another continues to rage in books and scholarly journals. Despite highly significant analytic and theoretical advances in the field, the dominant approaches presented here in one way or another neglect pertinent areas of analysis. The next two chapters outline the general parameters of an alternative approach that seeks to redress some of these analytical shortcomings while at the same time retaining its applicability to different political systems and phenomena.

Part II

The comparative study of politics

3   A synthesis

As chapter 2 demonstrated, there has been considerable debate among comparativists concerning the adoption of an appropriate approach to the discipline. In many ways this debate has come to resemble the "dialogue of the deaf" of a decade earlier between modernizers and dependency theorists.[1]

Each of these approaches has in its own way shed much light on previously unexplored angles, and each has deepened and enriched the level of analysis by its critique of the one before. But, as previously demonstrated, arguments over which line of inquiry best provides a method of comparison continue to rage in books, in university lecture halls, and in scholarly journals. As some of the quotations presented in chapter 2 indicate, at times the debate has lost sight of the issues at hand and has degenerated into one-upmanship and name-calling. Successive generations of scholars appear to have learned little from those who preceded them. Earlier state-centered analyses drew attention to the importance of political institutions and their forms, but their insights and contributions were largely neglected by the behavioralists. The behavioralists pointed to the significance of social forms, only to be overlooked by neo-statists.

What, then, is the comparativist to do? Which, if any, of the approaches to comparative politics is sounder as a framework for analysis? This and the following chapter seek to answer these questions, not by reiterating the strengths and weaknesses of the various approaches but by proposing an alternative framework for the study of comparative politics. As the following pages will argue, each of the existing approaches contributes something significant to further the study of the subject. Nevertheless, in their separate ways, they all ignore or overlook one or another crucial facet of comparative analysis. Here I do not attempt to devise an analytical framework that puts a definitive end to the debate. Instead, I draw on the insights provided by the various approaches to formulate, as far as possible, a comprehensive analytical framework for comparative examination. The goal here is to present more of a synthesis in order to address the analytical paucity left by other works rather than to outline a new approach from scratch.

An Alternative Approach

The main premises of the approach set out here are as follows: politics is neither strictly "political" nor "social"; it is both. The conduct and practice of politics is influenced by such factors as the nature and strength of existing political institutions, their democratic or dictatorial nature, their accessibility, their agendas, and the like. Also important are certain non-political factors such as the nature and the demands of social actors, their beliefs and their values, the institutions around which they cluster, the opportunity to use those institutions for political purposes, and so on. Comparative politics needs an analytical framework that takes into account both the political institutions as well as the social milieu within which politics takes place.

Nations assume their particular characteristics not just because of the political institutions that govern them but also because of the forces and institutions that exist at the social level. The interaction between the political and the social domains forms the crux of politics. There is a clear and undeniable distinction between "state" and "society"; yet these two phenomena are inextricably linked to one another.

State is the source from which all "official" political power emanates. It rules over society. Society, on the other hand, is comprised of a collectivity of people who are under the same form of political control and who share common modes of beliefs and behavior across long spans of time and space.[2] Both state and society are made up of and can be conceptualized as being two different sets of "institutions". State institutions are structured, perform specific functions, and have defined agendas, and their initiatives frequently result in tangible consequences. Their very existence and functions are specifically designed for the exercise of power over the larger society.

Social institutions, however, are largely amorphous and without clearly defined structural forms. They may and in fact often do have goals, but those goals do not necessarily entail the exercise of power. The functions they perform are often intangible, though their consequences are not necessarily any less significant than those performed by state institutions. Social institutions in one way or another reinforce group identity and solidarity, providing the web of bonds which, taken together, make up society.

What differs from one nation to another, and what must thus be the concern of the comparativist, is the manner and the nature in which the interaction between state institutions and social institutions varies across national boundaries.

The assumption that state and society are separate from each other rather than being entwined parts of a holistic system, as structural functionalists maintain, is a crucial departure from the approach proposed here. It is an inescapable fact that within any community of people, whether a tribe or a nation, there are some who for one reason or another are in control of resources through which they can affect the behavior, beliefs, and lives of others. Even in the most egalitarian settings, there are individuals or groups of individuals who stand out because of certain characteristics which distinguish them from others. In primitive societies such characteristics might have been bravery, physical stature, or a more gifted intellect. In the modern nation-state, these distinguishing characteristics tend to fall into three broad categories.

First, there are those who control or have access to greater or more profitable *economic* resources. These economic resources are often dispersed between the state and society, and the degree of access of either state or society depends on specific circumstances, abilities, and goals. Some states, particularly those inspired by Marxist doctrines, may desire to have a monopoly over all economic resources and activities, while others may seek to minimize their ability to control or to even regulate economic transactions.

There are also those who are in charge of or have access to *political* resources. These are public officials and government functionaries who, through the resources available to them, can regulate the behavior of others, extract resources from them, and enforce their will on social actors. Collectively, these officials and the mechanisms through which they perform their functions form the state.

Lastly, there are people who are in charge of defining and legitimating *social* resources. These social resources are the intangibles for which people in a collectivity or in groups long and which provide for them different means of identity. They include such phenomena as religion, values, and the various tenets of culture. The people who cluster around these social resources, and thus claim a common sense of identity, together form the society.

Politics involves the give and take and the exercise of power that goes on within the state and within society. But its scope and dimension extends further than that. Often overlooked by scholars, the dynamic nexuses between state and society are equally important, and in some instances are in fact more dominant, in determining the ultimate character and intrinsic nature of politics. Politics is, in brief, comprised of complex and changeable patterns of interaction between state and society. The exact nature and course of these interactions depend on the specific circumstances that may prevail in a given context, including the availability and the competition over valued economic, political, and social resources.

These patterns of state-society interaction may change over time, as may the composition of the resources which both state and society prize, the perceived or actual value of those resources, or the individuals who control them. There is, nevertheless, a certain degree of continuity and resilience in the ways that states and societies interact with one another over time. This interaction between state and society constitutes the pivotal point of focus through which comparative analysis can be conducted.

Central to the essence of comparative analysis must be the study of such phenomena as the emergence and subsequent evolution of state-society interactions, the resilience or changeableness of these interactions, their strength and consistency or their fluidity, their conflictual or consensual nature, their institutional bases and their valuative nexuses, and their ideological underpinnings. Within any given polity, these interactions are almost always highly complex and multi-dimensional, and by nature they differ from one national context to another. There are, however, broad similarities and parallels that may be found in state-society interactions across national boundaries and in select groups of countries.

It is through their respective institutions that a state and society interact. These institutions may vary in their structures, their names, and their constituent components from one nation to another. Furthermore, institutions with similar names and designations in different countries may perform very different functions. The institution of the political executive in one country may, for example, facilitate open political participation for those interested in being involved, whereas the same institution in another country may do everything possible to prevent any type of political participation from taking place.

Social institutions such as the family or religion may also play varying roles in different national contexts. What is important is that even in different national settings, state and social institutions constitute and provide the actual forums and the tools through which state-society interaction is made possible—an interaction which is, by its nature, different from one polity to another.[3] Regardless of their names and other designations, therefore, the various relationships that state and social institutions have with one another, and the overall context within which those interactions take place, are crucial to understanding politics.

State

The functions of the state, or more specifically of state institutions, can be classified into four broad yet intertwined categories. They comprise regulation, extraction, enforcement, and the setting of the public agenda.[4] To begin with, states regulate public behavior and thus modify the social setting, both intentionally and unintentionally. Every state has a set of goals and agendas. Regardless of what these agendas may be, whether economic, social, or political, their pursuit requires that the state regulate some types of public behavior, restrict or ban others altogether, and encourage still others. These functions of the state directly affect the ways in which certain social groups go about their daily lives. Still other groups may be indirectly and inadvertently affected and their lives consequently altered, even if the ensuing alterations are only minimal and their effects not readily apparent.

An example would be the launching of a road construction project by the state. The specific intent behind the construction of the road may be to facilitate better lines of transportation and communication to the marketplace for farmers and others living in rural areas. But the construction of the road may have several unintended consequences as well. Other social groups such as merchants and migrant laborers may find the new road beneficial for their own economic purposes. The road may also facilitate travel for other members of the community, or it may make road banditry, previously unknown, a common type of criminal activity. Roadside vendors and guest-houses may prosper economically and thus change their social and cultural outlook. The road can also make it easier for the government's tax collectors or its rural development officials to visit the peripheral areas, thus touching the lives of those who might not otherwise have been affected. This example demonstrates how one specific regulative act—the building of a road designed to influence the lives of farmers—can potentially have numerous other unintended consequences as well.

Another function that states perform is to extract resources from society. This may be in the form of collecting tax revenues or other types of material goods, or calling on the services and expertise of social actors for furthering state goals. Again, resource extraction by the state impacts society both directly and indirectly. Public service by the head of a household, for example, influences not only his or her life but also those of other family members as well. Similarly, the extractive relationship that the state has with the larger society involves more than just extraction (in terms of employment) and exploitation (in terms of natural resources). The relationship involves a complex web of interactions, some directly between the state and social actors and some indirectly. Certain relationships may also evolve among social actors themselves based on their respective dealings with the state. Compulsory education laws, for example, dramatically alter traditional patterns of interaction between educational establishments on the one hand—schools, universities, and adult literacy and vocational training centers—and various strata of society on the other—school-age children and young adults, adults seeking to overcome illiteracy or acquire more skilled training, and their teachers.

Closely related to the extractive functions of state are those of enforcement. States often extract goods and services in order to more effectively enforce their agendas. This in turn points to the interpretive functions of the state. States clarify and give expression to the "public agenda". The manner of enforcement and the types of institutions involved in enforcing state agendas depend on the nature of the agendas involved, the resources available to the state, the targets of those agendas, and the overall nature of the relationship that exists between state and society. State agendas may reflect popular sentiments and thus be easily enforceable. At times, however, states may set and define agendas for the public regardless of the public's interests or demands. Non-democratic governments frequently herald and pursue their agendas under such euphemistic banners as the "people's will" or some loosely defined "greater good". If the prevailing social circumstances prompt popular resistance to the state's agendas, then enforcing these contentious agendas would depend on the state's resolve and on the strength and reliability of the resources at its disposal.

It is important to realize that states function not just in relation to the society over which they rule but also in relation to other states. States are not alone; they operate in an international context comprising other states. In addition to the domestic environment, a considerable amount of state energy is directed towards dealing with other states. These international functions of the state are parallel to the domestic ones, and states pursue international agendas just as they do domestic ones. They extract goods and services from domestic resources and at times even from international ones (e.g. the relationship between a powerful country and its satellites) in order to enforce their own agendas. Insofar as agendas are concerned, states try to pursue policies that enhance their position vis-à-vis other states. In so doing, they influence—or at least try to influence—the conduct of other states as well as that of their own citizens. Almost every state, for example, imposes heavy penalties on those accused of compromising "national security".

The institutions through which states interact with one another and with their own societies are numerous and varied. These state institutions take the form of decision-making bodies, belong to the bureaucracy, or are part of the military and the police force. The institutions within the state that make decisions have historically been divided into three broad categories: the executive, the legislature, and the judiciary.[5] Whether dictatorial or democratic, made up of a presidency or a monarchy, comprising a parliament that is active or one that is politically marginal, or having a meaningful judiciary or only a nominal one, the decision-making institutions of state principally define, set, and enforce the state's agenda. In the international arena, they represent and defend the state among other states, while domestically they claim (rightly or wrongly) to stand for the good of the public.

There are instances where those state institutions that are specifically designed to implement and to enforce, most notably the military, assume decision-making functions also and essentially run the state. This is mostly the case in military-based regimes. To enforce and implement their decisions and the agendas they set, non-military states rely largely on civilian bureaucracies as well as on coercive institutions, namely the civil service, the police, and the armed forces. The military maintains domestic order and defends against incursion by other states. The bureaucracy, meanwhile, implements laws and regulations, regulates public behavior, and extracts goods and services from society and from other available resources.

State institutions provide the pivotal links between those in positions of power and authority and the rest of society. They are the principal mechanisms through which the state communicates with society. These institutions are often shaped and their functions are guided by the ideological orientations and the biases of those who are in control. While their powers and their specific roles vary within each political system, they all perform essentially the same functions across the board. The effectiveness of these institutions and how they go about performing their functions depend upon their resources, their goals, and their general relationship with society.

It is through these institutions that political actors engage in the act of government, through which the game of politics is played out. Providing the structural foundations of the political system, they are central to its political stability or vulnerability.

State institutions, and with them those in positions of power, face the possibility of collapse and overthrow in three broad circumstances: (i) when they are weak and vulnerable due to internal or external pressures; (ii) in instances when states lack widespread legitimacy in society or at least among politically relevant strata; and (iii) when they are unable to withstand challenges from collective or individual groups within society.[6] Social circumstances and conditions are equally as important in bringing about the collapse of states. Dynamics within society can significantly influence not just the viability of states but the general manner of their conduct and their performance as well. The central task of state institutions is to achieve some sort of working arrangement with society, be that arrangement coercive or consensual. This they cannot possibly do without regard to existing characteristics within society, particularly in reference to the social institutions around which much of the life and identity of social actors revolve. It is thus important to focus attention not just on the state and its institutions but also on society and the institutions attached to it.

Society

While state institutions are of crucial importance in influencing politics, it is largely through their interactions with social institutions that the exact nature of political life and the "how" and "why" of politics is determined. Social institutions, as mentioned earlier, do not have the structural manifestations that state institutions do. They are, rather, intangible phenomena that endow a community of people with a collective sense of identity. This collective sense of identity may revolve around a number of diverse factors. A common set of beliefs or a common ideology, shared experiences and sentiments, common rituals, shared ethnic lineage, a common attachment to a geographic area, or similar racial characteristics can all serve as seeds from which social institutions grow and evolve. Within any one society at a given time, there may be several social institutions in existence simultaneously, often overlapping and at times reinforcing each other.

Because they are sources of collective identity, social institutions may, and in fact often do, vary from one nation to another. A socially based phenomenon that may be highly consequential in one society may be only minimally relevant in another society, and completely non-existent in still others. In a racially diverse society for instance, each race may serve as a separate and pivotal social institution in itself. Such may not necessarily be the case in another society—a racially homogeneous one, for example—in which the institution of race may play only a muted role. Some of the social institutions that are most commonly found in different societies, albeit with varying degrees of influence, include family and kinship, tribe, religion, race, and ethnicity. Social institutions are important signposts and blueprints for identity and behavior. Although most are intangible and do not necessarily result in the birth of actual structures, they can be extremely influential in the lives of social classes and groups. A prime example is religion and the tremendous influence it plays in society in general and, in certain instances, for the political actors who seek to manipulate it for political purposes. Nationalism and tribal allegiances are similarly intangible in nature but, in some societies and political settings, can have very pronounced consequences.

Within a given society, the importance of one particular social institution may vary with time. Social institutions are passed on to and are perpetuated by successive generations. In the process, they are invariably modified. Religion can be viewed differently by those living in periods of uncertainty as opposed to tranquility. Racial identity can have different levels of significance for those living in racially tense times as opposed to periods of racial harmony. The same holds true for other social institutions such as the family and kinship, ethnicity, or particular sets of values. Consequently, the political significance of social institutions, and the context within which they interact with state institutions and with political actors, varies over time. A particular social institution that is highly politically significant at one time may be politically marginal at another. State institutions may find a social institution that was once an obstacle to their functions no longer an impediment but even perhaps a source of expediency. Changes and alterations within one institution are also bound to affect the way that the institutions from the other side deal with it. If religion becomes politically oppositional, then state institutions may in response modify themselves in order to contain the ensuing threat. If a tribe stops being supportive of a regime and launches a secessionist movement instead, state institutions alter their functions in order to meet the challenge. When racial tensions flare up, the state strengthens its regulative and enforcing capacities to maintain order.

The flow of different influences between state and society is not only bottom-up, from society to state: it may also occur in the opposite direction. Particular policies pursued by states may weaken, placate, antagonize, or strengthen specific social institutions. State agendas may call for the total abolition of certain social institutions that are political nuisances—religion or ethnicity, for example—and the encouragement of others that support specific goals. Political goals and initiatives that are carried out by state institutions are as instrumental in affecting the social order as are the workings of social institutions in influencing the political environment.

State-society nexus

The relationship between state and society, or more accurately between their respective institutions, is often part of a recognizable and regularized pattern of interaction. At least while there are no changes in the functions and the relevance of the institutions involved, there is a more or less clear pattern in the ways that state and society interact with one another. At any given time, state and social institutions perform specific functions in relation to each other. The state's agendas, its abilities, and the general prevailing political environment define all state initiatives that influence society. Barring sudden and unexpected changes, a state's pattern of conduct in relation to society can be safely predicted based on knowledge of its institutions and their abilities and agendas.

The manner in which societies interact with states, meanwhile, can be discerned through an understanding of the prevailing political culture. Political culture is "all the publicly common ways" of relating to the political establishment.[7] It is that aspect of the popular culture that deals with politics, or, put differently, it is the collective perceptions that people have of politics.[8] Political culture defines the general boundaries within which society at large and social institutions in particular relate to politics. But the connections between political culture and social institutions do not end here. It is through social institutions, and often because of them, that specific traits within the political culture develop. Social institutions are mechanisms for collective identity, and part of that identity is formed in relation to existing political circumstances. Thus, social institutions and political culture are often intricately intertwined. Equally important are the ways in which the expression of political culture is frequently facilitated through social institutions. Such phenomena as religion, race, ethnicity, kinship, and nationalism, all of which involve collectivities of people and their sentiments, provide excellent opportunities through which people can make their political views and perceptions known. As with the relevance and functions of states and social institutions, political culture also changes over time. But so long as the major tenets of political culture remain constant and predictable, so does the overall manner in which society relates to state.

Conclusion

Comparative politics needs to examine the forces at work both within society and within the state, and, more importantly, the resulting inter-relationship between them. Emphasis on the state alone overlooks the importance of social dynamics and their potential consequences on politics. But the opposite approach, viewing politics in terms of the workings of a holistic system—in the structural-functionalist sense—undermines the significance of independent and autonomous actions, such as the formulation and enforcement of agendas, by those in positions of political power. While social *or* political dynamics may be of singular importance in particular cases, it is the interactions between states and societies, and their mutual exertion of countervailing pressures, that form the core and essence of politics. All states and societies have institutions that are attached to them, and all state and social institutions interact and result in politics. These are phenomena that are universal to all political and social settings and that can thus be comparatively applied to seemingly different cases. More importantly, it is in these very interactions and in the workings of social and political institutions that a thorough understanding of a nation's political life—one that does not neglect crucially relevant but non-political forces—can be reached. It is to the elaboration of this theme that chapter 4 turns.

4 State and social institutions

A major theme of this book is its definition of politics as events occurring within the state, and within society, as well as between them. It is, by and large, this interaction between the two plains that has escaped the careful attention of most scholars, with much of the emphasis having been put on either the state or society and rarely on the nexus connecting them. There are two defining characteristics of both the functions of states and societies and of the nature of the interaction between them. First, as chapter 3 pointed out, both states and societies are made up of institutions that serve as their building blocks and constituent components. It is through these institutions that the interaction between state and society is made possible. Thus, the role of state and social institutions is pivotal in determining the very nature of the political process. Building on the arguments of the previous chapter, this chapter examines the role and significance of state and social institutions. Chapter 5, in turn, presents a more comprehensive framework for comparative analysis.

State Institutions

Every state is comprised of a variety of institutions through which its agendas are determined and implemented. From the conduct of international relations to dealing with domestic forces within society, from implementing laws and regulations to controlling or indirectly influencing the economy, states perform a wide range of functions. At the risk of repetition, it may be worth reiterating here some of the main characteristics of states set out earlier. State may be defined as "the source from which all official power emanates", power, that is, which is exerted in relationship to society. Regardless of the ideological views of its individual leaders or the overall premises on which their rule is based (i.e. the regime), all states basically perform the universal function of exerting control and power over society. What varies is the nature of the relationship that states and societies establish with one another. States also operate internationally, exerting power and in turn being influenced by other states and by multinational, non-state agencies such as private companies and various international organizations.

This relationship with society and with other states or non-state agencies is discharged through a variety of specialized institutions, each of which, depending on the structural complexity of the state, performs one or more specific tasks. This chapter examines states and their component institutions in comparative perspective and analyzes the nature and the causes of the diversity which marks their relations with society. Before doing so, however, it is important to examine the very processes through which state institutions are initially established—i.e. political institutionalization—as well as the processes through which they grow in strength and complexity—i.e. political development.

Political institutionalization and development are the logical complements of one another. The former occurs first and, at some point, it may be followed by the latter. A sharp and clear distinction needs to be drawn between political institutionalization and political development. Admittedly, the terms used to denote the phenomena for which they stand are somewhat arbitrary and have at times been used interchangeably, although the phenomena themselves are quite different. Political institutionalization must take place in order for political development to occur. However, political development does not necessarily occur simply because there has been political institutionalization. The importance of this distinction extends to more than a choice of words or concern with jargon. Despite many scholarly inferences to the contrary,[1] the two phenomena are actually different. Whereas political development carries with it a normative connotation, as will be discussed shortly, institutionalization does not.

Institutionalization, consolidation, and development

At its core, political institutionalization is the most fundamental stage of the state-building process, referring to the "effective establishment of governmental authority over society through especially created political structures and organs."[2] It involves nothing more than attempts by the state to give institutional resonance to its exercise of power. In Huntington's words, institutionalization "is the process by which organizations and procedures acquire value and stability".[3] It involves neither democracy nor any other less coercive political system, nor any other type of rule which may somehow be considered as normatively better. This normative quality is a characteristic of politically *developed* rather than *institutionalized* states. Political institutionalization is merely the establishment of a state institutionally. I have elsewhere elaborated on the phenomenon thus:

> *institutionalization* needs to be seen as precisely what it stands for: the penetration, both objectively as well as subjectively, of society by existing political institutions. The degree to which a particular system is institutionalised depends not on the extent to which it corresponds to democratic rules and practices but on its success in penetrating the

various levels of society, hence resulting in popular compliance with the body politic, whether voluntarily or through an actual or perceived threat of coercion. Thus institutionalization involves more than the mere mechanical penetration of society by various governmental organs and institutions. It carries with it an implied emotional and ideological acceptance, whether forced or voluntary, of the credibility of institutions which emanate political power.[4]

Political institutionalization refers to the establishment, arrangement, and codification of the various institutions of the states, often through constitution-making or another constitutional mechanism. Once this initial phase is over and as political consolidation sets in, path dependence steadily takes over and institutions tend to develop an inertia of their own. The state develops a set of "rules of the game", a code of conduct which may be implicit in its behavior or may be explicitly spelled out in a constitution or in other official documents of the same sort. Once this aspect of political institutionalization is complete, the state can then go about establishing actual institutional nexuses with society. Once political institutionalization is complete, political consolidation begins. Political consolidation refers to the operationalization of the institutions of the state both domestically and internationally. It revolves around the degree to which state capacity is developed in relation to domestic non-state or international actors, whereby the state can independently and successfully articulate and carry out its agendas in both the domestic and the international arenas.

This is where political development comes in. *On a purely organizational and structural level,* there is little difference between a politically institutionalized and consolidated state and one that is politically developed. Both have a number of highly specialized institutions whose functions are central to the continued viability of the state. This is the important contribution that scholars of comparative politics in the 1960s and the 1970s made to enhancing our understanding of both political institutionalization and political development.

To the likes of Leonard Binder,[5] James Coleman,[6] and Samuel Huntington,[7] political development revolved around the institutional characteristics and capabilities of the state. The linchpin of the concept for these and most other authors was the capacity of the state to satisfy socially generated demands for increased political participation and mobilization. "Modernization means mass mobilization", Huntington wrote, "mass mobilization means increased political participation; and increased participation is the key element of political development".[8] Political development was thus seen as the process of "admitting all groups and interests, including newly recognized interests and new generations, into full political participation *without* disrupting the efficient working of the political system and without limiting the ability of the system to choose and pursue policy goals".[9] In this sense, political development was perceived as a multifaceted process, a "syndrome".[10] This syndrome involved not just the organizational differentiation of the state or its capacity to integrate, respond, and adapt, but also its ability to ensure the equality of its citizens.[11] What grows in political development is power and capacity, both within the state and among the various strata of society. Political development entails the distribution of power between state and society, and within society, while the stability of the state is kept intact.[12] Although these scholars carefully avoid taking their argument to its logical conclusion, their definition of political development comes extremely close to that of democracy.

All states, despite their uniqueness and individual differences, have certain common characteristics. All are made up of institutions and component structures, all structures need some institutionalization in order to function viably, and, appearances notwithstanding, states remain essentially weak unless they undergo political development, which is defined here as the measure of the strength and capacity of the regime rather than just the state itself. As the discussion on political development just illustrated, however, even attempts at focusing on the state alone necessitate that forces and nuances within society also be taken into account. At any rate, politics by definition involves far more than the mere study of the ordinarily political. The state itself, the manner and nature of the state's interactions with society, the mutual flow of influence between state and society, the means and mechanisms through which state-society interactions take place, and the changeableness of these linkages all form the crux of political analysis. Thus, an adequate understanding of politics cannot be attained without reference to society, or, more accurately, without examining the components and functions which, in totality, make up society.

Society, it was earlier argued, is comprised of a series of "institutions". The following section examines these social institutions and their relationships with the state, which is itself comprised of a variety of institutions. Such an examination necessarily entails an in-depth analysis of political culture as well, for political culture provides the contextual framework within which state-society interactions occur. Societies and political cultures are each unique in their subtle nuances as embedded in their respective historical and national experiences, in their cultural values, and in other similarly unique characteristics.

Social Institutions

Like states, societies may be conceptualized in terms of their composition by various institutions. Unlike state institutions, however, which are more rigidly defined in their structural characteristics and their specific functions, social institutions are more loosely structured and perform their functions more subtly. Despite these differences, social institutions are, nevertheless, the counterparts in society of the institutions that comprise the state.

Conceptualizing societies in terms of clusters of social institutions is nothing new and has been part of a long tradition of sociological analysis.[13] A few noted sociologists—Talcott Parsons and Anthony Giddens, to name just two—have even gone so far as to assert that "institutions are by definition the most enduring features of social life".[14] Yet despite its repeated utilization by a variety of scholars, or perhaps because of it, little consensus has developed over the concept's precise definition. At the most elementary level, the majority have perceived of social institutions as "the basic focus of social organization, common to all societies and dealing with some of the basic universal problems of ordered social life".[15] In this sense, social institutions—be they the institutions of family and kinship, education, ethnicity and race, or other means of social stratification—are seen as means through which "patterns of behavior" are regulated.[16] They constitute the "social matrix" within which members of society acquire their values and, consequently, aspects of these institutions are reflected in their personalities.[17] Institutions, it is widely agreed, refer to recurring or persisting patterns of behavior and interaction. Something that has become regularized is generally considered to have become "institutionalized". Thus, social institutions provide general methodical and valuative blueprints according to which societies behave and function, especially at "the collective level". They are, as some maintain, "a complex system of attitudes, norms, beliefs, and roles outlining what *should* occur to solve a societal problem".[18] Other scholars, while concurring with these general premises, emphasize the more restrictive attributes of institutions, perceiving them as mechanisms through which human behavior is patterned and controlled.[19]

Social institutions exert considerable influence over the values, orientations, and the general behavior of members of society. They provide the contours and the overall guidelines through which and because of which certain social norms emerge and in turn evolve. As Parsons observed some time ago, a society's institutions are comprised of "a complex of patterned elements in role-expectations which may apply to an indefinite number of collectivities".[20] When discussing social institutions, nevertheless, it is important to distinguish between those institutions that have primarily emerged out of and revolve around common values and shared orientations (for example, such institutions as money and property), as opposed to those which involve organizations and other forms of institutional collectivities, regardless of how amorphous and formless they may be.[21] These different types of social institution serve quite different functions. In the sense of collectivities and organizations, social institutions are invariably comprised of groups of members (e.g. family, church, etc.) who together hold certain common values and who, as a collective group or as individual members of a collective group, interact among themselves, with other social groups, and with the state. Normative social institutions, on the other hand, do not in themselves constitute segments or groups within society. Rather, they form those regulative values which govern and influence interactions among social groups and between them and the state. These are "norms that cohere around a relatively distinct and socially important complex of values".[22]

The focus here is on those social institutions that have an organizational or collective element. Without borrowing too heavily from the structural functionalists, of whom Parsons is one of the most notable, social institutions can be seen as amorphous structures that are comprised of groups of people brought together by a series of bonds and commonalities. These institutions govern and legitimize the norms and values of their constituent members.[23] The connection between social *institutions* and *groups* or segments within society is an intricate one. In the sense employed here, social institutions are made up of groups and segments that have certain bonds and ties in common. However, in itself, not every group of individuals is an institution. A group may be defined as "any collection of social beings who enter into distinctive social relationships with one another".[24] Institutions, on the other hand, entail "established forms or conditions of procedures characteristic of group activity".[25] Thus, members of a tribe or an ethnic population, a family, a religious sect, and other similar *groups*, all of whose orientations and behavior are shaped and influenced by virtue of their membership within that collectivity, belong to their respective *institutions*. Social institutions provide the general structural and normative context within which members of that institution, whether individually or in a group, formulate their thoughts and values, interrelate with one another and with others in society, and interact with the state. It is a "clustering" of these social institutions which, taken together, form the structural basis of society, providing among their members a common sense of identity.[26]

Several important questions arise here and need to be answered. Exactly what types and categories of social institution are there? How and why are they formed? What roles and functions do they play? What is their relationship to individual behavior and independent initiative? And, in so far as the focus of this book is concerned, how and why do they interact with institutions within the state? The precise nature of social institutions and the broad categories which they form depend directly upon the specific historical and actual circumstances that may exist within a given society. Institutions revolve around those social phenomena that bestow on a group of people a common sense of identity, and which, through time and experience, form the general contours of that group's orientations and activities. There are, consequently, some institutions that can be universally found in all societies—those of the family and religion being the most notable—while certain other institutions may be found only in some other societies. In certain instances, even if a specific social institution exists in form, it may not be as consequential to the overall life and conduct of society as the same institution may be in another society. Tribal and ethnic institutions, for example, form a pivotal and inseparable part of some African and a few Middle Eastern societies. An adequate understanding of these societies cannot possibly be attained without considering the role that tribal and ethnic institutions play in them. But it would be almost entirely meaningless to speak of the defining social and political roles of tribal institutions in Western liberal democracies, for example. Each society needs to be examined individually to see what institutions it is comprised of, the specific functions they perform, and how important they are to the society's overall life and its conduct.

Nevertheless, it is not impossible to discern broad typologies of institutions (as the following sections attempt to do) that are most commonly found in societies, the historical evolution, normative values, and prevailing predicaments of which have some similarities. To begin with, there are certain "universal" social institutions that can be found in all societies. They include family and kinship, religion, and education.[27] There are other institutions that may be uniquely important to specific societies. Most notably, in countries where democratic political systems have not taken root and thus the divide between social and political institutions is much more clearly demarcated, the social institutions which revolve around tribal, racial, and ethnic identities often play a central role in giving direction to the social and political life of the country.

As was pointed out above, the initial development and evolution of social institutions directly depend upon those phenomena which bestow on a group of people a sense of collective identity and a common set of values and norms. Social institutions, therefore, can evolve around whatever factors the attached values of which a group of individuals, for one reason or another, wishes to maintain and perpetuate. Three basic, interrelated phenomena combine to make up a social institution: a group of people, all of whom are endowed with a sense of common identity, and who share and are bound together by certain norms and values. Thus, at any given point in the life of any society, a social institution may be about to emerge. Some institutions may take longer to form than others. Family institutions, for example, are formed almost constantly in all societies. Other institutions whose scope is wider and membership more disparate, such as ethnic or religious institutions, may be formed more slowly and may take considerably longer to mature. Nevertheless, given the appropriate ingredients and circumstances, there should be no impediments to the emergence of a social institution.

The cores around which social institutions evolve may be primordial in scope (the family or the tribe), or encompass a broader nucleus that espouses a specific set of values and thus fosters a collective sense of identity (religion, political parties, educational establishments, and the like). Most social institutions can become hallowed with time and their durability and persistence increase, along with what may be called "time-space stretch".[28] But mere historical longevity is no guarantee of the viability of a particular social institution. There may be circumstances, both social and otherwise, which impede or strengthen the viability of an institution. A political establishment, for example, may be bent on controlling or even destroying the institution of religion (as in the former Soviet Union), and that can significantly influence the fortunes of that institution as a whole and its individual members in particular. The very existence of education as a social institution—rather than as an auxiliary of the regime—is also directly dependent upon the policies of the state and the measure of independent autonomy which educational establishments enjoy. What is important is to examine the circumstances that allow some institutions to continue and flourish, and do so in a certain manner and at specific periods, as opposed to other institutions the importance and viability of which may be subsiding or even diminishing.

Another important attribute of institutions is the degree and nature of the influence they exert on the behavior and actions of their constituent members. Sociologists have long debated the constraints, or lack thereof, which social institutions impose on the norms and activities of their individual members.[29] By definition, institutions provide broad guidelines for thought and action for their members: most members of the same ethnic group have the same allegiances and loyalties; adherents of a religion generally hold the same values and engage in similar rituals; and members of the same political party almost always espouse the same ideals and goals. Nevertheless, while social institutions often "channel and control" individual behavior, there does also exist a good measure of "deviance" or at least autonomy on the part of individual members.[30] Institutions provide "constraints" and "incentives", but only that. They do not impose upon society immutable and rigid blueprints according to which everyone must behave and think. Human agency and independent initiative—choice—is an inescapable attribute of every society.[31] Offspring may go against family tradition; fellow tribal leaders may pledge alternate allegiances; co-religionists may think and behave differently; those registered with one party may vote for another.

Under particular circumstances and specific conditions, the actual role and importance of certain social institutions may decline. Due to broader social and cultural developments a religious denomination may dwindle in membership and lose much of its appeal (as was the case with the Dutch Reformed Church in South Africa in the mid- to the late 1980s); a trade union may become weak because of ineffective leadership or certain cultural traits, or due to economic conditions (as has been the case in the United States for a number of decades now); and various links between the government and the governed—as in corporatist bodies in Latin American countries or the institution of the *wasta* ("go-between" or social broker) in the Middle East—may lose their resonance in times of political upheaval and instability.

Conclusion

States and societies are both made up of institutions, and it is through such institutions that the crucial nexus between the two is made possible. Typical state institutions include those affiliated with the executive, judicial, and legislative branches of the government, among others, while social institutions, which are less easily discernible, are those that bestow on social actors their distinct senses of identity. Some social institutions are universal to all societies—chief among them the family, educational establishments and their products, and religion—and others are particular to specific societies—race, ethnicity, tribe, and others. Although the existence of a specific institution is important in itself, what also determines the character of a political system is the exact roles and functions that its various state and social institutions play in relation to one another. All societies, for example, entail the institution of the family. But family is a far more important political force in the Middle East than almost anywhere else. The political importance of religion also varies from one social setting to another, as does that of such universal state institutions as the military and the bureaucracy. Thus, the task of the comparativist is to determine both the precise nature of existing state and social institutions and to analyze their broader significance to the overall political nature of the system being examined.

It is within this context that the overriding importance of political culture becomes clear. How and why social institutions interrelate with one another is determined and influenced by the general culture. The relationships between social and political institutions, however, are shaped and largely determined by political culture. Social institutions, and the groups and individual actors of which they are comprised, behave politically within the general parameters set by the prevailing political culture. Nevertheless, just as the self-regulating nature of social institutions is not always a straitjacket constraining the behaviors of subgroups and individuals, neither is political culture an immutable determinant of political views and orientations. Both phenomena allow for what at times may amount to considerable deviations from the norm. It is to the examination of political culture that chapter 5 turns.

5 A framework for analysis

As we have seen so far, comparative studies have undergone significant paradigmatic changes in recent years, ranging from the ideologically laden poles of the dependency and modernization approaches of the 1970s to the somewhat more neutral neo-statist perspective of the 1980s. Concurrent with this shift in analytical focus has been a re-emphasis on the inter-connectedness and the mutual influences and interactions between state and society. A number of other scholars have pointed out the relevance, indeed at times the inseparability, of culture to political analysis.[1] Some of the most prominent of these arguments were presented in previous chapters. Building upon a synthesis of these arguments and those of chapter 3, the present chapter will propose a conceptual framework for the study of comparative politics.

In constructing the arguments that follow, I take the "state-in-society" paradigm in comparative politics as a point of departure.[2] To date, the proponents of this paradigm have gone the furthest in presenting a balanced, carefully nuanced framework for political analysis that takes into account the mutual interactions of state and societal dynamics, including culture (albeit only indirectly). But their focus needs to be sharpened, as there are several crucial areas of analysis that they either have completely ignored or have under-emphasized. In order to acquire a thorough and comprehensive framework for comparative politics, analysis must go beyond states and society and their mutual social and political interactions. There are four additional elements that must also be considered. They include (i) culture in general and political culture in particular; (ii) political economy, especially in relation to the economic causes and effects of the state-society interaction; (iii) international influences, both overt and subtle, diplomatic and political and otherwise; and (iv) the grey area of uncertainty and unpredictability that is the inevitable outcome of historical accidents, individual initiatives, and unintended consequences. The role of culture in politics, this chapter will demonstrate, can be neither ignored nor over-emphasized. Instead, it needs to be analyzed within a holistic approach to politics that balances its influence with those of state initiatives, societal factors, economics, international influences, and accidental occurrences.

Before elaborating on the parameters of this approach, some of the main premises of the state-in-society paradigm need to be highlighted.

The State-in-Society Approach

In the past few years, as we have seen so far, a number of scholars have devised a variety of approaches for comparative analysis in order to address some of the glaring shortcomings of the dependency, modernization, and neo-statist approaches. Enunciated in detail in only a handful of publications,[3] the new approach places the focus of analysis on state-society interactions. The most systemic treatment of the approach is found in *State Power and Social Forces*, one of the editors of which is Joel Migdal.[4] In a book published in 1988, Migdal elaborated on the need to examine states and societies in tandem. "The model suggested here," he argued,

> depicts society as [more] a mélange of social organizations than the dichotomous structure that practically all past models of macrolevel change have used (e.g., center-periphery, modern-traditional, great tradition-little tradition) ... In this mélange, the state has been one organization among many. These organizations—states, ethnic groups, the institutions of particular social classes, villages, and any others enforcing rules of the game—singly or in tandem with one another, have offered individuals the components for survival strategies.[5]

Later on, in refining their arguments concerning the precise nature of the state's interactions with society, Migdal and his collaborators maintained that states are often constrained in their autonomy when it comes to dealing with society. Therefore, the relative "weaknesses" and "strengths" of the two entities must be sized up.[6] Analysis also needs to be "disaggregated", requiring the examiner to go below the surface of both state and society and to look at the more subtle interchanges of state-society interactions. One must further realize that "social forces, like states, are contingent on specific empirical conditions", meaning that "the political action and influence of a social group are not wholly predictable from the relative position of that group within the social structure".[7] "The political behavior of social groups", in other words, "tends to be context-specific."[8] Lastly, states and social forces may be "mutually empowering" and, in fact, seldom assume overtly hostile postures toward one another.[9] "The ability of any social force, including the state", Migdal argues,

> to develop the cohesion and garner the material and symbolic resources to project a meaningful presence at the society-wide level depends on its performance in more circumscribed arenas. In those arenas, it must dominate successfully enough (close to total transformation or, at least, incorporation of existing social forces) so as to be able to generate

resources for application in other arena struggles and, ultimately, the society as a whole. Whether any social force, from social classes to the state, will succeed as the basis for integrated domination is far from a foregone conclusion.[10]

The analytical merits of this latest perspective seem quite impressive and the approach appears, at least initially, to have filled the gaps left by the previous paradigms. Significantly, the approach points to the common denominator that all political systems in one way or another share, namely, the manner in which states and societies inter-relate. Politics may be, and often is, influenced by a variety of factors and forces, but its simple essence is the relationships that exist between those in power and the people they seek to govern. At its core, politics is made up of a series of interactions that occur within the state, and within society, and between the state and society.

Similarly, the new framework appears to be largely value-free, permeated by neither the conservatism of modernization theory nor the radicalism of the dependency approach.[11] It simply points to a number of structural and functional characteristics that it sees as responsible for bestowing on national politics their unique characteristics.[12] It also makes sense of the confusing array of political oddities that have appeared since the demise of the Cold War. States and societies may be "weak" or "strong" compared to each other, and their respective strengths and capabilities determine the nature and manner of their mutual interactions.[13]

Nevertheless, upon closer scrutiny, it becomes clear that the above approach also overlooks some of the basic premises of politics. It is unclear, for example, whether such factors as political and/or economic performance play any role in shaping state-society relations, or in bestowing on people specific perceptions about themselves or the larger polity in which they live. In other words, does culture play any role in determining the nature of state-society relations? Also, what about the economy? The economic agendas of the state, or of social actors, and the various consequences of the economic activities of both state and society (e.g. industrialization, consumerism, rising standards of living, etc.) have significant bearings on both domestic and international politics. Such economic factors cannot be ignored in any analytical formulations about the very nature of politics.

It is also relevant to ask whether there is not an underlying assumption of political and historical determinism in the state-in-society approach that points to a gradual evolution of political systems from one type to another. Can all of politics be explained through the mechanical interactions of state and society, or does the involvement of human agency introduce an inherent element of uncertainty into it? Social and political *actors*, we must remember, are *people* and *individuals* who do not always behave and react as expected. Thus to assume that there are immutable "political laws" that provide an analytical explanation for everything is, at best, optimistic. By its nature, politics contains an element of randomness, one that is often overlooked by political scientists. Some of the proponents of the state-in-society approach have touched on this issue, though only briefly and not from the same angle as that proposed in this chapter. "Political behavior and the power capacities of social groups are contingent, at least in part", one has claimed.[14] But there are instances, although they are rare, when politics is more than just "contingent" and is outright random. Any approach to politics must take the possibility of this randomness into account.

In short, the state-in-society approach needs certain refinements and modifications. There are a number of features to this paradigm that make it an attractive framework for political analysis. But, as the preceding pages demonstrate, some clarifications of its core principles are definitely needed. The next section looks at the various components of politics and proposes a conceptual framework, with culture as one of its primary elements, which outlines the possible interactions of each of these components in shaping and influencing the domestic and international politics of a country.

A Sharper Focus

In understanding and conceptualizing the political characteristics and dynamics of a polity, the focus must be on six distinct and yet highly entwined planes of analysis. They include the state; society; political culture; political economy; extra-national influences and forces; and random occurrences. Purists are unlikely to welcome this call for a multi-disciplinary paradigm. However, it is difficult to arrive at any comprehensive and accurate understanding of comparative politics without examining the combined effects of all of these seemingly disparate fields. States do not operate in a vacuum. They operate in relation to other states as well as with their own and other societies. These interactions are facilitated—and take place within the context of—existing national and political cultures. State and social actors each have their own social standing, political priorities, and cultural peculiarities. One of the elements that shapes and determines these characteristics is the economy. Thus the economic axiom of state-society interactions cannot be ignored. Also important are the extra-national influences bearing on states and societies that emanate from other governments or from multinational agencies such as the International Monetary Fund or the World Bank, or are the result of larger movements that transcend national boundaries and local cultures (e.g. democratization, religious fundamentalism, cultural diffusion, etc.). Finally, there is a built-in element of uncertainty involved, a degree of chance based on such varied factors as historical accidents or the circumstances and opportunities that crop up and happen to be exploited by enterprising individuals. To conceptualize accurately the underpinning dynamics of a political system, therefore, attention must be focused on all six of the areas outlined above and on the ways in which they combine to give a political system its unique and individual characteristics.

The state

The state has not only long been a focus of scholarly attention, it has also been perceived as the ultimate institution responsible for bestowing on a system its essential political characteristics.[15] When, for a brief interlude in the 1960s and 1970s, the importance of the state was thought to have been eclipsed by those of society and of a larger "system", "neo-statists" asked for the state to be promptly brought "back in".[16]

There is, clearly, a danger in over-emphasizing the importance of the state at the expense of other equally pivotal political forces. Nevertheless, the analyst cannot ignore that center within the body politic which embodies a monopoly over official sources of power, to use Weber's simple definition of the state.[17] The position of the neo-statists is straightforward: within any given political system, there is a group of institutions and actors with powers bestowed by the state, and there are those who are largely recipients of this power. These institutions and groups may or may not act in concert with the rest of the polity; may foster a relationship with society that is conflictual or consensual; and may rely on varying degrees of subjective legitimacy versus objective force in order to maintain their position vis-à-vis the rest of the system. In one way or another, the role of the state cannot be overlooked or seen as part of a larger systemic whole in the sense that the "systems approach" claims.[18] Exactly what roles states play within given polities may differ considerably from one case to another. Some states may maximize their own powers in order to carry out far-reaching social and economic changes throughout their societies, as most communist and bureaucratic-authoritarian states tried to do in Eastern Europe and in Latin America respectively.[19] Others may facilitate the formation of a number of groups that seek to further their own corporate interests under a larger democratic rubric, as is common among the corporatist states found in northern Europe.[20] Still other states may relegate themselves to a largely regulative role, as most liberal democracies do, in order to ensure that the routinized flow of societal input into the political process is not interrupted.[21]

The discussion of the state in the above paragraph may be cursory, but it is sufficient to reveal the crucial points that analyses of comparative politics must entail. First and foremost, the analyst must determine exactly what role the state intrinsically—rather than episodically—plays in relation to the rest of the body politic. Is the state simply performing a regulative function (as in democracies), or is it trying to implement societal and/or economic changes (as in bureaucratic-authoritarian cases)? Is it fostering cooperation among contending corporate groups (e.g. in northern Europe), or is it ramming its own agendas through irrespective of the priorities that society may have? Does the state simply exist in a predatory capacity (as in the Democratic Republic of Congo), or does it sustain itself through the inclusion of mobilized masses into its own institutions (as in Iran and Cuba)? Once this overall role is determined, attention must focus on the institutions through which the state seeks to carry out its functions and agendas. Questions that must be asked include: exactly what are each of these institutions made of; how do they operate; what are their capabilities; do they tend to rely more on force than on a sense of legitimacy to operate; are they based on and in turn do they follow a specific doctrinal blueprint—socialism, for example—or have they evolved in response to prevailing past and present circumstances; and so on?

With these questions answered, the level of analysis must then be taken one step further by looking into the ramifications of the workings of each of the state's institutions. States operate at two levels. At one level, states operate amongst other states, as the dependency approach compellingly and convincingly argued. At another level, states operate in relation to society. Naturally, this state-society interaction has several consequences, some of which may be political, some social and/or cultural, and still others economic. The analyst must examine not only the ways in which states operate, but, equally importantly, the larger effects of this operation on such diverse facets of life as politics, economics, culture, and society. Put differently, both the structures and the functions of the state need to be analyzed.

The role and importance of the state is all the greater given its special position in the world system and in relation to its own society. Whether older or newer, authoritarian or democratic, ideological or non-ideological, most of the states in the developing world have been crafted in relatively recent historical time periods: most contemporary states of the Middle East came about between the 1920s (Turkey and Iran) and the 1940s and the 1950s (Iraq, Syria, Lebanon, Jordan, Israel, and Egypt); in South and Southeast Asia from the 1940s to the 1960s (India, Pakistan, Indonesia, Malaysia, and Sri Lanka); and almost all of Africa since the 1960s and the 1970s (Zimbabwe, Djibouti, Eritrea, and South Africa being among the latest).

Compared to most states in Europe and North America, these and many of the other states in the developing world are relatively young, having come about not so much through evolutionary, historical processes but often as a result of deliberate and rather sudden political crafting. Consequently, these states have assumed a special posture toward their societies, often feeling less constrained by the forces of tradition and heritage, being more zealous in their promotion of various domestic and/or international agendas, and much more directly and purposefully involved in their national economies than their know-how or capabilities allow. Put differently, the state in the developing world has occupied a special place in relation to other states and its own society by the very virtue of being of the Third World.[22] These are states for which maintaining political power is often a crusade and a struggle, not a by-product of historical evolution and maturation.[23] These are also states that strive to effect purposeful and calculated change in their societies, often fighting the forces of history and tradition. That some are swept aside by the very forces they engender—as happened most dramatically in China, Ethiopia, and Iran, among others—only demonstrates the ineptitude of the state's stewards and the inherent dangers that they face. And now that democracy is once again in vogue and when politicians are clamoring to be labeled as "democrats", the task of the state in the developing world is all the more difficult: how to survive if one is not democratic? And, if one is in fact a democrat, how to maintain the many delicate, fragile equilibria on which such a system relies? Especially in looking at the developing world, the state must be an even more focal point of analysis than might otherwise be the case.

Society

The above discussion implies that society is always on the receiving end of the state's powers, an implication which is both inadvertent and not universally valid. There are instances, as in communist and bureaucratic-authoritarian cases, in which society's powers have been emasculated to the point of making social actors and institutions merely passive recipients of the state's powers and agendas. In these cases, the political powers of the state are often based either entirely on brute force or on a combination of force and psychological manipulation. Society either is forced into institutional submission, or, as the circumstances and capabilities of the state may dictate, is fooled into it (in which case often an "inclusionary" polity results). A combination of state coercion and societal apathy frequently results in an otherwise institutionally weak and unpopular regime being kept in power. Military dictatorships rarely rely on much more than brute force to stay in power, as any victim of Argentina's "dirty war" can remind us. But there are politicians who seek to enhance their repressive rule through personality cults or other populist mechanisms. The penalties for non-conformity are likely to be extremely stiff in both cases. But while in exclusionary cases the state simply excludes society from the political process through repression, in inclusionary polities it represses but at the same time includes and co-opts large blocs of society within itself. In either case society is something for the state to reckon with. Which one dominates the other, and at what particular historical moment this domination takes place, varies from case to case. In fact, there are as many "strong societies and weak states" as there are strong states and weak societies, and there may even be cases in which neither the state nor society can effectively interact with the other over a reasonable period of time (witness the demise of political regimes in Somalia, Ethiopia, Liberia, the Sudan, Rwanda, and Angola).[24]

The above discussion is not to be taken as implying that society's political significance can only be summed up in the context of its overt, direct relations with the state. What happens within society itself can also have considerable political significance in its own right. Various groups or institutions in society may jockey for position amongst themselves for greater societal power and privilege, as, for example, religionist and secu-larist activists are currently doing in many countries of the Middle East.[25] There are also complex webs of social interaction that give society its over-all character and a sense of individuality. In some political systems, there may be a large gap between the cultural dispositions of society and the institutional configurations of the state. Again, examples from the Middle East come to mind.[26] In these cases, society may have non-political prio-rities and agendas of its own that greatly determine the state's behavior toward it in both the long and the short term. These characteristics, not all of which may at first seem politically relevant, in turn combine to influence the ways in which state and society relate to and interact with one another.

Of course, there is a point in social analysis at which the political scientist must draw the line; not everything that happens in society—a certain type of dance that becomes popular, for example—has any intrinsic political relevance. It is precisely this deciphering of the political relevance of various social phenomena that is the political scientist's main challenge. Never-theless, while not everything that happens in society is politically important or relevant, a lot of it is. The task is to decide which social phenomena, institutions, and forces are politically relevant and which are not.

In comparative political analysis, society must be examined not in only relation to the state but also as an entity in itself, one whose constituent institutions are politically relevant both on their own and when they come into contact with state institutions. Society needs to be viewed neither as a passive recipient of state power, although in some cases it may be, nor as its holistic extension, which some of the proponents of the systems approach claim it to be.[27] Analyzing society is not, therefore, radically different from analyzing the state. The central features to consider are simple enough: what are the institutions that make up society and what is the political relevance of each of them? What is the exact nature of the interactions, both at an institutional and a functional level, that take place between society and the state? Societies are by nature changeable. Which changes, and how many of them, are state initiated, or endogenously initiated, and what are their overall and more specific political consequences? In what instances and under what circumstances are societies politically passive in respect to the state, when are they cooperative, or when do they rebel? When and how does a society mold its state, or a state mold its society? Do the two remain oblivious of each other, or do they develop a routinized, consensual, and equal pattern of interaction?

These questions are not meant to be definitive points around which ana-lysis must revolve. Rather, they are intended to present general guidelines to consider in looking at social institutions, their possible political relevance, or their other relevant characteristics. Of particular importance are the nature and operations of various social institutions; the routinized patterns in which these social institutions interact within themselves and with the institutions of the state; the underlying reasons for and the ramifications of

processes of social change; the causes and effects of society-wide dislocations; the nature, extent, and consequences of social cleavages along ethnic,
religious, class, and gender lines;[28] and the less pronounced, more subtle
changes that take place in society's relations with the state over time.

Again, societies in the developing world by their very nature require special attention. These societies change rapidly. Moreover, sometimes they
may be subdued by an authoritarian state, while at other times they may
become highly volatile and rebellious. At times they are so fragmented as to
paralyze any power that attempts to govern over them (Lebanon in the
1970s, Yugoslavia in the late 1980s, and Burundi and Rwanda in the 1990s),
and on other occasions they may act as cohesive units. At times they may be
taken in by the rhetoric and propaganda of the regime in power (Peron's
Argentina), and at other times they may develop into a civil society and
become a vehicle for democratization (in East and Central Europe in the
1980s). Because of the changeability of their relations with the state over
relatively short periods, the potential political significance of developing
societies is all the more pronounced as compared to those in Western
Europe and North Africa.

As in the earlier discussion, the features mentioned here are meant to be
general pointers of where to look rather than a definitive list of analytical
dos and don'ts. Nevertheless, no matter how brief this list may be in relation
to a particular setting, two inescapable factors immediately become clear.
First, society is by its nature an important ingredient of politics and must
be included—or at least considered—in macro-level comparative political
analyses. Second, there is more to society than a mechanical collection of
institutions, individual actors, and groups who interact amongst themselves
and between themselves and the state. There is an additional normative
context, the political culture, which also influences the ways in which state
and society relate to one another. In short, political analysis must go
beyond the simple, objective circumstances of society and must take into
account its subjective, cultural dispositions and priorities as well.

Political culture

One of the important areas that the state-in-society approach has not
explicitly taken into account is political culture, although there have been
implicit assumptions about its relevance in some of the studies utilizing the
perspective.[29] As mentioned earlier, this lack of attention is part of a fairly
long tradition in political science in which culture in general and political
culture in particular has not been taken seriously.[30] For political scientists,
culture has often been a slippery phenomenon, more a by-product of larger
political developments than a determining force by itself. Depending on
their field of expertise, area specialists are also likely to ascribe different
degrees of political significance to culture. For example, culture has long
been an inseparable feature of Middle Eastern politics, especially since the

1960s, whereas it played little or no role in the bureaucratic-authoritarian regimes of Latin America or in their collapse.[31] Clearly, an expert on the Middle East will have a much harder time ignoring the region's cultural influences on politics than a Latin American expert would.[32]

In my advocacy of the importance of culture to political analysis, I propose a middle line. In so far as politics is concerned, I maintain, culture is not always a stand-alone phenomenon: it can neither make nor break politics by itself. In fact, politics being the art of the possible, culture is often molded and shaped by the powers of the state. Nevertheless, culture does form an overall framework within which communities and societies formulate their symbols, thoughts, and actions, interact with one another, and form opinions toward those in power. Therefore, all macro-level political analyses that concern state-society relations must necessarily consider the overall valuative context within which societies operate—namely, their cultures. In particular, attention must be paid to a polity's political culture, which is comprised of cultural norms and values that specifically govern state-society interactions.

In non-democracies, there are often sharp differences between the public manifestations of political culture ("regime orientations") and the real, private feelings that people have about politics ("political orientations").[33] Making such a distinction is not always easily possible in non-democracies, as the absence of open political forums and such mechanisms as elections make it all but impossible to quantify or empirically analyze popular political perceptions. It is no accident that the celebrated book *The Civic Culture* was based on largely empirical observations in a number of democracies.[34] Nonetheless, the analyst must see whether there is indeed a distinction between regime and political orientations, and, if so, where the centers of gravity of each of the poles lie. This entails an investigation of the various other phenomena that give rise to political culture, some of which may be unique to a particular country (a traumatic, historical experience such as a totalitarian interlude or a revolution, for instance), and some of which are found more universally (childhood socialization, education, political experience, etc.). Once the overall features of the political culture have been identified, the task must be to find out which of these features complement and which contradict the normative premises on which a political system is based. From here, one can examine the possible causal relationships that may exist between facets of the political culture on the one hand and the overall nexus between state and society on the other. Is the regime in power in harmony with the prevailing political culture of the masses? If not, is it being undermined as a result? Is the regime attempting to carve out a political culture of its own, or is it slave to the cultural dispositions of the people who will settle for nothing less than the full gratification of their political ideals and beliefs?

But culture does not always have to be overtly political for it to be politically relevant. There are many subtle and pronounced aspects of culture that can have great political significance without being in any way political. The neo-Confucian element in Southeast Asian cultures, for example, has long resulted in a remarkable degree of political stability and cohesion in Singapore, Hong Kong, South Korea, and Taiwan.[35] In the Middle East, cults of personality have similarly benefited from Islam's tendency to glorify the individual.[36] Moreover, a pervasive spirit of social and cultural inequality, running rampant despite Islam's pretensions to egalitarianism, is largely responsible for the maintenance of highly corrupt monarchical institutions throughout the Arabian peninsula.[37] Reverence for elders in Africa goes a long way in accounting for the political longevity of figures such as Leopold Senghore, Jomo Kenyatta, and Julius Nyerere, although that is not to minimize their acumen at manipulating other political and cultural forces.[38] And, in Latin America, who could deny the political importance of the *caudillo* mentality, especially given the military's intense political tenure in the 1960s and 1970s?[39] Cultures in all forms and everywhere provide the norms and values, customs and habits, symbols and means of expression, according to which people think, behave, and live their lives. Some of these norms and values are consciously picked up and manipulated by politicians who seek to enhance their popular appeal and legitimacy, while others provide more subtle emotional and psychological links between political actors and the ordinary masses. Therefore, it is not always easy to determine where popular culture ends and political culture begins, but both can have significant overt or more subtle political ramifications.

Political economy

Political economy is another area that the state-in-society approach overlooks but needs to consider more closely. More specifically, analysis needs to focus on the economic ramifications of state-society interactions, as well as the larger economic context within which these interactions take place. This is not, of course, a theme that the comparative literature has overlooked entirely.[40] In fact, Rueschemeyer and Evans, two of the original proponents of "bringing the state back in", argued persuasively in the early 1980s that in order to "undertake effective interventions" in the economic realm, "the state must constitute a bureaucratic apparatus with sufficient corporate coherence" while "retaining a certain degree of autonomy from the dominant interests in a capitalist society" to be able to pursue a consistent policy.[41] In a later collaborative work, Rueschemeyer, Stephens, and Stephens argued that state power is only one of "three clusters of power"— along with class power and transnational structures of power—that may result in the emergence or demise of democracy in the process of capitalist development.[42] Ultimately, the questions that comparative analysis must answer in this regard are how much economic power and/or autonomy the state and society have in relation to one another, and how their economic power capabilities affect their respective agendas and their interactions.

State and social actors compete, at times violently, for access to and control over various economic resources. These contests may occur at a variety of levels, from the top, national level—where the state tries to regulate the overall economic picture—to highly local levels, where state agencies or officials interact economically with individuals and other social actors. The nature and outcome of such contests largely determine the degree to which state and society can act autonomously from each other and, in turn, influence one another. The number of possible scenarios is rather limited: an affluent society (in comparison to the state) and a largely regulative state; a state that has successfully taken over the economic resources of society and now controls most market forces; and a state that tries but has not fully succeeded in taking over the economic resources of social actors and the market competition between them. These scenarios are often better known by their corresponding labels: advanced capitalist economies; socialist economies; and mixed economies, respectively.

In the first scenario, social actors have acquired considerable control over economic resources. This degree of societal affluence, itself the result of a historical progression of market forces, is made possible and is maintained through economic competition among the social actors, and the best the state can do is to play a largely regulative role in the economic agendas of the various social actors. In his insightful treatment of the subject, Barrington Moore has shown how in eighteenth- and nineteenth-century Europe the bourgeoisie, through its increasing economic might and autonomy, was able to press demands upon states that at the time were only just becoming aware of the importance of market forces.[43]

What evolved, most purely in the young United States, was raw and savage capitalism, fuelled by its two quintessential elements: the incentive and the opportunity to compete. But as the hard lessons of the 1930s were to demonstrate, capitalism can run into serious problems if left completely to itself, and successive capitalist-run societies saw the intervention of the state into various economic fields. Some states in Europe went overboard, to the point of becoming fascist and corporatist (Germany, Italy, and Spain), only to be dramatically altered later.[44] Others (Britain, the US, Switzerland, and Scandinavian countries) gave themselves extensive regulative powers within the economy and sought to fill the economic voids to which capitalism would not, on its own, pay attention (social security or unemployment benefits, for example).[45] In essence, capitalism in these countries has surpassed and overcome its brutish phase and, in comparison with its development elsewhere, has currently reached a certain level of maturity. The economic interactions between the state and society take place within the context of advanced capitalism, though they still revolve around the basic question of economic autonomy: social actors want as much autonomy as possible in order to allow market forces to yield the highest results, while the state seeks to ensure that the proper areas of the economy remain regulated.

This is not a scenario that is applicable to the advanced capitalist nations of Europe and North America alone. The same process has occurred in East Asia and Latin America, although under decidedly different historical circumstances. Here the state initially assumed an over-arching, bureaucratic-authoritarian format, excluding the masses from both the political and economic processes but instead promoting "patterns of capital accumulation strongly biased in favor of large, oligopolistic units of private capital and some state institutions".[46] At times out of necessity and at other times because it simply wanted to, the state embarked on ambitious processes of economic and infrastructural development, a task at which it was initially fairly successful.[47] But these experiments in state-sponsored capitalism often had peculiar results. The authoritarian state was always careful not to give too much autonomy to social actors, seeking to ensure that economic liberalism did not necessarily translate into political liberalism. At the same time, it reveled in laying down the economic and infrastructural foundations for further capitalist development.

In itself, there is nothing particularly damning in the pursuit of authoritarian capitalism. What often dooms authoritarian capitalism is the way in which it goes about its business. In East Asia (Singapore, Taiwan, and Hong Kong) and in Chile, where Pinochet's army rule was a one-man show and the Chicago Boys ran the economy, the armed forces as a corporate unit largely stayed out of economic affairs, allowing considerable policy-making discretion to civilian economists.[48] But elsewhere in Latin America—especially in Argentina, Brazil, and Uruguay—colonels and generals suddenly became economic policy-makers, and in the span of a decade or so ran their countries' economies into the ground.[49] But by the time authoritarianism collapsed in Latin America in the 1980s, it had already left behind a capitalist legacy and an infrastructure (though very poorly managed under the military) that was second only to that of the newly industrialized economies of East Asia. At present, therefore, the economic interactions of state and society in East Asia and Latin America (especially in South America) revolve around largely the same set of premises as those in other advanced capitalist economies: the degree of economic autonomy of the social actors versus the regulative reaches of the state.

The same fate has befallen the formerly socialist economies of Eastern and Central Europe, although in their case it is much more difficult to disentangle the many intrusive control mechanisms that the state once imposed on social actors. In the socialist scenario, the state, advertising itself as the dictatorship of the proletariat, sought to "guide" society through historical stages—i.e. take over and control it—by directly owning, in theory at least, all sources of economic production. It thus devised a comprehensive ideological blueprint and a highly penetrative bureaucratic apparatus, not to mention a uniquely efficient police force, in its self-proclaimed march toward eventual "liberation", economic and otherwise. The whole point of the venture, or at least its inadvertent outcome if not its purposeful goal, was to minimize any potential areas of autonomy that society might develop vis-à-vis the state, especially in the economic sphere, to which particular ideological significance was attached. In such a scenario, therefore, the economics of state-society interactions, as in other areas, were singularly one-sided, controlled, dominated, and overwhelmed by the state.

Any doubts about the extent of the state's economic shadow over society were allayed *after* the dismantling of the socialist state, when despite the unceremonious collapse of the state, the economic legacies it had fostered for over seven decades still linger.[50] The lingering economic legacy of the socialist experiment is as pervasive in East and Central Europe today as were the foundations of capitalism in South America after the demise of authoritarianism there a few years earlier. Reconstituting the economic aspects of the state-society relationship—by transforming the state's economic role into a largely regulative one, giving autonomy to market forces, etc.—is no mean feat, especially given the over-arching nature of socialist rule. Nevertheless, it is difficult not to take note of the new trajectory of political economy in formerly socialist countries.

The final scenario involves mixed economies, those odd and often confused cases where, theoretically at least, control over economic resources is divided between the public and private sectors. In these mixed economies, found in most developing countries—especially in the Middle East and Africa—the state seeks to foster market economies while still retaining control over most major sources of production.[51] In Latin America in the 1970s and 1980s, when most of the region's countries also had mixed economies, the state often sponsored joint industrial ventures with foreign and domestic investors (called parastatals) in an attempt to ease some of its own burden for economic growth and development.[52] Nevertheless, by their very nature states with mixed economies are highly constrained in their economic and political maneuverability. On the one hand, the state must cater to and placate the consumerist yearnings of the middle classes who, if left economically unhappy, are quick to blame the state for their deteriorating circumstances. On the other hand, the state is often beholden to special-interest elite groups whose investments help support the domestic economy. There is also the stigma attached to too close an identification with foreign investors, few of whom, even in the neo-liberal environment of the 1980s and 1990s, would find favor with intellectuals and most other members of the educated classes in the developing world.

Added to these are further structural limitations that states with mixed economies face. Unlike socialist states, mixed economy states do not have a coherent and comprehensive ideological blueprint for the economy. Instead, their overall economic programs often derive from a mixture of some planning, catering to this or that elite group, and, at times, joint ventures with various multinational corporations. The state also lacks the necessary resources to carry out its economic agendas fully and thoroughly, with the eventual results often falling far short of the intended goals. This hybrid form of economics, which may be best described as one of state socialism and societal capitalism, is rampant in the Middle East and, though to a somewhat lesser extent, in Africa.

All mixed economies invariably give rise to an expansive and highly active informal sector, and any visitor to the developing world will be immediately struck by the vibrancy of a thriving street economy. But, in the Middle East especially, there is a sizeable portion of the formal economy that continues to operate outside the government's purview. In fact, much of the formal economy in the Middle East—especially that involving the exchange of goods and services among non-governmental actors—retains an astounding level of informality and, therefore, autonomy from state regulations and other forms of government interference. This widespread informality of the formal economy has much to do with the phenomenon of the "bazaar economy".

The bazaaris, many of whose economic activities fall outside the formal sphere and are rarely ever regulated by the state, engage in capitalism par excellence, subject at most to unofficial rules and conventions formulated by their own guilds and associations.[53] Despite the seemingly small scale of their operations, most bazaari merchants are often inordinately wealthy, so much so that some can at times corner the entire market in a particular product (say, onions or tires), and by so doing significantly influence the supply and price of a commodity throughout their city or even the entire country. In turn, the raw and unregulated capitalism in which the bazaaris engage has a multitude of facets and dimensions, spilling over into other informal and at times even formal economic spheres. The state, meanwhile, is often largely powerless in dealing with the bazaaris as it has neither the resources nor the political will to break their considerable economic might. What results, therefore, is a savage capitalism operating at the societal level side by side with a timid socialism at the national level espoused by the state.

The situation in Sub-Saharan African countries is somewhat different. By and large—with such exceptions as in Kenya and Zanzibar, and to lesser extent Ghana and Ethiopia—an independent, politically autonomous merchant class has not developed in black Africa. Some classes do exercise a measure of autonomy from the state: the merchant communities (Bamilke) in Cameroon, the ubiquitous "contractors" in Nigeria, and the *magendo* (people at the upper end of the economic scale who are a "mirror image of the informal sector at the lower end") in Uganda, Ghana, and Zaire.[54] But there is nothing similar to the Middle Eastern bazaar economy in Sub-Saharan Africa, and the many, bustling open-air markets that are a consistent feature of Africa's urban landscape do not afford opportunities for an economically and politically affluent merchant class as such to grow.

In many African and non-African examples, nevertheless, society does exercise some autonomy from the state, at times in fact to the point of making the country as a national unit dysfunctional. But this autonomy is due to factors that are largely non-economic. In Western Europe, societal autonomy grew out of persistent demands for political space by various social actors. In South America and Eastern Europe, society gained autonomy (although in places the process continues to face obstacles) after the rolling back of states that had previously sought to overwhelm and subdue it. In the Middle East, in cases where autonomy from the state does exist, it is the prerogative of a distinct social class (the bazaaris) and its successive layers of clients, in relation to which the state is often ineffective and almost a non-factor. In post-colonial Sub-Saharan Africa, however, class factors have been less important than other systemic economic and sociocultural dynamics. Often, they tend to result from inherent institutional weaknesses by the state on the one hand and society's multiple fractures (along ethnic, linguistic, cultural, and at times racial lines) on the other hand. In short, a major obstacle faced by African states is incapacity (or timidity) in relation to society. Moreover, the prevalence of a stagnant "semicapitalism" in much of the continent has greatly hampered the ability of either the state or society on its own to successfully meet the challenges of development.[55] As a result, the economic nexus between state and society remains small and relatively insignificant. In most of today's Sub-Saharan Africa, therefore, with the notable exception of South Africa, where the maintenance of apartheid entailed significant economic advantages for the white minority,[56] political economy does not play as influential a role in state-society relations as have such non-economic factors as ethnic and cultural heterogeneity. In Migdal's terms, most African societies may be considered "strong" compared to the states which rule over them. However, this strength is not based on the social actors' greater access to economic resources. Rather it has more to do with the state's inability to tackle the challenges it faces from a deeply divided society.

International influences

Neither the inner workings of the state nor those of society, nor even their mutual interactions, occur within a vacuum. Inevitably, at times even reluctant actors within the regional, international, and even global community, states and societies cannot escape the variety of extra-national influences that come from beyond their own borders. The sociologist Anthony Giddens goes so far as to maintain that "globalization" is inherent in the socioeconomic structure of contemporary capitalism and this, he claims, has come about as a result of the "transformation of space and time". More specifically, globalization refers to "action at a distance", the intensification of which in recent years is due to the "emergence of means of instantaneous global communication and mass transportation".[57]

> Our day-to-day activities are increasingly influenced by events happening on the other side of the world. Conversely, local lifestyle habits have

become globally consequential. Thus my decision to buy a certain item of clothing has implications not only for the international division of labour but for the earth's ecosystem.[58]

Receptivity to influences from abroad and in turn the ability or willingness to generate such influences depend on a number of factors. Most notably, they include a country's position within and posture toward the larger international community; its ability or desire to project "hard" and/or "soft" power abroad; the extent to which social and cultural change has enhanced a society's attitudes toward outside influences;[59] and the nature and extent of political and societal means (state policies, electronic and printed media, satellites and computers, etc.) through which these exogenous influences are filtered, packaged, and disseminated throughout society. In Iran, for example, the government jams satellite television transmissions in a losing battle to keep out the corrupting influences of Western norms from Iranian living rooms. In Tunisia, e-mail was not available for some time due to political considerations. And in China, private fax machines are banned because of their subversive potential. There are countless such modern-day Hermit Kingdoms, each battling integration for fear of loss of cultural identity or, more truthfully, political power.

Four general categories of extra-national influences that act on states and societies can be distinguished. They include the forces of international economics; transnational cultural movements or shared identities; international regimes, rules, and agreements that regulate some aspects of state behavior; and diplomatic and/or military pressures exerted by another country, directly or indirectly, designed to influence a specific aspect of domestic politics. These categories are not mutually exclusive of each other and often do, in fact, overlap. When in 1990 Iraq violated international laws and conventions by invading Kuwait, both the Iraqi and Kuwait states were subject to military and diplomatic influences from the so-called Allied Forces. International economics and military force have often gone hand in hand. The forces of international economics have changed the political landscape of countless countries, at times completely, since the earliest days of international commerce. The Opium War, the colonization of Africa, the adventures of the United Fruit Company in Central America, the overthrow of Salvador Allende in Chile, and the "liberation" of oil-rich Kuwait from Iraq (but not of oil-poor Bosnia from Serbian ethnic cleansing) are only some of the more dramatic examples of the power of international economics. More subtle influences abound in the international system. One of the reasons for the collapse of the Soviet bloc, for example, is the cumulative effects of the costs of its economic and military competition with the West. In recent years, several states in Latin America, the Middle East, and Africa have been encouraged (some might say pressured) by the World Bank and the International Monetary Fund to undertake economic stabilization and structural adjustment programs designed to improve public sector efficiency and the productivity of public sector investments, liberalizing trade and domestic investment policies, and reforming the institutional arrangements that support the readjustment process.[60] As a consequence of these policies, the domestic powers and role of many states have been somewhat curtailed, the bureaucracy reformed, and the overall size and capacity of the state reduced. Eager to embark on economic liberalization programs, post-transition democracies are especially likely to implement reforms plans, some of the more notable of which include those launched in Poland (the Balcerowics plan), Brazil (the Plano Collar), Argentina (under Menem), and Peru (under Fujimori).[61]

Transnational cultural movements and/or shared identities that transcend national boundaries can also significantly influence domestic politics. The appearance of political Islam throughout the Middle East from the late 1970s is the most dramatic example of such a phenomenon: an Islamic revolution was launched, won, and consolidated in Iran after 1979; the very foundations of almost all Gulf monarchies were shaken by Islamist oppositionists (e.g. the takeover of the Grand Mosque in Mecca in November 1979); President Sadat was assassinated by Islamist activists in Egypt in October 1981; Islam became a force to reckon with in Lebanon throughout the 1980s; Algeria was plunged into a bloody civil war by its military and the Islamic Salvation Front (FIS) beginning in 1992; fanatical purists called the Taliban captured power in war-torn Afghanistan in 1996; and, earlier that same year, even the virulently secular Turkey elected an Islamist prime minister (Necmettin Erbakan of the Welfare Party).[62] While in each case domestic social and political forces were at work, the cross-national spread, diffusion, and reinforcement of values were also of great importance.[63] Even more dramatic has been the persistence of cross-national ethnic identities throughout Africa, often with devastating consequences for the nation-state and its inhabitants. From the very start, one might argue, the currency of extra-national ethno-tribal identities doomed the nationalist project in Africa.[64]

The Uncertainty Principle

The last area of analysis to consider in conceptualizing the political characteristics and dynamics of a polity is what a number of theorists have called "contingency", which may, alternatively, also be called "randomness". For a long time part of some historically grounded political analyses, contingency points to the existence of those elements whose genesis and causes are not always empirically explicable; they are not quantifiable; and they are almost impossible to predict. As a factor of analysis, contingency (randomness) is elusive and evasive, a shadowy area where the best we can do is to offer educated guesses and recognize our limitations in precise, tangible, "scientific" measurement and reasoning. This is more than the "contingence" factor which some proponents of the state-in-society approach have mentioned (though not elaborated on).[65] Instead, this is an area in social analysis where a measure of randomness is both possible and probable, where something akin to "the uncertainty principle" of quantum mechanics prevails. In the life of every country—whether in its politics or its history, its society or its economy—there is a certain amount of unpredictability, a number of accidental or unintended occurrences that have little or nothing to do with the national, political, or historical "norm" of that country. Sometimes things can happen that have no causal relationship to political, economic, or sociocultural forces that exist in a particular society. All political systems and societies operate according to sets of rules and guidelines that can pretty much be accurately grasped and analyzed. But, by their nature, they also contain an element of uncertainty, when developments arise based on no rules or conventions, when society or politics assume directions that no one expected, when culture develops norms few thought possible, when history takes turns few ever imagined.

We must, of course, be careful not to stretch the boundaries of this accidentalism beyond reasonable limits. There are very broad and general limits beyond which random occurrences are not possible. Nevertheless, there is a general framework within which not every occurrence or development is predictable. To assume, for example, that China might tomorrow suddenly become democratic is unreasonable; but no one could scientifically account for Chairman Mao's political antics after the success of the Chinese communists in 1949 (not the least of which were the Great Leap Forward and the Cultural Revolution). In *A Brief History of Time,* Stephen Hawking offers a layman's definition of quantum mechanics that seems to fit this model perfectly:

> In general, quantum mechanics does not predict a single definite result from an observation. Instead, it predicts a number of different possible outcomes and tells us how likely each of these is. That is to say, if one made the same measurement on a large number of similar systems, each of which started off in the same way, one would find that the result of the measurement would be A in a certain number of cases, B in a different number, and so on. One would predict the approximate number of times that the result would be A or B, but one could not predict the specific result of an individual measurement. Quantum mechanics therefore introduces an unavoidable element of unpredictability or randomness into science.[66]

The uncertainty principle can be caused by any one of four inter-related and complementary factors: circumstances and opportunities; historical accidents; unintended consequences; and personal initiatives. Unforeseen circumstances and random occurrences—the element of chance—can potentially play a crucial role in the uncertainty principle. Circumstances and opportunities often arise that, if properly situated or exploited, may significantly change the political life or social direction of a given country. The circumstances in which a country finds itself can potentially, and often in fact do, have an important bearing on its politics and society. These circumstances may be due to accidental factors that initially have nothing to do with the country itself. The tragic example of the link between the Holocaust and Palestinian politics may better illustrate the point. Who could rationally explain Hitler's crusade to annihilate the Jews? There is no single social, political, or historical explanation for the Holocaust; the man was simply a pathological murderer. One can rationalize about the causes of the Holocaust, but the reason as to why it was carried out, and why it was carried out the way that it was, ultimately rests with Hitler himself. Some other political leader might have carried out the same murderous crusade, but most probably he would have either avoided it altogether or at least done it differently.[67] That some six million Jews perished and countless others were displaced throughout the globe was simply a matter of unfortunate chance, but still chance nonetheless.

But this poor luck on the part of the European Jewry has dramatically altered the life, politics, and society of not only Jews but also Palestinians in a way they could not possibly have fathomed before 1947. The irrational actions of a man in distant Europe, resulting in the misfortunes of millions of people, influenced life in Palestine in a way that indigenous Palestinian factors had little to do with. The unpredictable element of chance, or in this case horrendous misfortune, has played—or in the inter-war period did play—a determining role in the nature of Palestinian (and of course Israeli) politics, society, and economics. Hitler's madness alone is not responsible for every aspect of Palestinian life or politics since 1947, but the coincidental connection between the two is more formidable than may at first appear to be the case.

Closely related to the randomness of circumstances and opportunities that are thrust upon a country are the role of historical accidents. Especially in the contemporary era, rarely has an accidental historical act or a random discovery changed or fundamentally altered the political life of an entire country. Yet a credible argument could be made that the appearance of the Age of Revolution in Europe, and particularly of industrialization in England, was quite accidental and that such Asian countries as China or Japan were initially better situated to be the birthplaces of technological innovation and advancement.[68] As Henry Steele Commager reminds us, "we must avoid assuming that history is a kind of chess game with every gambit logical and planned".[69] But, he warns, we must also avoid "the other extreme, that of ascribing everything to accident or luck; we must avoid giving too much prominence to untidiness and disorder".[70] "Though accidents often change the pace or the pattern of history," he maintains,

> they rarely change it in any fundamental way. For the sophisticated historian remembers what is, after all, the common sense of the

matter, that there are always enough accidents to go around, and that accidents tend to cancel out ... It is premature and almost perverse to assign too much importance to what we determine the accidents of history.[71]

Commager's points are quite significant, but he goes too far in his warning. Likening history to a football game, he maintains that "a particular fumble rarely changes the course of a game, or of a season of games".[72] But that is precisely where he is wrong. A fumble by itself may not change a game, but an accidental injury resulting in the loss of a first-rate player might. History may not change because of an army commander's sneeze somewhere, but that army commander's death, or military brilliance or incompetence in a particular campaign, can indeed impact not only the direction of history but also the lives of those influenced by it. The mental instability of King George III, no doubt, for example, greatly influenced his choice of responses to the rebellious colonies in the Americas, as did the Shah of Iran's struggle with cancer in his attempts to save his collapsing dynasty in the fateful days of 1978 and 1979.[73] Accidents do matter. Political history is not made up of random accidents alone. There are times, however, when accidents and other elements that are matters of pure chance weigh heavily in determining a particular political outcome.

Similarly unpredictable are the important roles played by personal initiative and human agency. At whatever level of "the political" one looks—be it the state or society, political economy or political history—there is the undeniable constant of human thought and action, men and women who, either individually or collectively, are either the benefactors, or initiators, or recipients of political power. Even when political ideology, or custom and convention, heavily constrain the range of options open to human free will, there is still a degree if not of independence then of variance between one person's thoughts and actions and another's. How that initiative impacts politics— how the fluidity of human individuality results in a certain political outcome that would have been different had someone else been involved—that is where the uncertainty of politics lies, where no analysis, no matter how concrete, can adequately account for or predict a particular outcome with exact precision.

Politics becomes especially problematic when a person decides to "make history", when a Bonaparte attains power, a Khomeini tries to cling on to it, an Idi Amin enters the scene, or a Gorbachev worries about how future Russians will remember him. In such instances, politics becomes erratic, highly personalized and unpredictable. It has few or no set patterns, no over-arching guiding principles other than what the political leader thinks is prudent for the moment and at the time. This is not to imply, of course, that the unpredictability of individual initiative is something to consider only in political systems or eras when powerful personalities overshadow institutions and principles. The likes of Ataturk and Mao do have an easier time in taking politics (and with it history) into their own hands and shaping it in ways they like; and some have even been successful in such endeavors. But even within the institutional limitations that, say, Western political systems impose on their politicians, there is still much room for individual creativity, initiative, and uniqueness of impact. And one does not have to be a vain Lyndon Johnson or a British Iron Lady to put a unique stamp on politics. The many big and small decisions that are made by such uninspiring Western politicians as Presidents Carter, Bush, and Clinton in the US, Prime Minister Major in Britain, and Japan's many short-tenured prime ministers, are all in their own way unique. These decisions would most probably be different, even if only slightly, if they were made by someone else. The lowest common denominator of politics is human thought and action, and very seldom are the thoughts and actions of two people identical. In fact, when it comes to politics, particularly when the stakes are high, people's thoughts and actions tend to differ especially widely.

Analytical applications

The analytical utility of the approach set out above becomes apparent when it is applied to the various political, economic, and social and cultural phenomena that, in totality and in connection with one another, constitute politics. Politics is a multi-faceted realm in which a number of forces, disparate and often initially unrelated, combine to determine the nature and behaviors of state and social actors in themselves and in relation to one another. In one way or another, previous approaches to comparative politics have failed to provide proper and sufficient analytical guidelines that would take all such diverse components into account. For its part, although it is far more thorough than those preceding it, the state-in-society perspective fails to leave room for accidental occurrences or to take into account factors related to political economy and political culture.

The approach being proposed here, filling some of the void left behind by previous paradigms, casts an analytical net that, for now at least, appears wide enough to take into account the many forces and phenomena that make up politics. It also retains an internal logical consistency that enables us to point to the causal connections that may exist in seemingly unconnected political domains. This is a holistic view of politics in which six areas of analysis have been highlighted: state; society; political culture; political economy; international influences; and random occurrences.

The inner workings of each of these six areas, and the inter-relations between them, form the blueprint which comparative analysis needs to follow. This larger model can then be applied in order to examine a specific political phenomenon or event from a comparative perspective. The analyst must determine which of the six areas best explains the characteristics and underlying causes of his or her particular subject of investigation; which other areas were directly or indirectly involved or affected; and how that specific phenomenon, which might have occurred in only one area, impacts the larger picture. There are a number of phenomena that may be important and inseparable aspects of a particular political scenario, and each may belong primarily in one of the six areas. By their nature, however, many political phenomena go beyond the original area in which they were generated: political development, for example, may be initiated by the state but also influences society and culture, and involves elements of political economy as well.

If the analyst's job is to study political development in a given country, he or she needs to determine what state factors were involved (e.g. institutions and other policy-making mechanisms, intents and consequences, etc.), and how, if at all, such other areas as the political economy or political culture came into play or were influenced. This is not to imply that comparative political analysis has always to remain at the macro-level. Micro-level analysis of specific aspects of a particular phenomenon is possible under the same rubric, though the scope is much narrower and, naturally, more specialized. Instead of the larger processes and consequences involved in political development, for example, analysis would only focus on the highly specialized factors that are pertinent to the investigation. Nevertheless, the analyst must remain mindful of the fact that although a very specific phenomenon is being studied (in this case a particular facet of political development), there are other forces and factors that *may potentially* be of significance to the subject of investigation as well.

Conclusion

Building on the state-in-society approach to comparative politics, this chapter has sought to take the level of analysis one step further by proposing a more holistic perspective. To examine comparative politics, it argues, analysis must focus not only on the state and society but also on the additional areas of political culture, political economy, international influences, and "the uncertainty principle". As the general umbrella under which popular norms and values toward political objects are formulated, political culture plays a decisive role in influencing a society's interactions with the state and, in turn, the degree of success or failure a state may have in carrying out its social agendas. Similarly important is political economy, in particular the economic contexts and ramifications of the interactions that take place between the state and society. States and societies operate in a global arena in which other states and societies operate and where extra-national influences from economic centers and cultural movements, multinational agencies, and international regimes abound.

Lastly, attention has been drawn to a certain amount of built-in unpredictability in politics, a degree of deliberate uncertainty based more on the laws of probabilities and accidental occurrences than on any tangibly predictable phenomena based on the laws of politics, society, or economics. Politics is not in any sense mysterious or magical; it is not a discipline the study and examination of which is a matter of pure speculation or abstract philosophizing. Rather, it is not always wholly quantifiable or reducible to immutable mechanical laws and regulations. We must acknowledge that due to the involvement of humans in it—humans who by nature retain a degree of uniqueness and individuality—politics can potentially result in outcomes that are not always precisely predictable. Even culture—and cultural analysis—does not provide concrete rules for political conduct and/or analysis. In political analysis, as with physics, the best we can do is to present ourselves with a range of possible options and speculate about their potential outcomes.

As the above analysis demonstrates, examining and conceptualizing comparative politics is a more complicated venture than previously assumed. This chapter has by no means put a definitive end to the ongoing debate, but it has presented a modified methodology for the various areas of analysis upon which attempts to conceptualize politics must focus. The assertions made here enjoy neither the elegant simplicity of the modernization perspective nor the compelling convictions of the dependency approach. Neither, I think, do they have the straightforward logic of structuralism or the loud and supportive, at times violent, rhetoric to which culturalists point for validation. Politics is presented here as a messy, complicated, at times accidental and unpredictable web into which may enter a number of non-political forces and considerations. But that, unfortunate though it may be, is precisely what politics is. As our understanding of comparative global politics becomes more thorough and sophisticated, so must we accordingly modify our perceptions and presuppositions of what *politics* is and how we must go about understanding it. It is only logical to conclude, then, that progressively greater levels of analytical and conceptual sophistication—and hopefully simplicity—are to be expected in the future.

Part III

State in comparative perspective

6 Democratic states

The political transformations that were the catalysts of the new world order of the 1990s, as well as those which resulted from it, were both numerous and dramatic. Whatever the causes of the "great transformation" of the 1980s, classical typologies of states, and ultimately of various political forms, fell apart with the collapse of communism in Eastern Europe. The easily discernible "three worlds of politics", with their sharply divided patterns of interaction between their respective states and societies, gave way to a much more complicated set of political relationships. In the new era, the worlds of politics have not just changed but indeed become revolutionized, making it necessary to reformulate traditional notions of comparative politics. Neither states nor societies, nor in fact the relationships between them, can any longer be properly conceptualized within the context of analytical frameworks developed over the past forty years or so. As recent global events have demonstrated, such conventional labels as "democratic", "communist", and "authoritarian", or even different variations of them, are no longer strictly applicable. A new typology is needed to account adequately for the new patterns of relationships that have evolved during the "New World Order" between states and societies.

It is possible to distinguish four distinct though very broad types of state currently in existence. Based on their component institutions and the nature of their connections with society, these state types include First World democracies, which have much greater degrees of historical longevity; the more recent democracies that were born out of the democratization processes of the 1970s and the 1980s; proto- or quasi-democracies, in which such democratic mechanisms as elections and political parties exist but the spirit of democracy does not; and non-democratic states, which frequently take the form of either bureaucratic-authoritarian regimes or inclusionary populist ones. The first two types of state are democratic—i.e. they are marked by open and consensual patterns of interaction with their respective societies. In quasi-democracies, state-society interaction is rather minimal and does not extend beyond certain elite circles. Another category is made up of non-democratic states, although to some extent the inclusionary policies of populist regimes bestow on the population a perception of democratic participation. In both inclusionary populist regimes and authoritarian dictatorships, the flow of influence is one way, from state to society. Both are in essence "command systems", but their supporting mechanisms and the underlying dynamics of their interactions with society are radically different. Whereas inclusionary populist regimes *include* broad strata of society within their institutions, authoritarian dictatorships strive to achieve the exact opposite and seek to *exclude* as many participants from the political arena as possible.

State Classifications

Before examining each of these state categories in greater detail, it may be useful to look briefly at some of the other categorizations used to classify states. The categories of states mentioned above, it is important to remember, are based on the underlying relationships between various state institutions with the institutions of their societies. This is consistent with the definition of politics and the analytical framework set out in previous chapters. That the categories put forward here are distinctly *political*, however, does not necessarily preclude other standards for categorization. Depending on one's particular perspective, states may in fact be classified according to their general status within the international system, their economic capabilities, or, alternatively, their leadership. Classifications of states into "weak" and "powerful", "radical" and "conservative", "patron" and "client", "modern" and "traditional", or "developed" and "developing", to name but a few, have been particularly prevalent within the social science literature of the past few decades.[1] Two of these patterns of classification— one based on status within the international state system and the other on economic capabilities—have received greater attention than others and thus deserve closer examination.

Internationally framed classifications of states have been both more contentious and more prevalent. Dependency theorists are especially likely to classify states into such categories as "patrons" and "clients", or the "centrer" and the "periphery" respectively. It is, nevertheless, possible to classify states based on their diplomatic positions and initiatives without getting bogged down in ideological debates. Different states do undertake different types of action in the international arena, have varying goals and preferences, and exert different amounts of influence. In fact, Harry Redner has distinguished five broad types of state based solely on their status in the international arena. They include "autonomous", "community", "client", "independent", and "satellite" states.[2] Autonomous states are those with enough domestic resources and international clout to be able to act with full autonomy, both domestically and diplomatically. Though their numbers are few, the powers of such states are considerable. They include such countries as the United States, Japan, China, and to a lesser extent India.[3] Community states, of which those in the European Union (EU) and in the Association of South East Asian Nations (ASEAN) are the most notable, are those that "cannot undertake wholly autonomous activities out of line with their fellow members but act to a considerable degree in concert with each other".[4]

Client states, on the other hand, are economically and militarily dependent on more powerful nations, or, at the least, cannot ignore impulses emanating from them. Most states in the Middle East and in Latin America find themselves in this category, compelled by the force of circumstances to pay close attention to other, more powerful state or non-state actors.[5] Satellite states are in a more vulnerable position, though their numbers have in recent years greatly declined following the collapse of the Soviet empire. Some of the current satellite states include Lesotho and Swaziland (both dominated by South Africa), and, potentially, the former Soviet republics that are now members of the Commonwealth of Independent States— namely, Armenia, Azerbaijan, Belarus, Georgia, Kazakhstan, Kyrgyzstan, Moldova, Tajikistan, Ukraine, and Uzbekistan, with Turkmenistan being an "associate member" as of 2005—for whose allegiance the dominant powers of the region (especially Russia, China, Iran, and Turkey) often compete.[6] Lastly, there are some states which try to assert a measure of independence in the international sphere, though some are more successful than others. Austria, Venezuela, and Iran are three of the more varied examples of states that strive to attain diplomatic and economic independence vis-à-vis more powerful actors.[7]

Closely related to the diplomatic and international positions of states are their economic capabilities. There is, in fact, often a direct correlation between a state's diplomatic history and its economic prowess. More specifically, states can be classified on the basis of their economic accomplishments and the types of policies they adopt for attaining industrial development. An economic/diplomatic classification of states results in a five-fold typology: the industrial capitalist states of Western Europe and Japan, bureaucratic-authoritarian states, dependent states, nationalist states, and, for lack of a better term, states "in decline".[8] Industrialized capitalist states, found primarily in the democracies of the First World, invariably promote and protect private and corporate ownership in a free and competitive market with minimal interference from governmental agencies.[9] Bureaucratic-authoritarian states also strive to enhance the economic and industrial competitiveness of their countries, mostly under the auspices of capitalist development, although to achieve their goals they develop highly penetrative and often repressive mechanisms which seek to direct even the most mundane aspects of social life. Nevertheless, as a general rule, dictatorships have not been particularly successful in bringing about industrial development, and their economic success depends on existing social, political, and historic circumstances within specific countries.[10] Nationalist states are similar to bureaucratic-authoritarian ones in their industrial predicaments and economic aspirations, although they lack the bureaucratic-authoritarian states' intricate networks of coercion and sociopolitical manipulation designed for directing and guiding industrial development. They are, in essence, coercion-free capitalist states that are not yet fully democratic. India, Mexico, and Costa Rica are some of the more notable countries in this category.[11]

Dependent states, meanwhile, found principally in Africa, Central America, and the Caribbean, are those that rely primarily on the export of raw materials in order to sustain power structures that continue to remain weak and brittle. Their ruling classes are, consequently, relatively pliable and highly vulnerable to negative economic developments from abroad.[12] Lastly, there are states that appear to be in irreversible and chronic decline, both in their political power and in economic capabilities. Having achieved formal independence relatively recently, these states never fully attain sufficient power to repel potential challenges from the outside and from within their own fragmented and fractious societies. For them mere economic survival, never mind development, is a struggle. Examples of this group of countries include Uganda, the Democratic Republic of Congo, Ghana, Chad, and Cambodia.[13]

Such a typology of states is useful for measuring their comparative economic and diplomatic strengths and weaknesses. In particular, this typology helps us to clarify and examine the specific position of a given state within the international system. Though not inaccurate, such a categorization of states does not fully reflect the dynamic patterns of interaction that states assume in relation to their societies. As accurate as these categories may be in their own right, they deal with the domain of *politics* tangentially and only in so far as it is affected by economic or other international forces. With politics being the interaction that occurs between the respective institutions of state and society, comparative examination of it requires a focus on those functions and characteristics of various states and societies that are solely political. Economics, diplomacy, and a variety of other factors do indeed combine to form the complex web of interactions through which states and societies communicate and influence one another. But each on its own is only part of a larger whole. Classifying states by virtue of international status and capabilities may be analytically useful for specific purposes, but it is at best politically reductionist. What is needed is a more comprehensive framework within which the *political* relevance, place, and contributions of both states and societies can be examined.

The central question which comparative politics seeks to address is deceptively simple: how does a specific state influence a society and how does a specific society influence a state? The answer requires the provision of typologies of states and societies based on their mutually interactive relations. The different types of states outlined at the start of the chapter— First World democracies, new democracies, quasi-democracies, inclusionary populist regimes, and authoritarian dictatorships—are state types that tend to influence and interact with their societies in broadly identifiable and separate ways. In essence, our concern with these states revolves around their social significance, in the same way as focus on societies is centered on their impact on the state. This chapter focuses on the three democratic varieties of states—viable, new, and pseudo-democracies—with non-democratic states the subject of chapter 7.

First World Democracies

Compared with other states, the democratic states of the First World are the oldest, most stable, and by far the strongest in terms of their capacity to mobilize, manage, and even extract social and economic resources from their societies and from other states. Nevertheless, neither their age nor their patterns of development and evolution are by any means uniform. The present uniformity that exists among First World states was preceded by a tumultuous political history wrought by unpredictable oscillations, the violent overthrow of power, and foreign occupation. First World democracies are an essentially post-World War II phenomenon. The historically most resilient democratic states of the First World number only a handful, among them Britain, the United States, and Switzerland. Almost none of the other European countries, even those which at some point were democratic states, have had a continuously democratic political history. The fascism that swept across the continent in the 1920s and 1930s destroyed some of the working democracies and devoured others under the weight of occupation.[14] It was only after the military defeat of fascism, coupled with the social and cultural upheavals which accompanied the whole experience, that democratic states were carefully engineered throughout the continent. So far, these democracies have proven remarkably resilient, pre-dating most other contemporary state types.

To a large extent, the enhanced capabilities of the democratic states of the First World are derived from the close and highly integrative nature of their relationships with their societies. By nature, a democratic system is one that freely facilitates the expression of demands and initiatives from members of society. For a viable democratic polity to thrive and to survive, the institutions and the underlying premises of both the state and society need to mutually reinforce one another. So far as the democratic state is concerned, the links that bind state and society together appear in the form of a series of highly evolved and complex political institutions designed to formulate and to give expression to the popular will. These are institutions upon which the very foundations of the state depend, the most crucial of which include legislative and judicial bodies, the executive, and the various branches of the bureaucracy. While these are institutions that are commonly found in all types of systems, what makes them uniquely important for democratic states is the principal functions which they perform. In democracies, legislatures and judiciaries are designed to ensure a regular and unimpeded flow of public input from society into the state. In dictatorial and populist regimes, however, they perform markedly different functions (see below). Democratic executives are also uniquely different from dictators and populist demagogues, as they are elected by popular mandate and are constrained by the wishes of the electorate. The whole system is based on a constitutional blueprint that is also popularly upheld and, in fact, at times even cherished. These characteristics of democratic states result more or less in their fusion with society, and, combined with features endemic to democratic societies themselves, almost inextricably bind the two together. This social permeability of democratic states, particularly those with greater historical and cultural resonance, in turn bestows on them an unparalleled measure of stability and strength.

A closer examination of various institutions in democratic states sheds more light on the underlying causes of their comparative strength. Not only do the prevailing social norms—as formulated within the context of political culture—lend added support to the executive, the legislative, and the judicial institutions of democratic states, the unique features of these institutions themselves greatly enhance their resilience. As mentioned earlier, democratic legislatures and judiciaries are primarily designed to be interconnecting links between state and society.

Legislatures

To varying degrees and in one form or another, legislatures generally perform three broad functions in all political systems. They serve as "advisory boards" to the executive; legislate and make laws; and provide an institutional forum through which societal interests and demands are represented within the state.[15] It is these latter two functions, those of legislation and representation, that form the very essence of democratic legislatures and which provide for them (and consequently for the larger state) a solid and self-perpetuating basis of support.[16] Far from performing "advisory" or other perfunctory functions, democratic legislatures are invariably deeply involved in the actual process of politics, whether by influencing and determining government policy or by facilitating channels of societal participation in the state. Whereas in dictatorial and populist regimes the functions of legislatures are mostly those of legitimization and mobilization respectively, in democratic states they have wide latitude in their powers and obligations.

Through their representative functions and their links to the larger society, democratic legislatures provide means of access for the recruitment and socialization of political leaders and elites. Most such legislatures are empowered to select, approve, question, or pass votes of no confidence on heads of government and their cabinet members, while others control finance, question ministers, debate issues, and critique policies.[17] Legislatures in democratic states carry forward the political process either by actively launching policies and legislation, as in the United States, or by assuming a more reactive role vis-à-vis the initiatives of the executive, as the

"Westminster-type" legislatures of Britain, Canada, New Zealand, and Australia do.[18] They are all nevertheless, in one way or another, integral and vital institutions without which democratic states cannot fully function.

The judiciary

Judicial institutions play a similarly paramount and important role in the viability of democratic states, one which, significantly, they do not play in non-democratic states. In all political systems, the judicial branch performs both a societal as well as a political role. At the societal level, all judiciaries adjudicate between members of society by mandating and interpreting laws and regulations. This function is standard to all judicial systems regardless of the type of state to which they belong, although their legal dictums and interpretations can vary significantly depending on different national and historic traditions and social and cultural patterns.

What does differ enormously from one type of state to another is the specific *political* role that judiciaries play. In non-democratic states, judiciaries are designed to prevent unsolicited inputs and other expressions of opinion regarding the political process. They are essentially protective institutions that use existing laws as weapons to guard against potential demands for political participation emanating from within society. During the tumultuous political events in China in spring 1989, for example, the judicial system sought vigorously to protect the Chinese state from social demands. Many of the student protesters who had gathered in Tiananmen Square to voice opposition to government policies were quickly arrested and found guilty of having engaged in "anti-state" crimes.[19]

Judiciaries in democratic states serve almost diametrically opposite functions. A telling contrast to the Chinese case would be the US Supreme Court's upholding, in 1989, of the right of American citizens to burn the American flag if they so wished: democratic judiciaries protect society from possible encroachments from the state, as opposed to the other way around. Their principal aim is to keep the powers of the executive in check and to ensure that the political liberties and rights of those in society are not abrogated. More specifically, democratic judiciaries assume four political responsibilities: they engage in judicial reviews and interpret the constitution; arbitrate between the state's various institutions; provide general support for the polity; and define and protect the political liberties of individuals.[20] Throughout, the democratic judiciary maintains strict independence from possible influences by the executive, though the executive does, in most cases, appoint the higher echelons of the judicial branch.[21]

Executives

Equally instrumental in determining the very essence of democratic states are their executive institutions, namely the head of government—who may alternatively be designated the head of state—and the successive echelons of administrators and bureaucrats who operate under his or her command. The nature of the executive branch correlates directly with the prevailing nature of politics and the relationship between state and society. The more consensual and frictionless the interaction between state and society—i.e. the more democratic the political process—the less dictatorial and centralized the executive tends to be. However, when the relationship between state and society is a conflictual one and dictatorial traits dominate the political arena, the state tends to be less restricted in its powers and more intolerant of diverging tendencies. Indeed, in most non-democratic polities, it is often nearly impossible to distinguish between the executive and the state. Most non-democratic executives view themselves as, and many often indeed are, *the state*. In contrast, the democratic executive's functions are only one of a whole array of functions that the state performs, albeit an increasingly central one.

Democratic executives are "creatures of society" and are elected and limited by it.[22] Whether presidential or parliamentary in character, the executives of democratic states are restricted in the scope of their powers and in their tenure in office by legal and constitutional restraints. In recent years, the executive branch of democratic states has consistently grown in power and autonomy as compared with other institutions, due largely to the increasing importance and complexity of the fields of responsibility within the executive's usual purview, such as international diplomacy, public administration, and military policy. The decline in the comparative powers of legislative institutions has been particularly noticeable.[23] Yet despite this relative predominance of democratic executives, their essentially constrained nature within states remains unaltered. As two authors on the subject have noted, "in democracies, as in no other political regimes, the command structure is carefully circumscribed and meticulously surrounded by institutional safeguards against those who trespass into areas of decision making outside their allotted field or who attempt to use short cuts in making decisions."[24]

Other components

In order to carry out policies and initiatives, executives in all states need to rely on a variety of bureaucratic and administrative networks and agencies. For democratic states, however, bureaucracies pose a peculiar dilemma. Particularly in more advanced and powerful states, bureaucratic agencies tend to have an inherent tendency to engage in a certain amount of autonomous policy-making when the opportunity arises. Thus traditional distinctions between rule-making and rule application, or even between *political executives* and *professional administrators*, can at times become disconcertingly blurred.[25] The pervasiveness and the unimpeded proliferation of bureaucracies, even in the most libertarian of states, have only compounded the potential problem of undermining due processes of democratic decision-making.[26] The fusion, and at times confusion, of executive and bureaucratic duties and responsibilities is even more probable in parliamentary systems, particularly in Japan and Britain, where few differences separate the top echelons of the bureaucracy from members of the legislature.[27] Nevertheless, the dominance in most First World democracies since the 1980s of the so-called, and unrelentingly conservative, "New Right", of which Prime Minister Thatcher and President Reagan were the most colorful representatives, has to a certain extent curbed the seemingly unabated growth of bureaucratic powers. The precise effects of the phenomenon of the New Right on the powers of the state are difficult to gauge. While figures associated with the New Right have been extremely persistent in their calls for minimalist states, they are also determined to enhance the state's military capabilities. They have also sought to use state institutions to push through their own conservative agendas. Nevertheless, the "anti-statist" predisposition—or at least rhetoric—of the New Right, coupled with its general mistrust of government bureaucracy, and calls for a return to a freer market economy, have somewhat curtailed the growing powers of administrative networks since the 1980s.[28]

A further reason for the institutional resilience of democratic states is the corporatist underpinnings which most tend to have. Corporatism, in its broad sense, denotes the convergence of varied and disparate interests within and alongside a state for the furtherance of common goals that happen to coincide. It involves the "joining of public agencies and private interest groups in the making and implementing of governmental policy".[29] The intimate and multifaceted interactions between societal and state actors in democratic polities often facilitate the emergence of a "democratic corporatism", although, as will be shown later, non-democratic states can also assume corporatist features. Although there is no definitive correlation between industrial capitalism and democracy, today's First World democratic states invariably preside over highly developed capitalist economies.[30] Advanced capitalism gives rise to special interest groups, who cooperate among themselves, as well as with the democratic state, in order to further their interests. Corporatism and consensus democracy can thus potentially become logical extensions of one another.[31] Consequently, such polities are endowed with yet another set of institutions which provide the critical means of nexus between an open and democratic state and a supportive society. By virtue of their goals and their functions, meanwhile, the emerging "corporate" institutions are neither strictly societal nor exclusive components of the state. Instead, they transcend the state-society divide, assuming and absorbing features and functions of both and in the process reinforcing their other attributes.

Lastly, the pivotal role of constitutions in maintaining the overall structure of democratic states, which are inherently reliant on highly artificial and carefully engineered political arrangements, cannot be overlooked. The general parameters of the state, the extent and manner of its interactions with society, and the functions of its central institutions are often detailed in constitutions, whether written or unwritten. "Constitutions", wrote S.E. Finer, a noted British scholar of comparative politics, "are codes of rules which aspire to regulate the allocation of functions, powers and duties among the various agencies and offices of governments, and define the relationships between these and the public."[32] They are "power maps" that outline the "territorial distribution of power within the nation-state".[33] Their role is, consequently, of insurmountable importance in democratic polities, where the institutions of the state perform clearly defined functions and are subject to close scrutiny by each other and by society. "Constitutionality" has thus become an inalienable feature of almost all democracies, even for those, like Britain and Israel, which do not have clearly spelled-out, written constitutions.

But not all constitutions are democratic. Some outline political systems that are blatantly non-democratic, while others are in reality "fictive" and merely give the illusion of democracy.[34] For a constitution to be democratic, it needs to guarantee equality to all citizens before the law and in their access to means of political control. A democracy, in other words, "cannot allow a constitutional distinction between citizens and subjects, or between first- and second-class citizens".[35] Moreover, democratic constitutions identify factors that will enable society to interact freely with and in turn influence the state. This is ensured through such constitutional provisions as the rights of assembly, the free expression of political views, *habeas corpus*, and protection against unwarranted state actions.[36]

No matter how comprehensive or grandiose in their enumeration of civil and political liberties they may be, constitutions are meaningless if they are not reinforced by supportive social and cultural milieus. Throughout the 1960s and 1970s, for example, liberal democratic constitutions were found in almost every Latin American country. Few, however, ever gained much social and cultural resonance while the region's bureaucratic-authoritarian regimes remained in power.[37] There needs to be a widespread societal consensus, as well as a meaningful and deep political commitment, towards the desirability of the core principles of a democratic constitution for it to become a meaningful political frame of reference. For democratic constitutions, remaining viable necessitates nothing less than an "effective majority agreement on the great issues".[38]

New Democracies

Inherent in democratic states, as the above discussion shows, are a number of features which automatically enhance the strength and durability of these as compared to other state types. Democratic polities are comprised of pervasive and far-reaching institutional links arising from both the society and the state, which foster among them a routinely harmonious and stable pattern of interaction. In turn, popular legitimacy is fostered and democratic institutions and practices become increasingly acceptable to the various strata of society. Particularly in the industrially advanced nations of the First World, the economic successes of democratic states only accentuate their incomparable levels of popular legitimacy and social acceptance. Moreover, the very self-regulating and restraining mechanisms, which so greatly limit the scope of actions and powers of democratic states, help endow them with a rather self-perpetuating character. State leaders and actors may change frequently, but despite the political demise of leaders, and, indeed, precisely because of the regular nature of such events, the democratic state remains remarkably stable.

The challenge of survival

Not all existing democratic states are so uniformly stable. Neither, for that matter, have all democratic experiences in the past been unqualified successes.[39] In particular, the newer democratic states that have begun appearing around the globe since the end of the 1980s find themselves confronted with a series of debilitating and at times seemingly insurmountable obstacles that threaten their very foundations. Democratic states have not only proliferated throughout Southern Europe, Latin America, and now Eastern and Central Europe, but also begun, albeit timidly, to appear in parts of Asia, Africa, and the Middle East. Some of the more successful and notable examples of recent democratic states include Argentina, Brazil, Colombia, and Chile in Latin America; South Africa and Senegal in Africa; India and Sri Lanka in South Asia; Turkey in the Middle East; and the Baltic republics, Bulgaria, Hungary, and Poland in Central and Eastern Europe.[40]

Despite this unprecedented proliferation, however, these relatively recent democratic states face a host of difficulties in their quest for political viability and survival. These obstacles are numerous and varied, and can differ greatly depending on the particular state in question. It is, nonetheless, possible to discern certain broad factors which, to one degree or another, can pose potential threats to the emerging wave of democratic states. They include, among others, democratically uncommitted and uncompromising actors within the state, the fragility of systemic means of support for democratic practices and institutions (including, in some instances, corporatist ones), and lack of supportive political cultures and other society-wide facilitators to democracy. The fledgling democracies of Nigeria, Pakistan, and Peru fell to coups by the military and the president respectively, and, particularly in the years following their initial establishment, the democratic systems of Argentina and the Philippines—especially during President Aquino's term—faced constant threats from elements within the armed forces.

Social structures and cultural values are of paramount importance in lending support and acceptability, not just to democratic states but indeed to all types of political arrangements that involve continuous interaction between state and society. As earlier discussed, democracy involves a measure of fusion and synchronization between state and society. This necessitates a widespread, if not necessarily uniform, commitment by most or all social strata to democratic institutions and practices. Society must not only support a democratic state but, more importantly, give it overwhelming support. Many of the newer democratic states, however, preside over societies the characteristics of which make the generation of such support extremely difficult or at best tenuous. This is not to imply that there are always democratic elites who try to lead undemocratic masses by the nose. Politicians may become democratic only when it suits their needs, as some of the examples of communists-cum-democrats in Eastern Europe have shown us. By the same token, traditions of consensus and tolerance can be found in many pre-industrial societies, even if the gap between village democracy and pluralism at the level of the nation-state may prove difficult to bridge. There are, nevertheless, certain social and cultural features that can hamper the viability of democratic states.

Perhaps most crucial is the absence of a political culture and social values that are supportive of democracy. Political culture is comprised of the totality of popular attitudes and perceptions towards the body politic. Since the newer democratic states are *new*, and preside over societies that do not have experience with this particular brand of polity, their normative support base is not as fully developed and reliable, at least initially, as they may need it to be. Democracy requires the active participation, commitment, and consensus of those in society. Especially in nations where democratic experiences have been historical rarities, such essential factors may not be readily available and may have to be cultivated over time and through deliberate social engineering (in the same way as they were in Japan, for example). It is this reason—the absence of a widely held belief in democratic values—that often leads to the obsolescence of the thoroughly democratic provisions of newly devised constitutions. Widespread inequality and wildly unequal access to resources can also further polarize differences in political culture and, therefore, jeopardize a budding democratic state. Lastly, an emerging democratic state needs to have the determined support of a corresponding civil society that is pluralistic, autonomous, and vigorously organized.[41] A number of the new democracies, especially those in Eastern Europe, are supported by zealously democratic civil societies. Yet most of the societies in which democratic states have recently appeared, at least in Africa and parts of Asia, happen to be torn by extreme and at times violent factionalism and inter-ethnic or other forms of animosity.

Apart from social dynamics, there are a number of political variables that can also derail or at least drastically reduce the viability of democratic states. As in all other types of state, the role played by executives is one of critical importance in the conduct and the overall health of new democratic states. But in their particular case, the centrality of the leadership is even further magnified. Whereas a society needs to have a general consensus concerning the desirability of a democratic polity, the resolve and commitment of leaders to maintain that democracy must be absolutely unshakeable. Since, in these states, democratic principles and institutions are particularly fragile and have few or no historical precedents, the agendas and actions of executives are even more directly linked to maintaining the viability of the whole polity. The responsibilities of leaders are far more onerous in new democracies than in those in the First World, where systemic and routinized democratic procedures make undemocratic deviations far more difficult and unlikely. Leaders in the new democracies, however, need constantly to remind themselves of the need to reject temptations to resort to undemocratic means, to be willing to turn to non-partisan sources of legitimacy, to accept coalitions with disloyal opposition if necessary, and to refrain from abusing the coercive resources of the state in order to keep themselves in power. They must, additionally, be skilful enough not to subject the state to unnecessary crises that it may not be able to withstand because of its relative youth.[42]

Reorienting political priorities by making them democratic is also crucial. But it involves more than just obedience to democratic norms. While the state must reformulate its goals and guard against excessive centralization, it can ill afford to become too weak and therefore unable to deliver the social, political, and economic goods that members of society expect of it.[43] Poor performance on various fronts, in fact, is a frequent catalyst for the collapse, not just of democratic states but indeed of most others as well. Leaders in new democracies face an added dilemma. Their eagerness to maximize their legitimacy prompts many to place most of society's unsolved problems on their agenda simultaneously. In the process, however, not only do they find their initiatives subject to an array of previously non-existent democratic checks and balances, but, more importantly, they also increase the number of people for whom such reforms can have potentially negative consequences.[44]

The difficulties and obstacles that the newer democratic states face are numerous and varied in nature. Their success and continued viability is thus by no means a foregone conclusion. Some of these obstacles are similar to those that First World states faced in the earlier stages of their political development, though this is not to suggest that the successful evolution of democratic states in the First World is certain to be replicated elsewhere. Nevertheless, there do exist certain factors which can potentially help sustain the emerging democracies. A number of far-reaching and fundamental social and cultural phenomena have so far combined to underwrite the viability and resilience of the new democracies. To begin with, almost all of the new democratic states came into power after the humiliating and ruinous failure of other, non-democratic, alternatives. In their various ways, the military juntas in Latin America left as many scars as did the communist regimes on Eastern Europe. There is, in these two regions at least, a compelling imperative on both state and social actors to make democracy work and to help it endure and thrive. International and economic factors are also of critical importance. The international state system that has emerged since the end of the Cold War is one in which democratic states find supportive dynamics. The economic predicaments of Latin American and Eastern and Central European states, and their dependence on economic aid from First World democracies, also serve as strong incentives for remaining democratic. For Europe's new democracies, the desire for greater integration with their more affluent and stable neighbors to the west provides added motivation.

Pseudo-Democracies

A number of Third World polities, both old and new, have embraced the principles of political democracy and, on the surface at least, are endowed with all the features and institutions which make up democracies. Nevertheless, despite all the political trappings of democracy, the essence of this particular form of polity does not penetrate throughout society. The political establishment remains essentially detached and isolated from social currents and nuances, operating by its own rules and largely managing to avoid extensive and meaningful contact with the masses or popular classes. At best, the democratic state skims no more than the tip of the societal iceberg, including with itself sociocultural and economic elites but not much more. These are Third World political systems that are democratic in appearance but not in substance, in institutions but not in spirit. These are, awkwardly put, pseudo-democracies.

What distinguishes pseudo-democracies from First World or other viable democracies is not their relative youth or their geographic concentration in one particular region. Among them are polities that are both old and young and they are found throughout the Third World.[45] The distinguishing characteristic is the absence of civil society, which is key to the birth and the continued existence of viable democracies. Its absence in pseudo-democratic polities makes the practice of politics for the most part socially vacuous and meaningless. As a social and political phenomenon, civil society entails the political self-organization of society, a largely spontaneous and haphazardly orchestrated move on the part of the populace to bring about and sustain a political system which is at once both democratic and based on the collective desires of the populace. In a polity in which civil society pervades, therefore, not only is there a determined effort on the part of society to maintain the democratic political order but also there are a number of supporting social and cultural phenomena which keep democracy intact and meaningful. The political culture is democratic, and the society as a whole has a vested interest in protecting the democratic essence of the system. None of these support mechanisms exist in a pseudo-democracy, however, and the distance between state and society is wide enough to allow the state to operate without close and intimate attention to the society.

The empty democracy

Pseudo-democracies do, nevertheless, have all the window-dressings of democracy, the most notable of which are constitutional governments, political parties, and regular elections. These are not by any means dictatorial regimes and their political arenas do, in fact, involve a genuine measure of democratic give and take. However, an unmitigated elitism permeates the system. As in Taiwan, India, Turkey, and Kenya (as well as Japan), in a number of pseudo-democracies the pivotal political forum for state-society interaction is often in the form of a single, dominant political party, one within which political contests revolve around personalities rather than principles, factional quarrels rather than policy differences. Even in polities in which there are a number of political parties vying for greater popular support, as in the Caribbean and in some Central American countries, their purview does not quite reach beyond the ranks of the social and economic elites.

Political parties may be voted in and out of office, but to the larger population they hardly mean much more than their acronyms and their colorful banners and symbols; presidential or parliamentary candidates frequently take turns in getting elected to office. Even if the voting is not rigged and is free of manipulation or fear and intimidation, the citizen casting a vote is unlikely to be aware of the issues for which his or her candidate stands, and these will most likely not be too different from those supported by other candidates. Voting becomes perfunctory and devoid of substantive meaning, as do most other rituals associated with the practice of democracy: marches and rallies, canvassing, waving banners, etc. Once the hype is over, democracy is largely forgotten about until the next election. Society ceases to have any meaningful impact upon the workings and the conduct of the state. Democracy is forgotten, not because the new guardians of the state are necessarily opposed to it (which they may indeed be) but because of the pressing nature of all the other concerns which society faces. Unemployment and declining living standards, crime and other societal conflicts all soon divert popular attention from the field of democratic politics, which to most looks remote and beyond reach.

Besides an inherent democratic elitism that bestows on the system a semblance of democracy, pseudo-democratic polities embody a number of other characteristics which set them apart from praetorian regimes. In stable praetorian polities, the absence of institutional means of participation in state affairs enhances the possibility of sudden eruptions of built-in political tensions from below. The state may be strong, but the broader foundations upon which it relies are at best tenuous and dependent on the unimpeded maintenance of coercive relations with society. Given the appropriate social and political conditions, such as unity and resolve among various social classes and the weakness and vulnerability of the state, revolutionary uprisings and other mass-based revolts are endemic possibilities with which praetorian regimes must contend.[46] Pseudo-democracies, however, are for the most part immune from the possibility of revolution and violent overthrow, for they not only enjoy a greater degree of societal legitimacy but, more importantly, provide safety valves for political aspirations through elections and other democratic rites. It is, in fact, not the state which has the potential of being considered illegitimate but rather those political aspirants and groups that seek to employ extra-institutional means in order to attain political objectives. Everyone may be aware of the elitism of the state and the corruption which often permeates its many echelons, but few would go so far as to endorse guerrilla warfare against the state. The polity as a whole and the state in particular rest on a cushion of popular consensus and legitimacy. In pseudo-democracies, democracy may not have much of a political meaning for society but it does, nevertheless, have deep emotional resonance among the populace.

Pseudo-democracies may be immune from revolutionary overthrow, but they are inherently susceptible to ideological and other populist movements. By definition, a pseudo-democracy, while embodying such institutional mechanisms of democracy as elections and legislatures, tends to lack meaningful legitimacy among the citizenry. The system may be democratic in name but it remains elitist in nature. Within this type of set-up, it is perfectly feasible for an individual or a political party with a populist platform to come to the political fore by mobilizing a vast pool of the electorate that had hitherto been largely ignored or taken for granted. Hitler's rise through the Weimar Republic beginning in 1933 and Juan Peron's election to the Argentine presidency in 1946 offer two extreme examples of populist movements arising within pseudo-democratic systems. In most existing pseudo-democratic polities, the political elite exercises enough control and discretion to prevent the unchecked ascent of populist elements from within its own ranks or from the outside. Nevertheless, there is always the possibility of such a development, especially at times when the ostensibly democratic system fails to live up to its political and/or economic promises. In all the pseudo-democratic political systems found around the world today—from Africa (Botswana, Kenya, and Tanzania) and Asia (Sri Lanka, India, and Bangladesh) to Latin America (Nicaragua, Honduras, Costa Rica, and the Caribbean)—the difficult realities of political and economic life make the rise of institutionally based populist movements a real possibility. All that is needed is for a demagogic politician, armed with a popular ideology, to step into the political arena and address the politically alienated and economically depressed masses.

Conclusion

Recent global transformations have necessitated the use of a new classification of the international state system, one based not on economic accomplishments or ideological blueprints but rather on the nature and type of relationships between state and society. Within this new framework, this chapter has examined the various types of democratic state, some of which have far greater socio-cultural and historical resonance than the others do, some that are relatively recent creations, and a few that are far more democratic in name and appearance than in substance and spirit. Democracies are not all of the same ilk. It would be stretching the limits of analysis beyond any degree of reasonableness to lump together such varied and yet "democratic" states as, for example, Germany, the Dominican Republic, and Argentina, in which the democratic states are sustained by quite different systemic, historical, political, and sociocultural dynamics. To conceptualize such differences among democratic states more satisfactorily, this chapter has proposed dividing them into viable, new, and pseudo-democratic varieties, the crucial distinguishing factor between them being the nature and intricacies of their relationship with their respective societies.

At the crux of every democracy, regardless of the national character of the state in which it may appear, is a routine, regularized, and unadulterated process of political input from social actors into the state. There are, however, significant differences in the imperatives that compel social actors to ensure the maintenance of the system through their political inputs, in the composition and agendas of the politically active social strata, and in the degree of social resonance that the democratic state has within society.

The trichotomous division of democracies into First World, newly established, and "pseudo-" varieties is not the only method of distinguishing between the different forms of democratic regime. Democracies have frequently been divided into presidential and parliamentary, representative and direct, and consociational and consensus varieties.[47] Some scholars have also differentiated between "elite-" and "mass-dominated" forms of democratic rule in the Third World.[48] Each of these forms of classification sheds significant light on the intricate dynamics that characterize the different varieties of democratic regime. The classification devised here, however, attempts to go one step further by examining the "social basis of democracy", to borrow a phrase from Barrington Moore.[49] The social and cultural imperatives that cause state and society to establish links and connections with each other are of great significance. In fact, the social and cultural basis of the state-society nexus supersedes in importance such other political factors as elite consensus, political institutions, or the precise forms that citizen participation may take. Each of these factors is quite important in its own right, but even more significant are the underlying reasons why citizens decide to make an input into the democratic system. It is here that the crucial, society-based differences between viable democracies and pseudo-democracies come to light.

Not all states foster or are part of a coercion-free, consensual relationship with their societies. Whereas all democratic states, regardless of their subtle defining characteristics, are based on some sort of routinized electoral arrangement with their societies, there are a number of states that view almost all types of societal input into the political process as potential threats to their survival. These are states that are in one way or another non-democratic, and, as in populist instances, may at best temporarily manipulate society into believing that it is operating within a democratic environment. Nevertheless, even such inclusionary regimes are reliant on popular manipulation and coercion rather than genuine consensus and acceptance. These non-democratic types of state are the focus of chapter 7.

7 Non-democratic states

The fact that democracy seems to have appeared in historical "waves", not all of which have lasted,[1] is compelling testimony that democratic regimes are neither natural nor sustainable through purely political means alone. Most political systems, in fact, at least up until relatively recently, have been more prone to centralizing power and trying to rule over society than to fostering a routine process of political give-and-take. That democracy as a political system is considered normatively "better" than others does not necessarily result in its appearance and endurance around the globe. In its most basic form, in fact, politics has often been defined as a contest over power.[2] In a significant number of countries, this contest over power is far more likely to be praetorian, brutal, and even violent than consensual and democratic. Even if such extremes as brutality and violence do not mark the state's relationship with society, a majority of political systems continue to be marked less by democratic premises and more by state attempts to either manipulate or repress society's political yearnings.

This chapter focuses on the two predominant types of non-democratic state that continue to exist in a number of countries, namely, inclusionary populist and bureaucratic-authoritarian ones, and examines the different institutions through which they govern and the patterns of relations they tend to establish with their societies. Neither variety, the chapter will conclude, can indefinitely sustain itself in power—as democracies can—as their bases of power frequently tend to be weak and their legitimacy fragile.

Inclusionary Populist Regimes

Closely resembling democratic states but not quite democratic are those states that aim specifically to foster populist and inclusionary policies. In fact, populist regimes contain several characteristics that draw them far closer to authoritarian and indeed totalitarian regimes than to democratic ones. Due to their structural set-up and the specific ways in which their institutions maintain themselves, populist regimes endow society with an illusion, or at best an overly exaggerated perception of, democratic participation. These are states the continued existence of which calls for an *inclusion* of the "masses" into the political process. They espouse populist policies and claim, often in vitriolic rhetoric, to lead on behalf not just of "the people" but indeed of the downtrodden and the disinherited, the "shirtless ones", as Juan Peron called them. This catering to the masses is not necessarily democratic but is often manipulative, attained not by free choice but instead by a careful forging of circumstances in which participants are used as tools for particular political ends.

Despite the inclusionary state's banners and dogmas, "the masses" are an end in themselves. As in authoritarian dictatorships, populist states often set specific and frequently intractable agendas for their society. Unlike authoritarian states, however, populist regimes seek to implement and to further their agendas not through sheer coercion but rather through cultivating mass-based support from within society. To do so, they develop highly penetrative infrastructures and institutions that allow them access to the various layers of society, and this, combined with the rigid dogmas which most embark on, means that they tend to adopt increasingly totalitarian policies. The distinction between inclusionary populist and totalitarian regimes, therefore, is often a matter of degree rather than being based on the nature of their institutions and functions. That is why the term "regime", which conveys a certain measure of totality, more appropriately describes these types of states.

It is almost exclusively in the developing world that inclusionary populist regimes and authoritarian dictatorships crop up. They are invariably in relatively young states, and thus need to be examined within the context of such processes as political development and institutionalization. Their relative youth and lack of institutional history makes them comparatively weak, particularly when they seek to govern older, fractious, and consequently stronger societies. When democratic and consensual interactions between state and society do not exist, the state, which has a monopoly over such means of coercion and manipulation as the armed forces and the media, is likely to opt for one of two courses of action: either it can force society into submissive compliance through force, or it may try to persuade (and manipulate) some if not most of the social classes into complying with its goals and agendas.

Both the submissive compliance and the manipulated mobilization of society require the existence of state institutions that are viable, solid, and penetrative. The quest to develop and to put into operation a variety of institutions—be they old or new, pre-existing or newly concocted—thus becomes a central part of the political process in both populist and authoritarian regimes. Where populist, inclusionary regimes in particular are concerned, the significance of state institutions often seems to be overshadowed by the more dramatic effects of mass participation. It often appears as if it is not the various institutions of the state that are actually in control but, rather, that real influence lies with seemingly spontaneous masses and their charismatic leaders. In fact, the most crucial factor in sustaining a populist regime, especially in its most ideal type, is not the degree to which its institutions remain viable but instead something that is quite amorphous and intangible: the strength of its leader's charisma. Reinforcing this are the particular political and social conditions that prevail in most parts of the Third World which, to varying degrees, encourage the rise of charismatically based polities.[3]

Politics of inclusion

In populist inclusionary regimes, the masses find themselves immersed in the beliefs and the mission of their leader, believing, however misguidedly, in his promises and rhetoric. "The Cause", the passion of the masses, becomes all-subsuming. The personality of the leader and prevailing social and cultural forces play especially pivotal roles in the emergence of charismatic rule.[4] Charismatic leadership requires three elements: a devoted mass of followers; a leader able to fulfill a charismatic role; and conditions conducive to a leader-devotee relationship. The charismatic leader constructs a new political universe in which he himself stands in the middle, surrounded and supported by the masses. He destroys the old order and builds a new one.[5] He becomes the object of much devotion, and the masses find solace in the ideals of the movement he comes to personify.[6] His message is simple, his plans bold, and his mission popular. He speaks the language of the average citizen and does so plainly and directly.[7] He understands the shared anxieties of the people and their feelings of personal inadequacy which arise from social and cultural turmoil.[8] But not only does he understand them, he in fact alleviates such miseries through political inclusion. Collective political participation assumes soul-saving functions, few participants realizing that they are, as one observer has commented, "little more than a cheap means to achieve political acquiescence".[9]

Specific social and cultural factors are also necessary for the success of inclusionary political phenomena. Charismatic political leadership tends to appear in the context of undemocratic and unevolved political institutions, during times of extraordinary transition and social disquiet, and in cultures in which the concept of a cult of personality is not generally viewed with suspicion. During times of uncertainty and social and cultural unease, people are drawn to those who stand firmly and who claim to have all of the needed remedies. The charismatic leader becomes the most important symbol of unity, long-lost self-assertion, and consensus on national objectives. "For those confused by changing values, he is the link between the old and sanctions the new."[10] Hero-worshipping becomes the political order of the day, embodying an ironic appearance of democracy which, once its façade is removed, is anti-democratic to the core.[11] People follow their hero, to whom they may even ascribe mythical qualities, not merely because of his promises of national salvation but, when in power, because he includes them in the political process. Just as they rush to adore him, he empowers them by opening the previously closed doors of the body politic.

Having previously been brutally excluded from the exercise of politics, people in inclusionary systems find themselves an integral part of the political process, and in turn bestow unmitigated legitimacy on their leader, together with their adoration. Symbolism becomes all-important. Goals must be constantly striven for, be they actual or contrived. Success in achieving these goals means bringing to an end the conditions that originally gave rise to charismatic rule and, as a result, an end to the charismatically based state itself. "Charismatic movements", in the words of one observer, "must founder in the face of success. When the crisis has passed, for whatever reason, the followers regain their sense of control, their sense of personal efficacy, and the leader recedes into the psychic shadow."[12]

What happens to the populist state then depends on the force of existing circumstances. Some conjure up perpetual crises, even going so far as to wage or to prolong wars in order to keep public fervor at a high pitch for as long as possible. Iran's bloody war with Iraq lasted for eight years; Cuba's war of words with the United States, like those of most other post-revolutionary states, shows few signs of letting up.[13] Other states, as Weber theorized, may turn instead to increasingly bureaucratic mechanisms to continue supporting themselves and may eventually lose their populist and inclusionary garb.[14] Still others, it is hypothetically possible, may see one charismatic leader replaced by another, although that would depend on an unlikely ability to maintain high levels of mass devotion over long periods of time.

Charismatic leadership, and along with it inclusionary states, are, nevertheless, at best only impermanent means of political control. They inevitably give way to routinized and more institutionalized forms of politics. While in power, however, inclusionary populist regimes thrive on the incorporation of politically significant social strata into the political process. One or more segments of society, often those who were particularly disenfranchised before the populist regime came into power, are especially targeted for mobilization. They become, in essence, the most "included" segment of the politically active, the "foot-soldiers" of the inclusionary state. However, despite appearances, this concerted and unbridled flow of mass input into the political process is not always spontaneous and uncoordinated nor, in fact, is it always voluntary and purely out of devotion. The populist state may, initially, not have a very highly evolved degree of institutionalization, but, from the start, it has very clearly defined and pointed agendas. As a result, it cannot afford but to micro-manage politics. Its lofty ambitions include closing the once enormous state-society gap, fostering a new political culture, and, consequently, creating a "new man". Politics becomes a form of religion:

> New political forms are developed that have the effect of providing for the continuity, meaning, and purpose of an individual's action. The result is a doctrine that is in effect a political religion ... The effects of political religion are such that they strengthen authority in the state and

weaken the flexibility of society. Hence it becomes difficult to change from autocratic to more democratic or secular patterns of political organization and social belief.[15]

Within this context, even collective behavior, seemingly spontaneous, becomes part of a carefully staged program of mass political inclusion. The regime cannot fully trust the unpredictable impulse of the masses, nor can it resist the temptation to impose subtle yet tight controls over their actions. Through the official party or through neighborhood committees, the state orchestrates—or perhaps as its leaders would like to see it, "channels"— mass-based displays of support for the political establishment. As one observer has noted, Cuba's post-revolutionary, inclusionary regime engages in precisely this type of machination of collective behavior:

> What may appear to the untrained eye as an immense sea of anon-ymous faces of persons temporarily detached from their customary social relations to participate in the jurnadas of the revolutionary calendar is instead a publicly acknowledged, carefully rehearsed, and studied choreographic exercise of groups who are firmly attached to existing institutions and occupy specified and lasting niches.[16]

In instances where populist regimes do receive spontaneous and unsolicited public affection, it is difficult to assess how much of it is genuine and how much a product of fear of abstaining from political participation. Clearly, populist regimes, by virtue of opening previously shut political doors and including the masses within the regime, do cultivate a considerable measure of sincere support and inspire countless loyal followers. No one can deny that such groups as the Hitler Youth in Nazi Germany, the "shirtless ones" *(descamisados)* in Peronist Argentina, the Youth Pioneers in Kwame Nkrumah's Ghana, and the "disinherited" *(mostazafan)* followers of Khomeini in Iran genuinely believed in their leaders and in the political constellation that they had created for them. But there are those who fear the possibility of negative sanctions if they refuse to become a party to the state's charades.

If not necessarily fearing outright imprisonment or dismissal from their job, everyone is at least mindful of the need not to cross the regime's many red lines. This is, admittedly, much more of a factor in totalitarian than in populist states, the former being far more coercive than the latter. Never-theless, there is always a possibility that opportunism may be at least a marginal motivating factor. Even the most egalitarian of regimes, of which post-revolutionary states are prime examples, reward their active supporters more positively than they do the rest of society. Some observers have even gone so far as to argue that "loyalty may be hypocritically simulated by indi-viduals or by whole groups on purely opportunistic grounds, or carried out in practice for reasons of self-interest. Or people may submit from individual weakness and helplessness because there is no acceptable alternative."[17]

Another element in perpetuating mass participation in populist regimes is the factor of imitation. Especially in a politically charged environment, where most members of society either are or pretend to be adherents to the day's "political religion", there are considerable psychological pressures to adopt the political values of the masses. Standing out as a non-participant among a sea of believers may be both materially unwise and psychologically troubling. As Eric Hoffer, a pioneer in the study of mass psychology, has written:

> The one-mindedness ... prized by every mass movement [is] achieved as much by imitation as by obedience. Obedience itself consists as much in the imitation of an example and in the following of precept.[18]

Organs of mobilization

Clearly, the mobilization of the masses, even with minimal interference from the state, necessitates the existence of an impressive array of organizational apparatuses and various institutions. It is true that in instances of charismatic rule, especially early in the life of a pluralist polity, much of the linkage between state and society is in the form of unspoken, emotional bonds that cannot be measured or quantified. But sooner or later such intangible bonds need to be made tangible and must be given institutional and organizational resonance. Devotion and loyalty may be essential to sustaining a political regime, but they are not sufficient. The inherent instability of a crowd only accentuates the need for a "guiding" force, a "vanguard" that can provide organizational cohesion to seemingly spontaneous manifestations of popular support for the state. Legislatures exist, and they do provide highly significant forums for grand oratory and the release of populist energies. But they do not in themselves generate and guide mass-based political enthusiasm. The bureaucracy does not suffice either, for it is a means of administration and not necessarily of mobilization. It has no overriding ideological agendas, at least ostensibly, and is designed for functions other than giving direction to mass movements. A more cohesive force is needed, one which can establish both ideological and institutional hegemony over the loyal masses and, in turn, help perpetuate the longevity of the state. Hence state-sponsored political parties are born.

It is in these regimes that political parties form an integral part of the governing apparatuses of the state. The reader must have noticed a conspicuous absence of any discussion of political parties in the examination of democratic states in chapter 6. The reason should be now obvious: in democracies, political parties arise from and are institutional manifestations of social (rather than state) phenomena. It is in non-democratic states that parties, if they exist at all, are part of the state. If not openly established and sponsored by those running the state, parties in non-democracies in one way or another still remain creatures of the political establishment. They are tools designed to further facilitate political control over society. But in democracies, their functions, nature, and, ultimately, direction are reversed; democratic parties are a means of access from society to state rather than representing the latter's control of the former. Parties are institutions that not only *express*, but also *channel*.[19] Of course, they perform both of these functions in *all* states. What differs is for whom they express—state or society?—and what they channel—societal energies or state directives?

The establishment of institutional networks by populist regimes is not as easy and uncomplicated as may at first appear. Contextually, inclusionary populism is antithetical to institutional organization. The masses will not always be as easily swayed to join a party, and to become active when they do join, as when they first became believers in the promises of the regime. To begin with, turning haphazard activism into organized mobilization is problematic at best. Moreover, as the goals of the populist state (and with it those of the charismatic leader) become altered or more realistic with changing circumstances, the initially enormous mass of followers can dwindle in numbers.[20] The social consensus regarding the state becomes increasingly narrow, though still sizable. Even if few in numbers, however, those who do remain loyal are die-hards and supply the regime with a vocal and active base of support. Their institutional forum is the official party; their ideology that of the government. The state-sponsored party serves four significant yet entwined functions: political institutionalization, legitimization, recruitment of state officials and future leaders, and the mobilization of popular support. In one way or another, these are all functions that the state initiates for its own benefit and that are aimed at society. Moreover, designed as all-encompassing institutions, most state parties in populist regimes are organized along rigidly hierarchical lines akin to the "democratic centralism" of communist parties.[21] This centrifugal characteristic is also meant to expedite a fusion of the state to societies that are torn by parochial ethnic and cultural tendencies.[22]

Totalitarian regimes

Finally, a word needs to be said about totalitarian regimes, which, as earlier maintained, represent the more extreme forms of inclusionary populist states. The basic underpinnings of the two state types remain the same. Both rely on the incorporation of broad strata of society into the political process in order to sustain themselves; both espouse dogmatic ideologies that promise to right the wrongs of the past; both embody a rigidly organized, state-directed political party; both are often headed by leaders who either are charismatic or aspire to cultivate charisma; and both try to maintain a siege mentality, a perceived state of crisis, through which they justify their rhetoric and their policies.[23] What varies between them is their intensity, and, consequently, their ensuing coercive nature. Totalitarian regimes are far more brutal and zealous in their pursuits than populist inclusionary regimes can ever afford or aspire to be. Significantly, totalitarian regimes strive to reshape the very fundamentals of life in their societies through massive dislocations of life, culture, property, and economy. They even seek to control the citizens' thought processes. The totality of life under the auspices of the state's ideology becomes so overwhelming that the average person loses his or her individual identity. The "mass man", as Hannah Arendt poignantly reminds us, is stricken by homelessness and rootlessness.[24] The crucial difference lies in the extent to which privacy is allowed by the government. Whereas inclusionary regimes seek to include and to infuse society within the political process, totalitarian regimes aim at nothing less than society's complete obliteration and total reconstruction anew. Totalitarianism's ideological agenda is, as a result, far more a crusade than anything else.

A summary list of some of the two state types exemplifies their differences. The more notable totalitarian regimes that have appeared within the past few decades include, among others, Nazi Germany, fascist Italy, Stalinist Russia, Maoist China, and, possibly, Khomeini's Iran. Populist states have tended to be decidedly less belligerent in their domestic, diplomatic, and ideological pursuits. They are also far more prevalent than totalitarian states. Most post-revolutionary states belong in this category, as do some of the more populist-oriented ones that have come about as a result of military coups. Most Middle Eastern states with successful coups in the recent past (Iraq, Syria, and Libya), much of post-independence Africa in the 1960s and the early 1970s, and a few isolated states in Latin America in the 1950s and the 1960s (Peronist Argentina, Cuba, and to a lesser extent Chile) can all be classified as inclusionary populist regimes. In these states there is a "mass man", but his individuality is not quite stolen, his identity reaffirmed, not overwhelmed and stripped.

Bureaucratic-Authoritarian Dictatorships

Democratic, populist, and totalitarian states all in some way closely interact with societies over which they rule, albeit in radically different ways. By various means, even if through blatant manipulation, these states aim to foster bonds of affinity and emotional identity with their respective societies. The functions, structural make-up, and institutions of bureaucratic-authoritarian states, in contrast, are specifically designed to regulate interactions between state and society and those within society itself. The relationship between these states and their society is completely different from those discussed previously.

All bureaucratic-authoritarian states, for one reason or another, assume an extremely hostile posture vis-à-vis their societies. Not only does the state not strive for mass incorporation and inclusion, it rarely hesitates to resort to coercive means in order to compensate for its depleted legitimacy within society. The polity can be best described as an "exclusionary" one. Society's inclusion in and identification with the state is replaced here with a violently enforced, highly authoritarian, exclusion from the exercise of all political functions. The state strives to create "a new situation of depoliticization, inertia, and atomization".[25]

Except for those few dictatorial states the policies of which are still being guided by the promises of communism, idealistic ideologies traditionally have not been a defining factor in the political configuration of bureaucratic-authoritarian states. Instead, the focus of these regimes frequently lies with the present and the immediate future, placing great emphasis on the prevention of impending crises, on national defense, and on economic advancement. This is not to suggest that dictatorial regimes are completely non-ideological; on the contrary, some espouse extremely dogmatic and Utopian doctrines with which they seek to enhance their popular legitimacy. Important as it may be, however, the state's creation of ideological strongholds within society takes a back seat to its economic performance. The viability and resilience of bureaucratic-authoritarian states depend not on the appeal of their dogmas but on their ability to deliver the goods and services that help keep society sufficiently politically complacent or obedient.

Political underdevelopment

Like totalitarian and populist regimes, exclusionary dictatorships need to be analyzed within the broader context of political development and of attempts by unevolved state structures to attain institutionalization. There is, in fact, a direct correlation between levels of political development, or lack thereof, and the degree to which a state freely interacts with society. Yet, equally important is the growth of state power and, specifically, an increased capacity by the state to develop and expand its sources of mutual access to society. A politically developed state is a strong state, but it is not necessarily a coercive one.[26] Despite their dictatorial nature, and in fact because of it, bureaucratic-authoritarian regimes tend not to be highly politically developed. They thus remain inherently weak and unstable.

Fraught with institutional "decay" and brittle structures, such states are frequent victims of forces that they themselves engender. Military coups and palace revolutions have long been endemic features of politically under-developed, dictatorial states.[27] The lack of political efficacy and the underlying instability of politically underdeveloped states is compounded and reinforced, and often caused, by extensive social divisions and cultural anomie. In essence, lack of political development is principally a product of a state that remains weak in comparison to society.[28] The state's desperate search for stability and for greater institutionalization prompts it to adopt and to rely on institutions that can maximize its survival and minimize potential threats from both the domestic (society) and the international environments. Military establishments and state-sponsored parties are two of the institutions most frequently used for this purpose and have, as a result, come to symbolize authoritarian dictatorships. Internally, meanwhile, these states are characterized by what one scholar has called the "politics of survival".[29] Frequent personnel changes, appointments and promotions based on loyalty as opposed to merits, and the utilization of a variety of "dirty tricks" predominate the internal workings of bureaucratic-authoritarian dictatorships, be they based on military *juntas* or civilian-controlled parties.[30]

The military

Military-based dictatorships were less prevalent in the 1990s than before, although only a few years earlier they appeared to be permanent political fixtures in Africa, Latin America, and the Middle East. The initial assumption of political power by the military establishment and the subsequent inauguration of an authoritarian state are dependent on a variety of factors, ranging from the nature of the military establishment itself to prevailing economic, political, and cultural circumstances. Broadly, there are three patterns of military involvement in politics. Some military establishments refrain from active participation in the political process but retain the right to exercise "veto power", either through overt means or behind the scenes. Such establishments play essentially the role of moderator in the government, influencing, particular, its policies and agendas.[31] The Turkish military, for example, politically intervened in 1980 in order to revamp the country's government machinery and to redistribute political power.[32] Other military establishments assume the guardianship of the political system, viewing their intervention as temporarily necessary in order to remove corrupt and unfit politicians and to reverse their misguided policies.[33] Such military regimes as inundated Latin America throughout the 1960s and 1970s were of this variety, driven by a belief that only they could rectify the numerous political and economic crises that beset the region. Lastly, there are those armed forces which view themselves as the rightful and natural inheritors of political power, using their tenure in office not only to ensure their political permanence but also to fundamentally change the fabric of the country over which they rule.[34] This has been the purpose of the Middle East's many military-based regimes, long in power in Sudan, Egypt, Libya, Syria, and Iraq.

But even if military establishments have a determined desire to intervene and, in effect, to subsume the political process, however temporarily, they cannot do so without the widespread existence of particular social and political conditions. For a military *coup d'état* to succeed, both the state and society need to have become highly fragmented, weak, dysfunctional, and vulnerable to outside penetration. The paralysis of civilian institutions, of course, is a powerful motivating factor.[35]

Within the context of unevolved and weak states, internal squabbles, con-stitutional impasses, and power vacuums following leadership successions can all have potentially serious consequences for the political process and can expose it to the threat of military takeover. Equally significant are pre-vailing social and economic anomalies. Military dictatorships are particu-larly likely to appear in countries threatened by sharp ethnic and regional cleavages that, if unchecked, could threaten national unity.[36] Under these conditions, the military is often prompted to intervene out of a sense of duty to the "motherland", because of its professional organization and unique command structure, and its monopoly over weaponry. Economic conditions too are not without importance, particularly in poorer countries that are dependent on the export of raw materials.[37] Military establishments not only seek to prevent a collapse of the national economy, but also, more realistically, strive to ensure that their own corporate interests are not endangered.

Bureaucratic corporatism

Despite a preponderance of conditions that give rise to the establishment of military-based authoritarian states, very few authoritarian states rely purely and solely on the armed forces to maintain power. It does not take long for generals-cum-presidents to appreciate the costs involved in ruling through sheer coercion and the need to complement the state's military and bureaucratic institutions with other support mechanisms. It is precisely this realization that has prompted most bureaucratic-authoritarian states to adopt corporatist practices and to cooperate with (though not co-opt) those social groups that they find economically and politically beneficial. These social groups differ according to specific economic and social conditions within each country, but they usually include members of the professional elite, industrialists, various non-political interest groups, and multinational corporations.

Corporatism offers three particular advantages for bureaucratic-authoritarian regimes. First and foremost, it bestows yet another instrument of social control on the state without forcing it to compromise its dictatorial hold on power.[38] This in turn lessens some of the burden placed on the regime because of its authoritarian policies and allows it to refocus its attention on other social groups, such as peasants and farmers, over whom it may not have such direct control. Third, and perhaps most important, since corporatization often involves industrialists and other groups with greater access to capital, it greatly enhances the state's economic perfor-mance. In fact, economic factors often provide a far more important impetus for corporatization than do political ones.[39]

There are, however, limits to how far an authoritarian regime can pursue corporatist policies. Rapid modernization and industrial growth, themselves products of corporatism, can upset the fragile working arrangements that have evolved between the state and its corporatist partners. Corporatist groups may gain enough autonomy to start voicing independent political opinions in the face of an inflexible political system. The state may also seek to impose a "purer" brand of corporatism and try to tighten its political domination, in the process unwittingly fostering oppositional alliances among previously divided groups. Former and present bureaucratic-authoritarian states in Iran, India, Egypt, and South Korea have all at one time or another experienced the ironies of corporatist arrangements.[40]

Communist regimes

A brief mention must be made of communist political systems, which, although at present numbering less than a handful, retain their somewhat unusual institutional arrangements and ideological content. A discussion of the state in communist countries was left to the end because of its very particular characteristics. Communist states' attempts to regulate all aspects of life invariably fall short of initial expectations—as made abundantly clear by the need for economic liberalization in China and Vietnam—and they are thus characterized by what could best be described as aspirational totalitarianism. They embody several features that make them at once totalitarian, populist, and bureaucratic-authoritarian. The totalitarian feature of the communist state stems from its ceaseless efforts at directing even the most mundane aspects of the lives of its citizens, falling only a little short of mind control. Nothing less than total and unconditional surrender to the communist system and its top leadership is acceptable.

Increasingly, however, both in the former Soviet-bloc countries as well as in the remaining communist states of China, Vietnam, and Cuba, total and utter devotion to the regime's political religion and its cult of personality have been toned down and replaced by more institutional means of political control.[41] The Communist Party has in fact always been, both theoretically and practically, one of the main supporting pillars of the state and its principal forum for interaction with society.[42] The legislature performs similar inclusionary functions, albeit to a somewhat lesser degree, and legitimizes, recruits, and socializes the masses into the political process.[43] But the system also tends to be highly authoritarian, often brutally so, and extremely elitist in its leadership. In China, with its population of more than a billion people, political power is concentrated in the hands of between twenty and thirty-five individuals.[44] However, in China as elsewhere, the powers and the position of the leaders remain relatively uninstitutionalized.[45] The degree of power the leader wields depends on such non-institutional factors as the relative strength of other top leaders, his age (since most communist leaders are relatively advanced in age), and even on the state of international affairs. A mammoth and highly penetrative bureaucracy, meanwhile, reaches into the innermost echelons of society in order to ensure compliance and the extraction of resources that the state requires.

Conclusion

Different states interact differently with society. The exact dynamics that shape this interaction depend on the agendas, resources, capacities, and structures of both state and society. The chapters in this Part of the book have identified five broad types of state, each with unique sets of characteristics and institutions: First World democracies; democratic states that are far more recent and thus not as solidly institutionalized; quasi-democratic states in which the mechanical manifestations of democracy—elections, parliaments, etc.—are not sufficient to foster a society-wide democratic spirit; inclusionary populist and totalitarian regimes; and bureaucratic-authoritarian states. States that are democratic contain institutions that facilitate a regularized and constant process of interaction with society through elections and other means of political participation. The legislative and judicial institutions of the democratic state are literally at the service of society, the former facilitating and the latter ensuring it. The democratic executive, meanwhile, comes directly from within society and remains answerable to it.

These arrangements are completely alien to non-democratic states, at least in practice if not in theory, for they either manipulate society or merely coerce it. The lack of opportunity to be constantly "refined" by society robs non-democratic states of a much-needed sharp edge. They become uncaring and unaware of the pressures within and the agendas that society wants to pursue. Society is subdued and its internal forces made subject to the wishes of the state. Even in populist regimes, in which the sentiments and desires of one or more segments of society are played up and ostensibly fulfilled, politically independent and self-generated pressures from society meet at best a muted and at worst a violent response from the state. The non-democratic state itself is not highly developed and, because this is so, it is susceptible to collapse. Its coercive arm, the military and the police forces, may have deadly efficiency and a fearsome reputation, but the state remains weak and vulnerable at its core, its immense political apparatuses crumbling under the weight of decay.

Politics, of course, requires political interaction with society, and different societies are governed by their own internal dynamics and characteristics. The complexities of the nature and institutions of the state form only half of the political equation. Society, too, has its own features, its own institutions, and its own forces. Examining politics requires more than simply examining the state and its institutions, nor does merely adding an examination of society and its institutions give a complete picture. What is necessary is to examine the types and the consequences of *interactions* between particular state and societal formations.

Part IV

State-society interactions: revolution and democratization

8   Revolutions

The appearance of revolutions and revolutionary movements in developing countries is a result of political, social and cultural developments and dynamics. More specifically, as discussed in previous chapters, the particular characteristics of states in the developing world, coupled with the larger consequences of social change, as well as the features inherent in political cultures, combine to give rise to conditions conducive to the outbreak of revolutions. Nevertheless, despite the widespread prevalence of such conditions throughout the developing world, revolutions are rather rare historical occurrences. Why, it is thus important to ask, have revolutions not taken place with greater frequency given the existence of their social and political pre-conditions? Moreover, exactly what social and political dynamics lead to revolutions, how do they do so, and at which specific junctures? It is to these questions that the present chapter turns.

Broadly, revolutions denote fundamental objective and subjective changes (i.e. both institutionally and culturally) in political arrangements and leaders, principles and orientations.[1] They entail the transformation of the very political fabric on which a government is based. Palace coups and changes in leadership and in personalities do not necessarily constitute a "revolution" in the fullest sense, despite what the coups' protagonists often like to think. Nevertheless, it is quite conceivable that a coup may set in motion a chain of events which may lead to the outbreak of a revolutionary situation. Compared to military coups, revolutions entail much deeper and more profound changes. They turn the world of politics around, change the basic premises on which political culture is based, and transform the larger implicit and explicit guidelines according to which political conduct is governed. In this respect, revolutions are distinctively political episodes, although their precise occurrence is brought about by a coalescence of not only political but also social and cultural factors.[2] As past and recent experiences have demonstrated, to say that revolutions are "political struggles of great intensity"[3] and that they invariably involve considerable violence[4] has become somewhat of a truism, although the decade of the 1980s did bear witness to the budding of "negotiated revolutions" in some parts of eastern Europe.[5] Yet by and large, revolutions still remain mass-based affairs of great magnitude, brought about and carried through by the mobilization of masses of people against specific political targets. Even Hungary's largely "negotiated revolution" was precipitated and in turn fuelled by frequent and noisy protests by thousands of Hungarians in Budapest and elsewhere.[6]

Causes of Revolutions

It follows that any credible attempt to explain revolutions needs to consider the conditions under which mass mobilization is achieved.[7] This includes an analysis of the prevailing *social* as well as *political* conditions that are conducive to the emergence of revolutionary mass mobilization. Revolutions are *political* episodes to the extent that they denote the institutional crumbling of an old political order and its replacement by new political objects, arrangements, and structures. Exactly how this collapse and the subsequent replacement are brought about are manifestations not only of political dynamics but also of all those other factors—such as social and cultural ones—which also influence mass mobilization and political activism. Thus to see revolutions as only political events is to grasp only half of the picture. Political dynamics need to be considered in conjunction with social and cultural developments.

Theories of revolutionary causation

It is within this multi-disciplinary framework that theories of revolutionary causation have generally been constructed and put forth. Ancient and contemporary scholarship bears witness to ceaseless and at times highly impressive efforts to examine the root causes of revolutions and to grasp the full extent of the social and political dynamics which result in revolutionary episodes.[8] Some of these theories have had greater explanatory success than others. Nevertheless, most theoretical explanations suffer from a number of highly significant analytical deficiencies.[9] To begin with, most existing theories ignore the inherently varied nature of revolutions and attempt to explain these diverse phenomena through one, all-embracing framework. What results is theories which in their attempt to find applicability to *all* revolutions become at best too generalized.[10] There is a need for both historical and contextual specificity. Revolutions vary from one another according to the different historical contexts within which they occur.[11] Thus a theoretical framework which explains the causes of, say, the French revolution may not necessarily apply to more modern examples such as the Vietnamese and Chinese revolutions.

Equal attention must be paid to the significant role played by human agency in revolutions, which is by nature reflexive and changeable. A theory of revolution needs to consider the intrinsic changeableness that is imparted to revolutions because of human initiative.[12] More than anything else, the actual success or failure of revolutions depends on the specific actions taken by revolutionary participants, actions that are inherently varied according to the context, the timing, and the manner of their execution.[13] The decisions that revolutionary leaders make, the manner in which those decisions are implemented and pursued, and the specific consequences that may arise from them differ from one case to another. It is precisely these vital details that make each revolution different from another one. Even in cases where deliberate attempts are made to emulate previous models, as, for example, Che Guevara tried to do in Bolivia, there are striking differences in the detailed mechanisms with which revolutions are carried forward. It is precisely this lack of attention to contextual specificity, at the heart of which is the variable nature of human conduct and initiative, that has led to the demise of so many emulative revolutionary movements around the world.[14]

In addition to their overly ambitious and thus highly generalized nature, most theories of revolution put too much emphasis on one aspect of revolutionary eruption at the expense of other, equally significant ones. Among the theories of revolution which in recent years have gained widespread respect and currency within the academic community, emphasis has been placed on the "dissynchronization" of value systems and the ensuing "disequilibrium" of pre-revolutionary societies;[15] on the inability of social actors to fulfill their goals and aspirations;[16] on the regime's lack of capacity to absorb emerging groups into itself,[17] or to mobilize them for its own benefit;[18] or on the state's inability to withstand the pressures brought on it by structural weaknesses and by class-based revolts.[19] In virtually all of these approaches, overwhelming emphasis is placed on one facet of social and/or political developments while the simultaneous contribution of other dynamics to revolutions is underestimated or even completely ignored.[20] In a few instances, emerging developments have forced a revision of earlier, one-dimensional theories.[21] But the tendency to give primacy to one aspect of analytical examination while underestimating the importance of others still pervades current scholarship on revolutions.

The study of revolutions, whether classic or contemporary, requires a multi-disciplinary, multidimensional approach. The dynamics that result in the appearance of revolutionary circumstances are political as well as social. Politically, the outbreak of revolutions requires a significant weakening of the powers of political incumbents and their growing incapacity to hold on to the state's institutions and its various other resources. These include loss of control of the means of economic hegemony over the general population; loss of control over the coercive organs of the state such as the army and the police and also over the state's propaganda networks such as the electronic and printed media; and a steady loss of privileged access to socially valued goods and institutions. In general, the primary pre-condition of revolutions is the loss of previously held powers and privileges on the part of the elite. This reduction in the elite's powers may be caused by any number of domestic or international developments that could adversely affect the powers of the state. Internationally, such a weakening could occur through inter-state disputes and military conflicts, or excessive diplomatic pressures or what may be termed "conditional relations".[22] Internally, the elite's hold on power may be weakened by such events as the death of a central, authoritarian personality, or excessive and naked competition over power resources. Concurrently, however, the political exigencies thus created need to be exploited by the efforts of groups that initiate specific acts in order to bring about the state's ultimate collapse. Unless and until such groups exist, and acquire powers sufficient to overwhelm those of the dying state, a revolution will not occur. In essence, revolutions are raw power struggles of the highest order: on one side is the political elite, in control of the state, its powers and privileges steadily declining owing to a variety of internal and/or international developments; on the other hand there are revolutionaries, increasingly belligerent and with more specific demands, gradually achieving enough size and strength to overpower and replace the elite.

These political dynamics cannot occur in a social vacuum. The growing momentum of the contenders for power, who are gradually seen as—and who come to see themselves as—revolutionaries, and the withering of the state, both take place within and in fact are precipitated by social and cultural dynamics. Social developments help in the structural weakening of the state in a number of ways. Most fundamentally, social change and industrial development lead to the creation of various social classes and values which the existing system cannot absorb into itself.[23] Thus, especially in modernizing societies, where new classes are continually emerging and where old and new values are in constant flux, the state assumes an essentially conflictual relationship with emerging social groups and seeks constantly to sever their access to sources of political power. Regardless of the eventual outcome of this state-society conflict, even if society has been subdued and subjected to the state's full control, the very existence of such an adversarial nexus weakens the basic foundations of the state and increases the likelihood of its collapse.

A more important contribution made by social dynamics to revolutionary outbreaks is in influencing the extent of popular support enjoyed by revolutionaries among the general population. By their very attempts to communicate with the masses and to get their increasingly revolutionary message across, emerging revolutionary groups employ various social media, some of which they may not even be aware of. The existence of a number of social and cultural factors can significantly enhance or curtail the legitimacy of revolutionary actors. Depending on the specific conditions within a given society, apathy and conservatism may drown a revolutionary group, condemning it to oblivion, with its cries of injustice and calls to revolt falling on ears deafened by passivity and contentment. By the same token, social conditions may invoke in people senses of injustice and deprivation, and nationalist and religious sentiments which make them highly amenable to revolutionary mobilization. The prevalence of specific social conditions that encourage revolutionary action, and the exact nature of the link between the existing conditions and the types of response evoked, are context-specific and vary from society to society. Nonetheless, in all revolutions social conditions influence the direction and nature of unfolding events, to the same extent as, if not more than, political factors.

As the above summary suggests, the causes, the course, and the outcome of revolutions in the developing world can be best analyzed through the adoption of a multi-disciplinary approach that takes into account both social and political forces. In contrast to the West, throughout the non-democracies of the developing world social and political forces confront each other nakedly, in their most brutal form, seeking aggressively to implant themselves and to supplant others.[24] This polarization is further accentuated by the fragility of norms that govern political conduct, underwrite social relationships, and support existing institutions. Within this context, while state-society links in non-democracies are more tenuous, their relationship with each other is a much more consequential one. In the developing world, changes occurring in the state can affect society far more dramatically than is the case in the West. Changes taking place in developing societies can have far more dramatic political ramifications than they would in Western countries. Examining revolutions in the developing world thus requires detailed analysis of political dynamics that lead to the state's weakness and to the emergence of revolutionary groups, in addition to the development of social and cultural conditions conducive to popular revolutionary mobilization. State breakdown is only one facet of revolutionary episodes. The social and cultural milieu within which it occurs is just as important.

State Breakdown

Revolutions are brought about through a confluence of political developments and social dynamics which weaken the powers of governing incumbents, and, at the same time, enhance the capabilities of those aspiring to replace them. The political dynamics at work involve the incumbents' loss of legitimacy, the growing weakness and vulnerability of the structures and the institutions they have at their disposal, and the concurrent activities of revolutionary groups aimed at exploiting these emerging exigencies and the resulting mobilization of masses toward revolutionary goals. Equally significant are the prevailing social and cultural conditions that are conducive to revolutionary mobilization, be they a general sense of deprivation among various social strata or disenchantment over prevailing cultural values. Also important are the means of access which revolutionary groups have to the general population, determined by either existing social organizations or alternative means of nexus that are specifically forged for this purpose.

It is only through the concurrent appearance of all of these dynamics, from legitimacy crisis and structural breakdown to revolutionary activism and mass mobilization, that a revolution in the fullest sense takes place. Otherwise, in instances where emerging political weaknesses and vulnerabilities are not exploited by revolutionary groups, or when self-proclaimed revolutionaries operate in a social vacuum and seek to overthrow a strong and viable state, what occurs is merely political instability and upheaval, but not revolution. It is important also to distinguish between a revolution and a palace coup, the latter resulting merely in a change of personalities while the former denotes an all-encompassing change in political arrangements, institutions, and practices. Coup leaders all too often proclaim themselves as revolutionaries and declare their reign to be the start of a revolutionary era. It was indeed a military coup that brought the Ethiopian revolution to a head and caused the dawn of the post-Haile Selassie era.[25]

The Ethiopian example has not been widely repeated, and the vast majority of military coups, especially in Latin America and Africa, result in a change of political personalities rather than of principles. Politicians are only actors in the political drama. Their replacement by other actors does not necessarily affect the outcome of the play. It is the institutions they create and occupy, and the ideologies and principles they espouse, that constitute the political drama itself and affect society at large. Revolutions involve changing not only political actors but the entire scenario on which the drama of politics is based.

With this in mind, it is important to remember that the key to all successful revolutions, the catalyst that sets in motion all the other dynamics which produce revolutionary circumstances, is the political incapacitation of the ruling elite. Revolutions are primarily developments that result from the political crises that engulf those in power. This centrality of state power arises out of the state's control of the various prized resources in society. Especially in the remaining non-democracies of the developing world, the state not only has power over the army, the police, and the bureaucracy, but also controls, directly or indirectly, various aspects of economic life, including resources, services, and general economic activity. In short, the state controls most if not all of the essential tools and resources that are necessary for running the country. Unless and until this control is somehow weakened and is transferred to power centers outside the state, then aspiring revolutionaries will not find sufficient resources with which to mount and to maintain a political takeover.

Causes of state breakdown in pre-revolutionary states

The political weakening of pre-revolutionary states can be caused by the appearance of three broad types of development. Most directly consequential in bringing about revolutionary situations, and by far the most common set of developments weakening state power, are those with direct negative bearings on the state's cohesion and organizational viability. These are developments that lead directly to the structural collapse of state organizations and institutions. Developments as diverse as wars, economic bankruptcy, or the death of a central figure in a personalized system are among those categories of events which can dramatically reduce the state's continued ability to control the resources needed to stay in power. Similar consequences may arise from partial and incomplete processes of political modernization, thus leading to over-stretched bureaucracies incapable of dealing with evolving circumstances, unfulfilled demands for increased political participation, and a general absence of society-wide political entrepreneurship. Lastly, there is the development of a situation best described as a "crisis of legitimacy", reducing the ability of state leaders to continue justifying their hold on power.

These developments are not mutually exclusive and, in fact, often occur in connection with one another. The relationship between crises of legitimacy and structural collapse is an especially strong one. In fact, these two developments are naturally interrelated and reinforce one another. This relationship of mutual reinforcement assumes particular importance in developing countries, where the very process of development can trigger crises of legitimacy for political incumbents. Questioning the legitimacy of political leaders is an inevitable consequence of the intertwined processes of industrial growth, social change, and political development. The "development syndrome" results in a widening of perceptions on the part of ever greater numbers of people and, therefore, an increase in sensitivities about possible alternative ways of doing things in most aspects of life.[26] What occurs is a "dissynchronization" between the values that state leaders hold on the one hand and those of the general population on the other.[27] More specifically, crises of political legitimacy arise when the claims of current leaders to power are based on socially unacceptable historical or ideological interpretations, when the degree of political socialization has not been sufficient to convince the people of the legitimacy of existing political arrangements, and when there is excessive and uninstitutionalized competition for power.[28]

In essence, legitimacy crisis arises out of inadequate and incomplete political institutionalization and consolidation, itself an inherent feature of non-democratic political systems.[29] Thus a structural analysis of the collapse of pre-revolutionary states must necessarily examine the legitimacy crises that concurrently accompany them.

A crisis of legitimacy

A legitimacy crisis is basically a crisis of authority. It signifies the inability of political leaders to justify their continued hold on power.[30] As mentioned earlier, legitimacy crisis is inherent in the process of development. However, a number of specific dynamics exacerbate the withdrawal of the proverbial "mandate of heaven" and heighten a regime's sense of illegitimacy among the population at certain historical junctures. The problem is one of inability to deliver the goods promised or in demand, be they economic, political, or emotional.[31] Lack of dynamic leadership and political acumen, continued and persistent demands for greater political participation or increased economic gratification, or a neglect or abuse of sources with symbolic importance, such as religion and nationalism, can all significantly accentuate popular perceptions about a state's illegitimate claims to power and unfitness to govern. Structural weaknesses in turn sharpen the potency of legitimacy crises by compounding the difficulties faced by supposedly incompetent leaders and by giving added purchase to people's negative feelings toward the state. Moreover, when prevailing circumstances allow, the sense of illegitimacy that prompts people to demonstrate their displeasure with state leaders has important consequences for mass mobilization. Here again, the relationship between structural variables and legitimacy crisis is crucial in pushing forward the eruption of revolutions.

Within the plethora of social and political developments that bring to a head the eruption of legitimacy crisis, the role of state leadership is central. This centrality arises from the fact that it is the legitimacy of state leaders that is at the very heart of legitimacy crisis. This propensity toward a sense of leadership illegitimacy is even stronger in non-democratic countries subject to intense social change, where, through diffusion or imitation, the populace is constantly striving to attain the political liberties prevalent in democratic polities. To varying degrees, non-democratic leaders need constantly to react to or at least to justify not abiding by the standards which underlie democracies.[32] It is no accident that revolutions have historically taken place in decidedly anti-democratic, authoritarian states.[33]

Within the specific context of the developing world, exclusionary regimes, which do not bother to mobilize popular support in order to justify their narrowly based sources of authority, are seen as particularly illegitimate and are most vulnerable to the outbreak of revolutions.[34] Such regimes are often based on the rule of a single, all-powerful political figure and have an increasingly narrow base of support. The blatant elite corruption that is frequently endemic to these states, their tight control over education and the press, the control of the economy by a few families, and their frequent neglect of national interests in preference to the interests of the superpowers, all combine to increase significantly the likelihood that such polities encounter crises of legitimacy.[35] Nevertheless, even these vulnerable political systems can stave off revolutions if they acquire the patronage of a sufficiently strong segment of the population, especially the middle classes.[36]

The relationship between state leaders and legitimacy crisis extends to more than the mere maintenance of popularly acceptable political practices and interpretations. State leaders can significantly enhance or harm their popular legitimacy depending on how they treat the various symbols that are held in high value by important social classes. Most notably, the state leaders' neglect or offensive treatment of nationalist values and sentiments, historical traditions and cherished cultural values, and religious beliefs and symbols can dramatically reduce their legitimacy. In order to bring prevailing social and cultural principles into concert with their political doctrines and ideologies, political leaders often interpret socially pervasive symbols in a manner that fit their own narrow purposes, regardless of how twisted or even offensive those interpretations may be. Interpretations ascribed in particular to specific historical episodes and to religious values are used extensively in augmenting the legitimacy of existing political institutions and practices.

Manifestations of nationalism tend to be even more influential in accentuating the popular sense of illegitimacy ascribed to state leaders in many non-democracies.[37] Colonial or neo-colonial relations generate the strongest sense of popular nationalism and are most conducive to legitimacy crises for colonial powers or their local proxies. Other forms of less dependent relationship are also instrumental in bringing into question the legitimacy of existing elites by heightening a perception of their subservience to foreign powers.[38] Nevertheless, the linkage between legitimacy crisis and nationalism is more than one of political sensitivity.

Nationalist sentiments can be offended through the appearance of economic and industrial subservience to a foreign country. State elites may effectively cultivate a sense of political nationalism and in fact exploit it to their benefit. However, the economic policies that they pursue, especially if their strategy of economic development is one of import-industrialization substitution,[39] can give rise to sentiments of economic nationalism and can discredit their legitimacy as genuinely national leaders. Intense propagation of Western values and norms and ensuing backlashes among social classes can have similar effects.

In addition to demands for greater political participation and the upholding of values with symbolic importance, crises of legitimacy can arise out of a government's inability to meet evolving economic demands and expectations. The inability to "deliver the goods", politically and emotionally, represents only two of the shortcomings that lead to legitimacy crisis. A state's inability to deliver more tangible goods, those which directly affect the economic well-being of the population, can have even more direct bearing on its perception as legitimate or illegitimate. Like anti-democratic, authoritarian states, those countries that are in a comparatively disadvantageous economic position are more prone to revolutions.[40] Not unlike growing demands for greater political participation, often arising out of diffusion with or exposure to Western political practices, the transitional nature of economic development breeds rising expectations, thus accentuating the legitimacy crisis of those regimes unable to meet such expectations.[41] In instances where "there is the continued, unimpeded opportunity to satisfy new needs, new hopes, new expectations", the legitimacy of political leaders is greatly enhanced and the probability of a revolutionary outbreak

is reduced to a minimum.[42] When there is widespread economic deprivation, however, whether actual or perceived, real or relative, the likelihood of
opposition to a state is significantly increased, especially when that state is
seen as an obstacle to continued economic mobility.[43]

Lastly, the sources and the means through which a sense of the illegitimacy of political leaders is instilled and popularized among the people are
important. A general feeling among a population that the political and
ideological justifications of political incumbents are unacceptable may
already exist. But how are these negative sentiments given sufficient potency
and direction to be usefully channeled into revolutionary agitation?

The issue is not merely one of overt revolutionary mobilization. Before
large-scale mass mobilization toward avowedly revolutionary goals can be
achieved, and even before the social and cultural conditions conducive to
mass mobilization can appear in a society, there must be voices of dissent,
no matter how faint and silent, bringing to light the illegitimate premises on
which the current leaders' rule is based. Legitimacy crisis is based on the
perception that current political values and practices are not legitimate
while certain alternatives ones are. It is more than coincidental that almost
all legitimacy crises that precede revolutions occur along with a general
"intellectual rebelliousness", a "foment of ideas" which sharply criticize the
status quo and propose ideological and valuative alternatives.

The proliferation of intellectual activities that occurred before the revolutions in France,[44] Russia,[45] Cuba,[46] Iran,[47] and Hungary,[48] to mention a
few, all had the affect of heightening popular perceptions of illegitimacy
attributed to incumbent states. All too often, these sudden outbursts of
intellectual activism are scattered, unorganized, and uncoordinated, without
a coherent doctrine or theoretical framework emerging until some time
later. In France, for example, there was little agreement before 1789 between
the many philosophers and physiocrats who were theorizing about such
concepts as liberty, political accountability, and egalitarianism.[49] Russia's
pre-revolutionary "foment of ideas" was expressed mostly through a highly
amorphous literary movement. In Cuba, what occurred was not a coordinated attempt to formulate a new theory, but essentially "a guerrilla war of
concepts, objectives, and abstractions".[50] And, in Iran, the evolution of
"political Islam" as an alternative frame of ideological reference was only
piecemeal and gradual.[51] What is important is the cumulative effects of
these alternative values and conceptual frameworks in undermining the
legitimacy of political incumbents.

Precisely why the flourishing of intellectual activity, which is part of the
process of legitimacy crisis, occurs before revolutions is related both to
social and to political dynamics. On the one hand, the characteristics that
are inherent in political cultures in non-democracies, coupled with the
intense social changes under way there, breed an environment which is
conducive to the appearance of intellectuals propagating comparatively
revolutionary ideas and concepts. In societies where merely speaking one's

mind or even satirical writings are considered "revolutionary" and sub-versive, any meaningful steps toward commentary and analytical writings can have a magnified social and political affect. At the same time, on the other hand, the structural weaknesses that engulf pre-revolutionary states add a special significance to the works of intellectuals and other men of letters. Even if purely artistic in value, the works of intellectuals in such an atmosphere add to the overall sense of skepticism regarding the legitimacy of the current order in general and that of the political establishment in particular.

The growing sense of unease with the legitimacy of the body politic is further compounded by the structural breakdown of the political system itself. A group of politicians who are unable to deliver the political, social, and emotional goods that are in demand are considered as even less justi-fied in their rule when the very organizations through which they govern start to break apart. Again, the contextual relationship between legitimacy crises and structural weaknesses assumes crucial importance. Revolutions, as mentioned earlier, are in large part a product of the break-up of the political establishment. Only after the state has already lost a substantial part of its coercive abilities as a result of various debilitating developments, such as military defeats or bureaucratic collapse, have revolutionary groups found an opportunity to carry forward their agendas and gain widespread popular support.[52] Reinforcing and in fact expediting this break-up is the popular perception of political elites as unfit to rule and unjust in holding on to the reins of power.

Structural collapse

In analyzing the structural break-up of pre-revolutionary states, equal attention needs to be paid to domestic as well as to international factors. With the growing complexity of evolving national agendas and international circumstances, economic and even political interdependence between modern nation-states has become an inseparable part of contemporary comparative politics. "Every modern state", it needs to be remembered, "if it is to be understood accurately, must be seen just as fundamentally as a unit in an international system of other states as it must as a key factor in the production of social and economic power within its own territorial purlieus."[53] Consequently, the types of developments and relations neces-sary for conducting analysis within pre-revolutionary states are not merely those between the pre-revolutionary state and society but also those between the state itself and other states.[54] Specifically, it is important to see what negative ramifications arise from a state's inability to meet the chal-lenges of evolving international circumstances as, for example, the French, Russian, Chinese, Iranian governments, and more recently those of the eastern European countries experienced.[55]

Various types of domestic development have the potential to paralyze pre-revolutionary states and subsequently to expedite the appearance of revolutionary movements. Such developments occur especially in relation to the state's organizations and its structures. Among non-democratic countries there are many with states that have variously been called "bureaucratic-authoritarian", "praetorian", "neo-patrimonial", or "Sultanistic".[56] For reasons that are discussed below, the structures supporting these states are particularly fragile and unreformable, and are, therefore, prone to being subsumed by revolutionary movements. Such states are inherently weak, for they cannot substantially penetrate their respective societies, regardless of their massive bureaucracies or the fear and awe they instill in their populations through their armies and secret police. The fragile and often compulsory bonds that link the state to society are easily broken when the very seams that hold the state together begin to disintegrate, and the social energy released through this severance often has devastating revolutionary consequences. It is not widespread poverty and misery but rather this endemic fragility of state institutions, and in turn their inability to control and to penetrate society, that is the most prevalent cause of revolutions in the developing world.[57]

Non-democratic states are particularly susceptible to revolutions because they tend to foster an atmosphere that politicizes grievances that may otherwise be completely non-political. Those who are excluded from the political process and are not recipients of its patronage are especially likely to blame the political system for shortcomings that may or may not be politically related, such as economic difficulties or sudden social and cultural changes that cause widespread disillusionment and resentment. Particularly in closed, authoritarian systems, state leaders are seen as the primary protectors of the social and economic good, the all-embracing force from whom all power emanates. Eager to ascribe to themselves all benefits accrued through their rule, they are similarly blamed in the popular mind for discomforts that may not necessarily be of their doing. Precisely because of this overwhelming role that they play in all the affairs of the country, or at least due to popular perceptions of such a dominant role, these elites represent highly visible and resented symbols of authority, targets that not only are easily identifiable but also serve to unify protesters with different grievances and different agendas.[58] Also important is the tendency of such states to valorize political opposition and, by virtue of their repressive character, to turn even moderate opposition into radical revolutionism.

Military dictatorships and bureaucratic-authoritarian states are not as susceptible to revolutions as are personalized political systems, although they are inherently just as unstable politically. The accentuated instability of personalized systems as opposed to bureaucratic or military dictatorships arises from structural characteristics as well as the functional attributes of the different systems. Structurally, the varying roles of the armed forces and the police in different systems are central to the extent to which they survive politically. In literally all non-democratic political systems, repressive organs such as the military and the police play a pervasive role in maintaining the status quo. In fact, coercive organizations in such systems tend to be the most sophisticated and organizationally viable of the institutions.[59] Nevertheless, in military dictatorships and in authoritarian bureaucracies, the police and the army are often more capable than in personalized systems of supporting the political order in times of crisis and turmoil. This discrepancy in the effectiveness of coercive organizations in maintaining the status quo arises out of the different structural relationships that they have with the various governing bodies.

In bureaucratic and military dictatorships, the army and the police are often the very organizations that occupy the seat of power and themselves form the governing elite. Even if these organizations are not directly part of the establishment themselves, the relationship between them and the ruling elite is much closer than in personalized systems. They have, thus, much more at stake in ensuring the survival of the political order than might be the case in different circumstances. Moreover, dictators in personalized systems often govern through creating and then manipulating cleavages between various organizations, even within various factions of the army, and are highly dependent on the loyalties they forge through patronage and manipulations.[60] They are thus constantly on guard against possible conspiracies or at least a waning of loyalties, loyalties that frequently wear thinner as crises set in.

Domestic developments are, nevertheless, only one category of events that bring about the structural collapse of an existing state. International factors can be just as influential determinants of the viability of domestic state structures and institutions. The prevalence of unequal economic and political relationships between governments in the developing world and the more powerful Western countries only heightens the sensitivities of developing political institutions to changes in the international environment. The extent of domestic structural responsiveness to international fluctuations varies according to the degree of economic and political dependence.

In overtly dependent developing countries, several factors make the domestic power structure particularly weak and exposed to revolutionary situations. To begin with, the over-identification of the elite with one or more foreign powers substantially increases their perceptions of illegitimacy in the public eye and makes it difficult for them to justify their rule on historical and nationalist grounds. More specifically, dependence on a foreign power reduces the political maneuverability of incumbent elites and circumscribes the range of their potential responses in times of crisis.[61] For the elite, the conduct of domestic politics becomes diplomatically conditional: domestic responses rely heavily on the diplomatic nuances of the more powerful state.[62] Thus pre-revolutionary states in Iran, in the Philippines, and in Hungary felt compelled, for one reason or another, to pursue domestic policies that were being explicitly or implicitly advocated by their much stronger patrons.[63] Whether under actual or perceived conditions, these states felt constrained in pursuing policies which might have otherwise helped them remain in power.

In instances of outright colonial domination, ruling colonial structures are not necessarily any less prone to revolutions than are weaker, dependent states. Like personalized and bureaucratic-authoritarian states, direct colonial rule often disperses economic and political privileges to very few elite groups, often to settlers, and thus generates considerable anger and resentment, especially among the middle and upper classes.[64] As if the granting of special privileges to visible minorities is not a sufficient pre-condition for widespread animosity toward the colonial establishment, nationalist sentiments and demands for political self-government further fan the flames of anti-colonial revolutions.[65] Moreover, like personalized states, colonial administrations inadvertently facilitate revolutionary mobilization in two important ways: first, they serve as highly visible targets for grievances that are economic and socio-cultural as well as political; secondly, they often function as unifying elements that draw together groups with diverse social, economic, and ethnic backgrounds whose unity might not have been as easily achieved otherwise.[66]

The external relations that can potentially lead to revolutions need not necessarily be of the type found between patron and client states. The outbreak of revolutionary circumstances in one country may lead to similar developments in another through imitation, instigation, or even contagion.[67] Insecure about the extent of their newly acquired powers and paranoid about the conspiratorial designs of outside forces, revolutionary states often try to foment revolutions in neighboring countries in order to enhance their own legitimacy and power base both at home and abroad. Similarly, domestic revolutionaries, for lack of indigenous role models or an ideology of their own, often idolize revolutionary heroes in other countries and try to follow their teachings and replicate their actions. Fueled by such revolutionary myths as Latin American continentalism, Arab unity, and Pan-Africanism, the "echo effect" of revolutions is amplified by the intense propaganda and repeated slogans of what is usually no more than a handful of guerrillas.[68] Also prevalent are the contagious effects of revolution in one country on events occurring in another, a development further fueled by the unrelenting propaganda of most revolutionary states and the tendency to imitate foreign revolutionaries. As the changes in the former Soviet Union in the late 1980s and their reverberations in the rest of eastern Europe demonstrated, also important are the cumulative effects of gradual changes in world-historical contexts. These accumulated developments often give rise to "slow, secular trends in demography, technology, economics, religion, and worldly beliefs that set the stage for the rise and decline of core hegemonic orders, which in turn create opportunities for peripheral and small groups to gather situational advantage and revolt."[69]

In so far as internationally dependent states are concerned, relations with a more powerful foreign patron can have either negative consequences for the viability of domestic structures or, as the case might be, a reinforcing, positive effect. For decades, for example, the overwhelming diplomatic force of the Soviet Union, backed up with military might under the Brezhnev doctrine, kept together the seams of eastern European regimes and repeatedly suppressed emerging revolutions such as that in Hungary in 1956 and the one in Czechoslovakia in 1968. In the 1960s, the Kennedy administration's policy of "Alliance for Progress" was similarly designed to contain the emergence of revolutionary circumstances in the Latin American continent.[70] This policy of containment was once again pursued with great zeal in the 1980s under the auspices of what came to be known as the "Reagan Doctrine". In speech after speech, President Reagan warned of "a mounting danger in Central America that threatens the security of the United States" and spoke of the necessity to contain it.[71] "Using Nicaragua as a base", he declared,

> the Soviets and Cubans can become the dominant power in the crucial corridor between North and South America. Established there, they will be in a position to threaten the Panama Canal, interdict our vital Caribbean sealanes and ultimately move against Mexico.[72]

The pursuit of a foreign policy thus shaped in turn resulted in heightened American economic, diplomatic, and even military presence throughout Latin America, from Mexico down to Grenada, El Salvador, Honduras, Panama, Colombia, Chile, Brazil, and Argentina. In one way or another, whether militarily or through economic aid, American efforts in Latin America were designed to strengthen incumbent states and to stem the tide of revolutions threatening the anti-communist governments of the region.[73]

Incomplete political modernization

States can lose a substantial degree of their cohesion and organizational viability not only through crises of legitimacy and domestic and international sources of structural weakness, but also through incomplete and partial processes of political modernization. Thorough and complete political modernization involves the progressive rationalization and secularization of authority, the growing differentiation of new political functions and specialized structures, and increased participation in the political process.[74] Non-democracies, however, are reluctant to open the system to unsolicited and undirected political participation and to reform other existing centers of power.[75] The negative consequences of skewed political modernization thus figure particularly prominently in non-democratic polities, where centralized political structures strive to pursue parallel but contradictory goals of increased consolidation and accommodative participation.

Political modernization is, in fact, politically inherently destabilizing, as it undermines loyalty to traditional authority, creates a need for new loyalties and identifications, and increases the public's desire for wider participation in the political process.[76] When demands for greater participation are not met, the accentuation of unfulfilled aspirations substantially increases the likelihood of political instability.[77] The absence of any meaningful means and institutions through which political objectives and demands for participation could be channeled only aggravates the inherent fragility of the system.[78] Even those groups which gain entry into politics do so without becoming identified with established political institutions or acquiescing in existing political procedures.[79]

Under repressive states, where political demands cannot be comprehensively formulated, much less expressed, the result is a further polarization of the inherently antagonistic relationship that in such countries exists between the state and society.[80] Moreover, partial political modernization further hampers the cohesion of the political system and impedes the growth of political entrepreneurship and national integration.[81] The political context remains hopelessly unevolved, exacerbating the rawness and nakedness with which political forces and dynamics confront each other. Such a persistent absence of "normative regulation of the means of competition", as one observer has put it, results in heightened political instability and a growing proclivity toward revolutionary eruption.[82]

Functional characteristics are just as important as structural attributes in determining the longevity of political systems. Personalized systems are comprised of highly visible, widely feared and resented, manipulative political figures whose longevity is determined by their vigilance, political will, and sheer wiliness. Patrimonialism pervades and there is a predominance of inter-elite and inter-organizational rivalries manipulated by the person of the ruler.[83] However, bureaucratic and military dictatorships, along with other types of "corporatist" state,[84] are more likely to extend patronage to the various social groups and try to incorporate them into the system.[85] The vulnerability of such states to widespread, mass-based revolts is thus reduced, at least so long as the extension of patronage continues uninterrupted and the popular goods in demand—political and otherwise—are delivered.

Revolutionary Mass Mobilization

The political dynamics that bring about revolutionary circumstances are by no means limited to the structural breakdown of pre-revolutionary states. Equally important are the deliberate efforts of avowed revolutionaries to overthrow the political order, as too are the situational possibilities that enable them to achieve the widespread support and mobilization of the masses. Revolutions, it must be remembered, are as much products of human initiative as they are the result of the political and structural collapse of state institutions and the elite that rule through them.[86] The existence of oppositional groups who specifically seek to exploit the state's mounting difficulties is an integral part of every full-blown revolution.[87] What varies from one historical example to another is the exact timing of the formation of such groups. Some revolutionaries pre-date the start of the state's structural difficulties, while others begin to collect into cohesive organizations *after* the state's atrophy has begun.[88]

The crucial difference, especially in so far as the starting point and the nature of revolutionary activism are concerned, is that some revolutions are *planned*, signified by the premeditated actions of revolutionaries based on previous calculations, whereas others are more *spontaneous*. Planned revolutions are typically formulated and carried out by revolutionary organizations which, due to the force of circumstances, rely on guerrilla warfare in overthrowing existing states. Thus the revolutions in Vietnam, China, Cuba, Algeria, and Nicaragua were all planned.[89] Spontaneous revolutions, on the other hand, acquire their leaders only *after* the revolutions are well under way. The revolutions in France, Russia, and Iran, and the ones that swept across eastern Europe in the late 1980s were all of the spontaneous variety. In all instances, nevertheless, the active initiatives of groups aiming to compound and exploit the political difficulties of states are essential in bringing revolutions to fruition. Otherwise, what results is weakened states, lingering and in disarray, but unopposed and unchallenged.

Manner of mobilization

Spontaneous and planned revolutions differ most significantly in the manner in which the revolutionary mobilization of the masses is achieved and in the role of the revolution's leadership cadre. In both types of revolution, the paramount weakness and vulnerability of existing political institutions are necessary pre-conditions. In planned revolutions, however, a clear, identifiable cadre of revolutionary leaders exists who seek to expedite the state's collapse through their activities. In the process, they hope, their stature and legitimacy with the public will increase, enabling them to augment their popular support and following. Such groups are actively revolutionary, both in name and in their goals, and seek specifically to bring about revolutionary circumstances. They in fact proclaim themselves to be "revolutionaries" long before actual revolutionary circumstances set in. In spontaneous revolutions, on the other hand, leaders of revolution ascend to that position gradually and only through the progression of revolutionary circumstances instead of the other way around. In planned revolutions, revolutionary leaders expedite the appearance of revolutionary situations. In spontaneous revolutions, it is through the progression of revolutionary developments that the ultimate leaders are determined.

In planned revolutions, the role and initiatives of professional revolutionaries are highly important. These revolutionaries do not by themselves necessarily "make" revolutions, but are instrumental in mobilizing, organizing, and arming supporters and sympathizers, who eventually become revolutionary masses.[90] Their specific purpose is to compound the structural deficiencies of the state by turning the political frustrations of the masses into organized revolutionary action.[91] In their efforts, self-proclaimed revolutionary leaders recruit an army of their own and wage a war aimed at overwhelming the state. They have two pressing concerns: the formation of an army that would at least be comparable in strength to that of the state; and the strategic and tactical maneuvers of this revolutionary army aimed at bringing about the state's military defeat. It is only through a successful combination of these two tasks that a revolutionary organization can succeed in overthrowing the state.[92] For reasons discussed below, the leadership cadre of this revolutionary army is frequently drawn from the ranks of the urban middle class, while the rank-and-file foot-soldiers, the majority of the troops, are made up of rural inhabitants and peasants.

Peasant-based revolutions

More than anything else, the efforts of revolutionary leaders aimed at mobilizing and directing peasant activism require a solid and viable organizational apparatus. In addition to an aroused peasantry, capable of being mobilized, guerrilla revolutions require a disciplined army and a party organization that can provide the coordination and tactical vision necessary for peasant unity and, ultimately, for control of national power.[93] Peasant-based revolutions depend directly upon the mobilization of peasants by revolutionary organizations, making the sheer availability and effectiveness of such groups a necessary pre-condition of revolutionary situations.[94] Spontaneous political acts by peasants have often forced a scramble for the mobilization and formation of its would-be leadership.[95]

The degree of interaction between peasants and the leadership, and the extent to which leaders can absorb the peasantry into their organization and expand their power base, determine the viability and success of the revolutionary movement. The absence of firm links between revolutionary leaders and followers, especially in guerrilla revolutions where planned revolutionary initiatives play an extremely important role, can substantially reduce a movement's chances of success.[96] Moreover, for guerrilla organizations to succeed in achieving their revolutionary goals, they need to have a sustained ability to recruit new members, to structurally and organizationally evolve and develop, and to endure the adversities of military confrontation with the state.[97]

Unlike the rank-and-file followers, the social composition of the leadership of planned revolutionary movements is often decidedly non-rural. It is, in fact, frequently the disaffected members of the middle classes, most notably urban-educated students and intellectuals, who occupy most of the leadership positions in guerrilla organizations. Disjointed processes of social, political, and economic development turn the middle classes into inherently revolutionary groups, groups whose oppositional inclinations are likely to rise along with their level of education and social awareness. Given their greater sensitivity to their environment, most revolutionary leaders in the developing world come from middle-class, intellectual backgrounds, especially from the ranks of students.[98] These are dissatisfied literati elites who have turned into professional revolutionaries. They have taken upon themselves the task of establishing solid revolutionary coalitions and alliances which not only can overcome social, ethnic, and economic divides but also are capable of eventually replacing the current regime.[99] In search of an audience willing to follow and to obey them, they most frequently find the peasantry.

The preponderant role of the peasantry in guerrilla organizations arises out of a combination of rural conditions that are conducive to oppositional mobilization, as well as from the political and ideological inclinations of revolutionary leaders themselves. To begin with, urban-based political activists are drawn to the peasantry by a number of practical political considerations. A lack of political penetration by the government machinery into distant towns and villages has in many countries resulted in the alienation of the countryside from the rest of society.

Despite detailed and large-scale control over various aspects of urban life, most governments in the developing world at best pay scant attention to the countryside and, for the most part, neglect not only the economic development of rural areas but their political pacification as well. Even in instances where concerted efforts aimed at the political mobilization of rural inhabitants have been launched, large numbers of peasants continue to remain outside the influence of what often turns out to be only half-hearted campaigns. The political vacuum thus created offers potential guerrilla leaders ample opportunity for recruitment and mobilization. In an environment of little or no official political presence of any kind, guerrilla leaders can not only recruit followers with relative ease but also conduct "revolutionary acts" which, even if only symbolically important, may have a magnified effect. For guerrilla organizations, mere survival can be politically as important as it is to win battles. In the eminently political types of wars they wage, for the guerrillas survival is a victory in itself.[100]

Another reason for the attraction of revolutionary leaders to the peasantry is the supposed "ideological purity" of peasants, brought about by their geographic and political distance from centers of power. Alienation from the world of state politics also entails ideological and valuative estrangement from the political establishment. Mao, who was perhaps the most astute observer of the peasantry's revolutionary potential, went so far as to label peasants (not the communist party) as "the vanguards of revolution", "blank masses" uncorrupted by the bourgeois ideologies of the city.[101] Moreover, not only is the peasantry ideologically unassimilated into the political establishment, its predicaments and objective conditions often closely match the revolutionaries' ideologies. Most revolutionaries declare their aims to be the alleviation of misery and injustice, poverty and exploitation, the very conditions which in one way or another pervade rural areas in the developing world. Coupled with greater possibilities for recruitment and mobilization, ideological compatibility with objective conditions draws most leaders of planned revolutions to remote rural regions and areas. There is thus a strong connection between the revolutionaries' ideology and dogma and circumstances prevailing in the countryside.

The development of the links that bond revolutionary leaders and guerrilla organization to the mass of peasants is important in determining the extent and effectiveness of revolutionary mobilization. The establishment of such means of nexus and the resultant mobilization are dependent upon several variables, some indigenous to local conditions and others dependent on the characteristics of the guerrilla leaders themselves. Chief among these determining factors are the degree of the hegemony of the local ruling classes, the nature and extent of rural coalitions and alliances, and the ability of guerrilla leaders to deliver the goods and services which others cannot. In most rural areas in the developing world, pre-capitalist, peasant smallholders, sharecroppers, and tenants are likely to enjoy cultural and social (as well as organizational) autonomy from ruling elites, despite their tendency toward localism and traditionalism.[102] This relative, built-in resistance to elite hegemony and consequently receptivity to ideological and organizational alternatives arises out of a sense of economic security and independence, inflated though it may be at times, vis-à-vis the more dominant rural classes such as big landlords and estate owners. The spread of capitalism and the subsequent commercialization of agrarian society are also important in bringing about peasant rebelliousness.[103] This increasing propensity toward revolutionism is not necessarily because of the increased exploitation of peasants, but, rather, it is derived from a general breakdown of "prior social commitments" to kin and neighbors and thus greater flexibility and independence to act as desired.[104] Even more important, however, is the extent of direct government control over a region, or indirectly through landed proprietors acting as government proxies. Favorable political circumstances, the most important of which are the existence of weak states, are crucial in determining the feasibility of revolutionary activism and possibilities for peasant mobilization.[105]

Another significant factor that can directly influence the success of guerrilla leaders in mobilizing peasants is the guerrillas' ability to deliver goods and services, both actual and perceived. People will join or abstain from opposition groups based on the rewards they receive, both individually and as a collective whole, rewards that may be emotional as well as material.[106] In specific relation to rural areas, revolutionary movements have won broad support when they have been willing and able to provide state-like goods and services to their targeted constituents. The establishment of "liberated areas" that are secure from government attacks, the provision of services such as public education, health care, and law and order, and the initiation of economic reforms in the form of land redistribution or tax reductions are particularly effective measures in drawing peasants closer to guerrilla leaders.[107]

The success of revolutionary groups in peasant mobilization becomes even more tangible when they provide local goods and services with immediate payoffs before attempting to mobilize the population for the more difficult task of overthrowing the government.[108]

The provision of goods and services may not necessarily be material. For most peasants and rural inhabitants, participation in an army-like guerrilla organization offers a way of escaping from disillusioning surroundings and finding purpose and meaning in a greater cause. Membership in an organization becomes an end in itself, a means to fulfill desires of assertiveness and beliefs in higher goals and principles. To command and in turn to be commanded, to hold a gun in one's hand, and to aspire to dreams and lofty ideals are often mechanisms through which peasant revolutionaries, especially younger ones, try to shatter their socially ascribed, second-class image, and, in their own world, attempt to "become somebody".

While planned revolutions frequently take the form of organized, peasant-based guerrilla attacks on specific targets, spontaneous revolutions are more elusive in their start and in their objectives, especially in their earlier stages, and tend to be centered more in urban than in rural areas. Spontaneous revolutions typically begin with a drastic decline in the coercive powers of the state, followed in turn by a simplification of the political process and the subsequent growth of polarization among various segments of society.[109] Political simplification and polarization are inter-related: the growing dichotomy of society into two crude and simplified camps of political "supporters" and "opponents" polarizes the political environment and leads to the politicization of traditionally non-political groups.[110] Crisis-initiating events, exacerbating responses by the state, and the increasing weakness of the elite in the face of the revolutionaries' growing momentum all combine to bring about a revolution.[111] In this sequence of events, political mobilization takes place outside the state's purview and, in fact, it occurs precisely because the state itself was unwilling or unable to sanction popular political participation. Precipitating events force the hand of those claiming the revolution's leadership mantle, prompting them to be more reactive than proactive in their maneuvers. These emerging leaders exploit rather than create the situational opportunities that arise as the revolution progresses.

The role and importance of revolutionary leaders and their actions in spontaneous revolutions cannot be over-emphasized. The significance of the role of leaders in spontaneous revolutions increases as the course of events progresses and as the revolution's features and goals become clearer. Leaders of spontaneous revolutions do in fact call the shots, but only *after* it becomes clear that they are indeed the ones commanding the adherence of the masses already protesting in the streets. How these leaders achieve their exalted position vis-à-vis the protesting masses depends on a number of developments. Most notably, they include a coalescence of their organizational and verbal skills, the cultural communicability of their revolutionary message

and ideology, and their effectiveness in exploiting the opportunities presented to them by the state's collapse. Also important is the viability of the
social and/or political organizations through which they establish their links
with the larger society and relay their beliefs and propaganda to their
ever-growing mass of followers.

Social organizations

It is here that the crucial role of social organizations in spontaneous revolutions becomes evident. The focus must be on the groups and classes that
comprise the strata of a society, the various groups that seek to overthrow
the state by mobilizing popular support, and the connections that are
forged or which already exist between the social classes on the one hand
and the opposition groups on the other. In planned revolutions, the links
between revolutionary leaders and the masses are established through the
political parties that have been established for this very purpose. The ideology, structure, and initiatives of these parties are designed in a manner not
only to capture political power but also to acquire popular support as a
necessary starting point. In contrast, in spontaneous revolutions avowedly
revolutionary organizations initially play only a marginal role and operate
on the fringes of the larger social and political setting. In fact, as exempli-
fied in one historical case after another, the revolutionary organizations that
evolve under the eventual leaders of spontaneous revolutions are initially
highly amorphous and rather unstructured.[112] Instead, it is through existing
social organizations that the necessary links between revolutionary leaders
and the masses are established. Even before having acquired the support
and sympathy of the population, the revolution's leaders are determined, by
virtue of their dominant position within society and by the strength of the
social institutions they have at their disposal.

Whereas the success of planned revolutions depends greatly on the viability of the political parties and organizations involved, it is mostly through
highly fluid, non-formal, and society-wide institutions and means of communication that the leaders of spontaneous revolutions communicate with
their emerging followers and push the revolution forward. Gatherings in
churches and mosques, tea-houses, community meeting places, social or
ritualistic ceremonies, and other occasions in which intense inter-personal
interactions at the local level are conducted, can all serve as instruments
through which messages and instructions can flow from revolutionary
organizers to street protesters.

The accessibility of various revolutionary groups to these instruments of
communication and mobilization determine which ones can call on the
most followers more effectively, enabling them to assume eventually the
leadership of a mounting revolutionary movement. Other factors significant
in the nexus between the leaders and followers thus established include,
among others, the depth and social salience of the informal and society-wide

institutions involved, the sheer numeric size and popular availability of these organizations, and their degree of immunity from government reprisals. Equally important are the ideological and strategic compatibility of these social organizations with those of the opposition groups. While priests and religious activists may fully exploit the advantages of churches and other religious institutions in communicating with the masses, for instance, communist activists, most of whom reject religious aesthetics on doctrinal grounds, are likely to shun their use and thus circumscribe the scope of their mobilizational efforts.

It is this differing role of social organizations as opposed to revolutionary parties that has led to a historical paucity of spontaneous revolutions in developing countries. Examples of planned revolutions spearheaded by guerrilla organizations, or at least intended revolutions, are prevalent throughout the developing world, especially in Latin America and Africa.[113] Planned revolutions occur most frequently where relatively strong (often military-based) states coexist side by side with bifurcated societies plagued by social, cultural, economic, and ethnic divisions. In such settings, revolutions could not possibly take place without the deliberate efforts of revolutionary organizations.

Spontaneous revolutions, however, require strong social organizations and comparatively homogeneous societies, characteristics that are not readily found in many developing countries. As it happens, throughout the developing world, the most viable social organizations that have not been fully absorbed into the state are religious institutions, especially those with a history of political independence. This is primarily why, in countries where spontaneous revolutions have recently taken place, as in Iran and in eastern European states, religious institutions have played a highly important role in the revolutionary movement.[114] Politically independent social organizations, of which religious institutions have been prime historical examples, have afforded emerging leaders of revolutions access to the popular classes, in terms of both communication and organization, and have enabled them to popularize their beliefs and propagate their revolutionary actions among the population at large.

Ideology

A final feature that separates spontaneous and planned revolutions is the role of ideology. Ideology plays a much greater role in planned revolutions than in spontaneous ones. Planned revolutions, by their nature, are far more dependent on the deliberate revolutionary mobilization of the masses than are spontaneous revolutions, in which state breakdown and mass oppositional activity largely occur spontaneously and with little encouragement from designated leaders. Ideologies therefore form an intrinsically more important part of planned than of spontaneous revolutions. Planned revolutions, brought on by the efforts of organized guerrilla organizations, are often guided by strict interpretations of specific ideologies. They are, in essence, as much *ideological* movements as they are *revolutionary*. Sponta-neous revolutions, however, initially lack ideological specificity, especially in their embryonic stages when revolutionary leaders have not yet been fully determined.

Leaders of planned revolutions know exactly what they want, i.e. to wrest political power, and have clear targets and objectives. In their pursuit, they develop or adopt an ideology most suited to their ends. In furthering their cause and their efforts, the adoption of an ideology by guerrilla leaders is particularly important in representing an alternative frame of reference to that of the regime. Since they do not hold power, revolutionary leaders must convince their audience that what they believe in holds greater promise than what the state has done. A revolutionary ideology is needed, therefore, to further the legitimacy of the revolutionaries and to delegitimize the views and beliefs of those in power.[115] In spontaneous revolutions, on the other hand, the ideology of the revolution becomes clear only with the emergence of its cadre of leaders. Most spontaneous revolutions are, in fact, free of any specific ideological character until well after the ultimate winners of the revolution have become clear and have established their reign over the country.

During the course of the revolution itself, different ideologies are as much in competition with each other as are various opposition groups who find themselves at the helm of a brewing revolution. For protesting crowds, and for the emerging leaders of the revolution themselves, an ideological under-standing of the revolutionary movement is summed up in dogmatic slogans promising vague ideals and rejecting the present. Specific doctrines with detailed outlines for future courses of action are conspicuously absent, at least until after one revolutionary group has completely dominated the movement. Even then, the ideological character of many post-revolutionary states does not become clear until well after their initial establishment. Post-revolutionary ideological orientations often emerge out of strategic, diplo-matic, and organizational considerations that may not necessarily be the original ones the revolutionaries held.[116]

Considering that spontaneous revolutions start out as largely non-ideological movements, the existence of precise factors and conditions that specifically facilitate mass mobilization assumes particular importance. A state's popu-lar social base among those it governs, its ability and willingness to use coercion to quell the expression of anti-state sentiments, and the degree to which the popular classes are allied together against the governing elite all determine the extent and depth to which a population is spontaneously mobilized against a political order. A most important factor is the extent to which various social classes have been co-opted into the state and identify with it both politically and valuatively. It is precisely those groups who are not incorporated into the system, who are often unidentified and alien from it, that are most amenable to anti-state persuasions.[117] They have very little or nothing at stake in the prevailing political arrangements, and indeed frequently view them as a source of misery and grief. Given the existence of favorable social and political circumstances, such as a permissive political environment and a general willingness to revolt, these groups waste little time in showing their displeasure at the state of affairs. Expressions of anti-state sentiments by one group are greatly strengthened when joined by those of other groups, enhancing the size and forcefulness of an emerging alliance united in its dislike of the prevailing polity. An alliance of the middle classes, who in the developing world are most prone to political opposition, and other, less well-placed social groups like the peasantry or the lumpenproletariat is particularly threatening to the political order.[118] Such a coalition not only enjoys the raw social and economic powers that stem from middle-class participation, but also has the numerical strength and size of the lower classes, who, not having much to lose anyway, are more prone to taking risks and partaking in acts of political violence.

Logistics

Also influential in shaping the depth and the nature of anti-state mobilization are a number of otherwise politically unimportant logistical factors. Variables that in one way or another affect popular conduct, such as the weather, the availability of recreational facilities, transportation routes, and opportunities for face-to-face communication all influence the extent of mobilization and the manner in which it comes about and is conducted.[119] Expressly political factors are equally important. The mere existence of anti-state grievances and sentiments is not sufficient to result in mass mobilization.[120] The political space provided by the state and by the efforts of existing or emerging revolutionaries is equally important. The extent to which the state is willing to use coercion to maintain itself in power, and capable of doing so, contributes most directly to the nature of oppositional mobilization. Often, pre-revolutionary states lack the strong willpower necessary to withstand the onslaught of an evolving revolution, wavering between which options to adopt and unwilling to bear the costs of heavy-handed repression. In other instances, where expressions of opposition are met by determined responses, only sympathizers are intimidated into silence and become passively obedient. For the most part, activists are not discouraged but are rather radicalized, and the political atmosphere is more polarized than stabilized.[121]

The breadth of mass mobilization is, in turn, determined by the existence of specific, society-wide conditions which are conducive to revolutionary developments. Several developments, not all of which are specifically political in origin and in context, arise within the larger society. They make various social strata prone to revolutionary mobilization and, concurrently, have the potential of further exacerbating the state's political difficulties. In a broad sense, these developments provide the contextual background within which the widespread mobilization of emerging revolutionaries is made feasible and takes place. More importantly, the consequences of these developments – or, at times, their mere existence – often serve as the main impetus for popular opposition against ruling elites, made possible by permissive political circumstances.

People will not revolt against a state unless there is a compelling reason for them to do so.[122] Political incapacitation by incumbent regimes simply provides the space and the breathing room necessary for the articulation and expression of political antagonisms. It is not, however, by itself a sufficient *cause* for the coordinated expression of anti-establishment sentiments by a reasonably large segment of the population. The specific sentiments and grievances that prompt populations into political activism *may be* political, but they may just as likely be non-political, at least in genesis if not in the actual form of expression. What is needed is a thorough examination and understanding of the underpinning characteristics and features, both political and otherwise, of societies in which revolutionary mobilization takes place. Then an identification can be made of those factors and dynamics which, individually or in conjunction with one another, invite an otherwise inert mass of people to demonstrate their collective displeasure when political circumstances allow.

Grievances

Three specific sets of developments in any society have the potential of leading to the mobilization of large numbers of people. They are, broadly, those developments that give rise to economically based grievances, to social and cultural grievances, and to political grievances. In their own way, each of these developments produces feelings of resentment and opposition against those who are popularly perceived as responsible for society's ills. Feelings of economic unease and grievance can potentially arise out of the many consequences of industrial development and technological modernization, such as scarcity of essential goods resulting from demographic growth, feelings of deprivation and inequality vis-à-vis others, and class structures conducive to antagonistic behaviour. Social and cultural grievances, meanwhile, become most acutely pronounced during periods of intense social change, particularly when prevailing social values become disjointed and clash with one another. Lastly, political grievances, which are frequent and which also form an integral part of almost all revolutionary movements, arise out of such developments as alienation and desires for wider participation in the political process, nationalism, and the growth of alternative ideologies.

In one way or another, various facets of economic development substantially increase the potential for widespread protests among the different social classes. The precise causal connections between economic development and political instability and violence are blurred and varied at best.[123] Nevertheless, under specific circumstances, the consequences of economic and industrial development may potentially be politically threatening to the state. At the most elementary level, industrialization expands the numerical size of some economic classes at the expense of others: rural inhabitants, most notably the peasants, find their numbers increasingly dwindling while the industrial and middle classes often rise steadily. Property-less and unemployed villagers mushroom into lumpenproletariat, and domestic migration becomes an uncontrolled, integral part of the development process. Depending on specific economic policies, traditionally based elites and upper classes are also often weakened, both politically and economically, and are replaced by newly emerging elite groups.

In most developing countries, it is thus not uncommon to find long-established landed or commercial elites and other aristocratic families who gradually fade into political oblivion and give way to new groups. These new social classes owe their status to modern economic relations such as banking, international trade, and modern industries. How these consequences of industrial development and economic growth on class composition affect the stability of political elites varies from one specific instance to another. Nevertheless, shifting class structures can, and in fact often do, influence the viability of a political system, particularly in cases where the state is dependent on and, in turn, patronizes a specific class. The close political and economic affinity of numerous developing states with one or more of the elite classes has frequently been one of the main sources of dissent and grievance on the part of both the public at large and emerging or existing revolutionary groups.

Another potential source of economic grievance that can increase the public's propensity toward revolutionary action is a feeling of deprivation from desired economic objectives. This syndrome is not unrelated to the development process and is, in fact, most accentuated in countries undergoing rapid economic growth and modernization. Modernization brings with it new needs, outlooks, and desires. It engenders new hopes and fosters rising expectations. Those who experience continued increase in well-being develop expectations about continued improvement.[124] In the promotion of society-wide economic grievances,

> the crucial factor is the vague or specific fear that ground gained over a long period of time will be quickly lost. This fear does not generate if there is continued opportunity to satisfy continually emerging needs; it generates when the existing government suppresses or is blamed for suppressing such opportunity.[125]

What occurs is a sense of economic deprivation, one that either is relative to one's past, or to future aspirations, or is a result of lesser current capabilities than before but higher aspirations for the future.[126] People who feel deprived and who are frustrated in their goals and aspirations have an "innate disposition to do violence to its source", which, especially in the developing world, is perceived to be the state.[127] In instances when the sources of deprivation are obscure and cannot be attributed to specific political targets, alternative doctrines and ideologies which justify violence gain increasing currency and appear as more and more plausible to ever-growing segments of population.[128]

Also related to the general process of development and more specifically to feelings of deprivation are growing rates of inequality among various classes. Economic inequality by itself does not necessarily lead to political violence, and the relationship between the two developments is context-specific.[129] In accentuated forms, however, inequality, whatever its causes, leads to a reduction of identification between the rulers and the ruled. In the face of continued immiseration and little or no identification between the body politic and the rest of society, widespread expressions of political discontent become highly likely.[130] In countries entangled in the complicated and multi-faceted web of industrial development, a variety of factors can potentially heighten existing economic inequalities and create new ones.

Unequal access to economically valuable goods due to social or political influence, especially those goods with a value that rises with the pace of industrialization, exacerbates differences in class standing, power, and prestige. The spread of commercialism across social and class lines polarizes competition over valued goods, especially those that are often in scarce supply, such as arable land and water. In instances where institutional means of competition are lacking and there are permissive class structures and political circumstances, the potential for political violence is greatly magnified.

Economic inequality can also arise from demographic growth, albeit indirectly, which similarly increases the scarcity of prized resources in both rural and, especially, urban areas. Although the connection between the two developments is not universal, under certain circumstances population growth severely strains state capabilities and can bring a state to the brink of collapse, as was the case immediately prior to the English revolution.[131] Reduction of state revenues and irregularities in finances, elite competition and turnover, and other difficulties associated with population growth may in one way or another propel a weakened state toward breakdown.[132] The connection between population growth, inequality, and revolutionary action is even more direct. As one observer claims, "given a finite set of resources, a bifurcation process takes place in which many persons have very little and a few persons have much. This process has been shown to occur in instances of mass revolution."[133] In fact, those revolutions that have involved the extensive mobilization of peasants have taken place in countries where there has been a scarcity of land and its concentration in strikingly few hands.[134]

The last category of economic grievances that can potentially lead to revolutionary mobilization stems from the predominance of particular class structures. These class-based dynamics may or may not be exacerbated by the industrialization process. The prevalence of specific structures and patterns of intra- and inter-relations within each class can significantly determine its potential for revolutionary mobilization. The middle and the lower classes, including the peasantry, are most directly amenable to grievances arising out of class structures and relations. As earlier discussed, the primary source of grievance among the middle classes in the developing world is the frustration of their aspirations and feelings of relative deprivation. In so far as peasants and other rural inhabitants are concerned, their revolutionary mobilization is most feasible when the peasant community as a whole is strong and they enjoy some degree of economic and political autonomy, and when landlords or proxies of the establishment lack direct economic and political control at the local level.[135] Peasants with smallholdings are normally conservative and quiescent, reluctant to risk losing their paltry goods and heavily dependent on wealthier peasants and landed upper classes.[136] Sharecroppers and property-less laborers, who have little to lose and much to gain by risking the adversities of violent action, along with middle-income peasants frustrated by their inability to break into the ranks of large estate proprietors, are most apt to partake in revolutionary action. An equally inert conservatism similarly pervades in the upper echelons of the industrial working class, especially among highly skilled technical workers who form the "labor aristocracy".[137] Having finally secured stable and relatively comfortable positions, skilled industrial laborers are less willing to engage in the risky and often violent political activities in which the lumpenproletariat readily participate.

Despite their important role, economic grievances are not the only category of dynamics that are conducive to mass mobilization. Society-wide grievances with deep roots among the population can arise out of the appearance of certain social and cultural factors as well. The many and varied ramifications of social change are examples of the developments that can propel an otherwise quiescent group of people into revolutionary mobilization. Socially aroused political opposition is often attributed to an absence of "harmony" between a "society's values and the realities with which it must deal".[138] Disparities between the way people feel and behave and their surrounding environment may indeed lead to their disillusionment and the subsequent focusing of their anger on political targets. But, at least in so far as developing countries are concerned, social antagonisms are more likely to arise out of an incoherence in the very values that people hold and cherish. Specifically, deeply felt feelings of trauma and anguish are likely to occur when the prevailing values of society themselves are sharply divided, incoherent, and at times outright contradictory. Social and cultural homogeneity is hardly evident in any contemporary modern society. In some societies, however, especially those undergoing rapid modernization and development, values are so disjointed and contradictory that valuative heterogeneity turns into what is almost completely separate and unrelated clusters of different cultures. When sufficient numbers of people subscribe to these differing value systems, and they all demand equal shares of the available cultural and political resources, then there is potential for violent action, especially if institutional, agreed-upon means of political competition do not exist.

The mutual incompatibility of desired and cherished values may not even transcend social and class lines. People who are constantly bombarded with ever-changing norms and values, especially in developing countries, can become culturally disillusioned and may, under the right circumstances, turn their anger on political objects. They become torn between the values that they have traditionally come to adopt, and those contradictory ones which they either feel compelled to adopt or willingly desire. The greater the intensity of the conflict among prevailing social values, the greater is the extent of individual and collective disillusionment, and thus the higher is the probability of politically threatening behavior. Similarly, the more acutely aware of the conflict between the values to be adopted, the higher is the people's disillusionment and thus the likelihood of their political activism. That is primarily why in the developing world, students and intellectuals, whose job it is to critically reflect on prevailing social values, are more prone to political opposition than are other groups.[139]

Lastly, a series of developments can give rise to politically originated grievances. Because those grievances that are derived from social and economic developments are expressed in political terms, it is frequently difficult to distinguish between singularly political dynamics which prompt mass protests as opposed to those with social or economic roots. Nevertheless, there are several explicitly political developments that are, by themselves, sufficient causes for widespread political mobilization. In fact, they are for the most part the same set of dynamics that bring about crises of legitimacy for incumbent elites and nullify their justifications for their continued hold on power. The same factors that lead to a state's growing political weakness have the potential of bringing about mass mobilization. They include, among others, growing demands for greater political participation, increasing awareness of nationalist sentiments, and the widespread acceptance of ideologies other than that of the state. There is, nonetheless, a fine and subtle difference between legitimacy crisis as such and politically induced mass mobilization. Legitimacy crisis is one of the conditions through which states are weakened and are pushed to the brink of collapse. It is only then, well after a permissive political environment has appeared, that the same set of factors that had led to legitimacy crisis results in mass-based revolutionary mobilization.

The depth and preponderance of one particular form of grievance throughout society is so important that it can directly influence the composition of the revolution's leaders and their followers. More than anything else, the leaders and followers of a revolutionary movement are determined by virtue of their relationship with the various sources of grievance that exist throughout society. Those who can most aptly discern the sources that aggrieve people, who are ideologically and organizationally capable of exploiting this anger, and who offer remedies or promises for their alleviation, rapidly ascend to the leadership of the revolution. At the same time, those masses who are most acutely afflicted by a certain form of actual or perceived misfortune, who are organizationally and situationally most accessible to groups promising to alleviate those misfortunes, and who are emotionally and valuatively receptive to the appeals and cries of revolutionary leaders, form the bulk of mobilized protesters. In short, the very dynamics that set in motion the onslaught of revolutions to a great extent determine the character and nature of their leaders and followers.

It is precisely for this reason that the overwhelming majority of participants in revolutions in the developing world are displaced and dispossessed peasants, disillusioned and unassimilated rural migrants, and the aspiring but frustrated segments of the middle classes. Given the right political circumstances, increased inequality and bifurcation due to a growing scarcity of goods or skewed commercialization can promote an appropriate environment within which peasants become politically active and mobilized. The discovery by self-proclaimed revolutionaries of the merits of peasant-based revolutions, derived either from practical realism or from doctrinal idealism, provides a nexus between the two groups that has been a recurrent feature of many revolutions. The less than successful peasant-based revolutionary movements that once flourished throughout Latin America attest to the centrality of bonds between peasants and guerrilla activists. The successful revolutions that occurred in China, Cuba, Vietnam, and to some extent in Nicaragua, all entailed considerable peasant participation.[140] At the same time, the cultural disillusionment, economic frustration, and political alienation of ever-growing lumpenproletariats can also turn them into readily mobilizable foot-soldiers for various revolutionary causes, the full meanings of which they may not necessarily grasp or even endorse. Their participation in revolutionary movements is not so much a result of deep understanding of and adherence to specific revolutionary ideals but more a result of their readiness and availability, both emotionally and organizationally, to partake in politically oppositional activities. Those who do hold revolutionary hopes and aspirations, and who do not hesitate to voice them, are mostly drawn from among the ranks of the middle classes. By virtue of their social and economic positions, their education and background, and their political aspirations, the middle classes are much better positioned to assume the mantle of a revolutionary movement, and when revolutions do occur, it is indeed the middle classes who are frequently in the forefront and are their most vociferous leaders. The politics of exactly what groups become mobilized and by whom is in turn determined by the prevailing social and cultural dynamics that bond the various social strata together.

Conclusion

Revolutions are clearly multi-faceted phenomena arising out of the interplay of an array of diverse political, economic, and social developments. They are, in the first place, products of skewed political development, of inherently unstable processes through which the body politic passes, voluntarily or involuntarily, on its way toward becoming a modern polity. Revolutions are, in essence, violent struggles aimed at achieving a fuller and more developed political establishment that is supposedly more capable of delivering popularly desired goods and services than those which the incumbent state can offer. This struggle is in fact a thoroughly political one, with its genesis, direction, scope, and magnitude all dependent on the specific political configurations that happen to prevail at the time. However, the contextual environment within which the willful leaders and the receptive audience of this struggle emerge is heavily influenced by dynamics which may be fundamentally apolitical, particularly those that are social and cultural or economic in nature. The polarizing effects of this contextual environment are all the more accentuated in the developing world, where industrial development, rapid urbanization, and intense social change simultaneously take place at a dizzying pace and breed an atmosphere that is highly conducive to the eruption of full-blown revolutions or at least to the appearance of revolutionary movements.

Where revolutions lead is a question largely dependent on whether they are more planned in genesis and execution or involve greater spontaneity. Planned revolutions are based largely on premeditated programs devised by willful revolutionaries who know precisely what they want and have a clear idea of the ways and means to achieve their goals. Their efforts are undertaken with clear goals in mind and, if successful, there is often little disparity between their previously proclaimed goals—apart, of course, from their boisterous and at times manipulative and false promises—and newly initiated policies. Spontaneous revolutions, on the other hand, are more often the outcome of developments that at first look hardly revolutionary. They involve neither formulated programs nor planned initiatives. Their leaders emerge relatively late, and the ultimate goals of those leaders are formed and pronounced even later. The revolution's goals and ideals are initially elusive at best, summed up in dogmatic slogans and vague promises. Each cadre of leaders promises such appealing alternatives to the status quo as democracy and equality, principles that are left open to differing interpretations once it is time for their implementation. In these instances, the ideals and purposes of revolutions often appear vastly different from their eventual outcomes, a difference which is the result of the inherent looseness of the revolutionary process itself rather than of sinister manipulation by revolutionary turncoats.

Nevertheless, with remarkable uniformity and regardless of whether spontaneous or planned, revolutions give rise to populist, inclusionary regimes. By their nature, revolutions involve the patronage of masses of people. The relationship between revolutionary leaders and followers is essentially one of patrons and clients, with the group most capable of catering to the needs and wishes of the widest spectrum of people emerging as their leader in opposing the establishment. Once the revolution has succeeded and formerly oppositional leaders become newly ensconced elites, their reliance on the patronage of the masses does not wither and is, in fact, in most instances accentuated. Their mandate is no longer to oppose the regime but to make good on the numerous promises they gave before the revolution's success.

The viability of the fledgling post-revolutionary order depends on a continuation of the mass patronage that the revolutionaries acquired before they attained formal political power. To sustain power, they now need to deliver the goods they promised, or at least to divert attention from them by fomenting popular anger against enemies of the new order, real or imagined. Diverting attention they indeed do, as the many instances of politically sanctioned post-revolutionary violence, wars, and other international disputes, and purges and the elimination of "counter-revolutionaries" demonstrate. But even if only symbolic, a token delivery of the goods promised is necessary to maintain the viability of the new system. The result is populist and politically inclusionary states, states that in one way or another allow greater participation in the body politic if not in the actual decision-making process itself.

It is here in these inclusionary, post-revolutionary states that revolutions meet an embryonic death. Various means of patronage such as economic reforms, programs for public welfare, and greater political participation, no matter how farcical and marginal, heighten the new regime's sense of legitimacy among the population and, at least so long as that legitimacy lasts, make it immune from another revolution. Moreover, post-revolutionary states, which in any event owe their very genesis to violence, feel less inhibited in using coercion in order to preserve their newly acquired powers than would otherwise be the case.

The constant identification of "counter-revolutionary" elements as the prime public enemy, the perpetual sense of being besieged and under threat from outside forces, and the unending rhetoric of denouncing the morbid past all make post-revolutionary states more prone to using violence against actual or perceived sources of opposition. Crushing those who oppose the new order is indeed one of the very sources upon which its legitimacy is based. In the many instances where generally accepted means of political competition are absent, the tendency toward violence and revolutions remains an endemic probability. Whether the new wave of emerging democracies in the developing world proves capable of stemming the tide of engendered instability remains to be seen. What is certain is the enduring likelihood of further revolutionary eruptions in narrowly based, delegitimized states promoting rapid social change and industrial development in the face of non-responsive and unchangeable political structures.

9   Democratization

In the mid- to late 1970s, dictatorial systems began collapsing one after another, first in southern Europe, then in South America in the early and mid-1980s, and in eastern Europe in the late 1980s and early 1990s. Eventually, national movements aimed at instituting democracy also bore fruit in a number of African countries—not just in South Africa but also in the continent's Francophone countries—and in South Korea. Even in the Middle East, a bastion of "authoritarian holdouts", demands for political accountability and democratic representation began to dominate the national discourse in Morocco, Algeria, Egypt, Jordan, Iran, and elsewhere. As more and more countries joined the ranks of democracies, Professor Samuel Huntington's declaration that a "third wave" of democratization was under way was indeed becoming prophetic.[1]

Gradually, however, the euphoria of global democratization gave way to a number of sobering realities. It soon became apparent that democratic *transitions* were only half of the equation. Equally problematic were the dilemmas involved in democratic *consolidation*. The new democracies were confronted with a plethora of economic and political problems with which they had to contend, many continuing to suffer from the squalid legacies of the authoritarian systems they had replaced. These included, among others, the challenges of economic liberalization and globalization, the modalities and procedures necessary for conducting elections and other necessary democratic practices, reformulating civil-military relations, and ensuring that democratic pacts and bargains were observed. This chapter focuses on one specific facet of democratic transitions and consolidation, namely civil society, and the pivotal role it plays in significantly influencing the overall nature of the transition process itself and the general character of the incoming democratic political system. It is by now a truism that the outcomes of the recent wave of democratization cannot all be considered to be equally democratic, some of the new states being truer to the spirit of democracy than others. There are various reasons for these differences, ranging from past experiences with democracy to the nature and intents of the actors involved, and the structural and institutional limitations and/or opportunities within which they operate. While each of these differentiating factors is in itself highly important, civil society plays a far more significant role in determining the overall character of the post-democratization polity.

This crucial role of civil society has often been overlooked by the literature on democratization, especially in so far as democratic consolidation is concerned. Despite the unprecedented proliferation of studies on democratization in recent years, there is little consensus in the current literature about the exact role of civil society both before and after the transition to democracy. Much of the democratization literature has either focused on the role of civil society *before* the actual transition from the non-democratic state was set into motion, or has overplayed the importance of political crafting and institutional consolidation in the post-transition phase.[2] Overlooked in the process has been the pivotal role that civil society in general and civil society organizations in particular can have in shaping the exact nature of the post-transition democratic state.

This chapter argues that the more truly representative, viable democracies that have emerged out of the recent transitions must by nature have a strong social and cultural footing among the social actors who were active in the transition. However, less representative, more restricted quasi-democracies are less culturally grounded and are more dependent on intra- and inter-elite political pacts than on sociocultural imperatives for democratic maintenance.

Democratic transitions are set in motion by the workings of two general sets of dynamics that could broadly be classified as either structural or cultural. All democratic transitions involve structural transformations, for without such changes the actual institutional mechanics of democracy—ranging from inter-elite pacts to constitutional guarantees—would not come about.[3] In such instances, democratization is often initiated from above and is set in motion, at least initially, as a direct result of changes and developments that are indigenous to the state.

Economic paralysis or political malaise result in state breakdown, or at best profound weakness, and compel old political elites to open up the political process and to accommodate other contending elites.[4] When the transition is complete, the new elites face the arduous tasks of democratic consolidation, chief among which are the politically hazardous neo-liberal economic reforms that almost all newly democratic states decide to undertake soon after assuming power.[5] But sacrificed in the process is the popularization of democratic norms and ideals among the larger population, a process that is made all the more difficult under worsening economic conditions, declining real wages, and the removal of many of the previous state's social security networks.[6]

Most post-democratic political elites are simply too preoccupied with institutional and economic concerns to pay sufficient attention to the popular norms that are beginning to take hold in their country's new, post-transition political culture or to worry about the larger population's general dispositions toward democracy. This is all the more important given that in these countries democracy has become a political and economic reality and is no longer an abstract, sought-after ideal. Many of the democratic states that have recently appeared in the developing world, therefore, face crises of social and cultural legitimacy and, as demonstrated most starkly in Fujimori's Peru and to a lesser extent in Turkey, remain susceptible to demagogic, populist, and at times outright anti-democratic movements.

Exceptions do exist, and such democracies as those found in Argentina, Brazil, Chile, and South Korea (as well as in Greece, Portugal, and Spain) all seem to enjoy high levels of cultural consolidation despite having come about as a result of negotiated pacts among elites. In all of these cases, democracy was initiated from above, but, sooner in some cases and later in others, it appears to have become culturally accepted and popularized among the various social strata.

For whatever reason, however, democratic elites do not always actively try to consolidate democracy culturally, or succeed in this attempt. The ensuing democratic system often ends up being comprised of largely isolated, elite groups whose main interests lie in securing their own positions within the new institutions of the democratic system (especially in the parliament, or in their own political party) rather than representing their constituents. Such an outcome has occurred in many of the ostensibly democratic countries of the developing world, both old and new: Kenya, Tanzania, Zambia, and Madagascar in Africa, to name a few; Costa Rica, Colombia, Panama, Peru, Nicaragua, and Venezuela in Latin America; Taiwan, India, Sri Lanka, Bangladesh, and Pakistan in South and Southeast Asia; and Lebanon and Turkey in the Middle East.[7] Democratic transitions from above, in short, face the *potential* (rather than inherent) danger of resulting in elitist, quasi-democratic polities that have all the institutional and structural trappings of democracy but lack a strong cultural component that would give them resonance in the different strata of society.

Not all democratic transitions are initiated from above, however, and there are some that come about as a result of societal pressures in general and civil society agitations in particular. In such cases, the incoming democratic system cannot help but have a strong cultural component, and it enjoys comparatively higher levels of popular legitimacy, and tends to be more representative of the broader strata of society. In these types of transition, the impulse to democratize begins not within the state but with non-state actors, some of whom ask specifically for democratic rights while others may have demands that are limited to particular issues. In either case, in the pre-democratization era certain societal actors begin to demand greater space and political autonomy, and many of them over time cluster into organized or semi-organized grass-roots movements and turn into civil society organizations.[8]

If these civil society organizations, which by definition must operate democratically internally, begin collectively to demand, and succeed in bringing about, a democratic polity, they themselves in turn become the societal and cultural cushions on which the new system rests. In a way, the new democratic polity is already culturally consolidated *before* the actual democratic transition takes place. Were this not the case, civil society organizations could not have gained enough support and momentum to force the authoritarian state to agree to democratic concessions. And now that broadly based, increasingly popular civil society organizations have finally succeeded in bringing about a democratic polity, they are not about to take their newly won liberties for granted or to allow democratic rights to be practiced primarily by specific elite groups. They seek to participate actively in the political process and to ensure the democratic and representational integrity of the system.

Viable democracies, driven by civil society, are comparatively rare, but they have come about in recent years in Poland, Hungary, and most notably in South Africa. These democratic systems are not only more truly representative of broader strata of society but, in fact, highly self-conscious. Eventually, such democratic systems may over time begin to be taken for granted by their citizens, as most long-established democracies often are. But in the years immediately following the democratic transition they are far more vibrant than quasi-democracies could ever hope to become, a vibrancy maintained by their very youth and popular legitimacy. In viable democracies, membership levels in political parties tend to continue to increase, voter turn-outs are relatively high, elections—both national as well as regional and local ones—are often hotly contested and taken very seriously, the media are free and by-and-large vigilant, and, frequently, a growing plethora of issue-driven grass-roots organizations spring up and help facilitate increasing levels of popular political input.

Civil Society and Civil Society Organizations

The concept of civil society has gained increasing currency in much of the recent literature on democratic transitions.[9] Despite considerable scholarly advance on the subject, a clear distinction has yet to be drawn between the concepts of "civil society" and "civil society organization". While inextricably linked, the two are distinct. In fact, civil society organizations, once they emerge, become permanent or semi-permanent features of the social landscape, whereas civil society may emerge immediately before and during the democratization process and later die out once the transition is over.

Civil society organizations are a part and sub-component of the larger civil society. A civil society organization could be any politically autonomous and independent group that can articulate and, in turn, further both a corporate identity and a specific agenda. In itself, such an organization may or may not be democratically inclined, although its very existence does to a certain extent bode well for democracy as it necessitates at least some rolling back of the powers of the state. Religious societies, ethnic and/or tribal confederacies, and women's groups are representatives of this type of civil society organization. On its own, a civil society organization—which may be found in any social setting—does not necessarily result in the increasing prevalence of demands for political space and representation among social actors. It simply has a corporate identity which it seeks to further. But when this civil society organization is one of a number of other, similar organizations that also begin to emerge within society, its social and political resonance becomes all the more pronounced.

The simultaneous emergence and/or operations of civil society organizations is likely to result in two concurrent outcomes: on the one hand, a self-sustaining and self-perpetuating momentum develops within society that makes it want to safeguard and maintain its newly won sense of autonomy from the state; on the other hand, the state finds itself increasingly on the defensive, and, if it is sufficiently vulnerable, it will be forced into giving democratic concessions to society. Why and how civil society organizations emerge and operate is context specific and a result of developments within society itself, or because of its relations with the state, or both (discussed below). In either case, a politically charged and politically laden civic sense overtakes a majority of social actors, compelling them, among other things, purposefully to seek democratic liberties and demand representational privileges. This is civil society, which is in turn the linchpin of a viable democracy.

The most apparent manifestations of civil society, as mentioned, are such pressure groups as Mothers of Plaza de Mayo in Argentina, Solidarity in Poland, and the New Forum in the former East Germany. These organizations may be diverse in intent and composition; in fact they may have nothing in common in so far as their stated purposes and agendas are concerned. But they all have one crucial common denominator: they are pressure groups pressing the state for greater autonomy and political space—*they demand democracy*. Social and political autonomy by such a self-organized group is of critical importance, but it is not enough. If we were to stop here, backgammon players in the tea-houses of the Middle East or every beer lover in Poland and former Czechoslovakia would have to be considered as progenitors of civil society. They are not. Neither is civil society made up of just any group that manages to exert pressure on the state for political cooperation or even space. Had this been the case, most corporatist institutions pressing demands on the state—labor or the Catholic Church in Latin America in the 1960s and 1970s—would also have to be considered as components of civil society, and that is not always the case.

Civil society gives rise to a very specific type of organization, one that is *social* in its genesis and composition but *political* in its agendas and initiatives.[10] It is an organization that is formed out of the independent, autonomous initiatives of politically concerned individuals. These social actors are united by a common concern, often rallying around a specific issue (greater political space or less literary censorship, for example). But irrespective of their specificities, if their demands on the state are met, they either directly or indirectly result in a greater opening up of the political process. Ernest Gellner has argued that civil society is primarily a liberator from the tyranny of social and cultural rituals.[11] But in addition to its social and cultural ramifications, civil society has a more pointed political function and agenda as well. Knowingly or unknowingly, civil society organizations are agents and proponents of democratization: the cumulative effects of their pressures on the state, at a particular moment of regime crisis, may be too much for political leaders, with exhausted legitimacies and few other non-coercive means of governance, to bear.

As argued earlier, transition to a viable democracy can be greatly facilitated by the prior existence of civil society. But civil society may not always usher in a democratic transition; the state may put up an effective struggle and hang on to the reins of power. A viable democracy necessitates civil society, but civil society in itself does not necessarily mean democratization. To have democratic consequences, civil society organizations must embark on democratizing themselves and the larger social and political environments within which they operate. Often with faltering steps and at times with vigor and determination, these soldiers of democracy march on, *and if successful*, they bring about a democratic revolution, one that may be either negotiated or as cataclysmic as any other revolutionary episode. The point to bear in mind here is the chronological order in which civil society and democratization take place: there are first social pressures for democratic openings; these pressures crystallize in the formation of civil society organizations that are democratic in nature and democratizing in pursuit; if these groups coalesce or on their own mount a political challenge that the state cannot fend off, then a successful process of democratization takes place. Once democratization has taken place, there is a more hospitable environment for even further civil society groups to take form and evolve.

How does civil society come about? A number of reinforcing and complementary social and political forces need to be simultaneously present for civil society and groups representing it to emerge. A praetorian political system is a most essential prerequisite, for democratic yearnings must first be formulated and then frustrated in an authoritarian setting for groups to look to alternative, non-state agencies for political expression. More specifically, the praetorian state and the larger society must operate in two different, mutually alien cultural realms. The average person must feel not just disenchanted with the state; he or she must feel completely detached from and in fact disgusted with it. There are no norms or values attached to the state with which he or she can identify, and there is a stark contrast between his or her overall cultural orientations and whatever it is that the state stands for. Examples would be states that seem to operate in a world of their own, detached from the cultural contexts of their societies, apparently unaware of or insensitive to social and cultural nuances emanating from below.

Within such a context, civil society organizations offer alternative, non-official, and therefore seemingly untainted forums and organizational alternatives through which social actors could mobilize and express their concerns about specific issues or toward politics in general. With the exception of Tito's somewhat charismatic rule in Yugoslavia, former communist states in east and central Europe fit this model perfectly, as do the many bureaucratic-authoritarian states that dotted Latin America in the 1960s and 1970s. If society is at its core religious, the state either is aggressively secular or is in fact deliberately anti-religious; if industrialization has not progressed to the point of overwhelming agrarian life, the state pretends to be industrially advanced and highly modernized; if society wants to be left alone and be subject to its own internal dynamics, the state seeks to penetrate and change it; if society wants to express itself politically and to participate in the system, the state subdues and controls it. At every turn, the state and society diverge and differ from one another. Nothing binds them but animosity and distrust—no political cultures that could be manipulated by politicians and bought by the people, no half-hearted democracies that could placate demands for real participation, no charismatic leaders who would find devotees among the masses.

But this is only the political half of the equation, an equation based on a clash of perspectives on the part of the state and those who see it as at best apathetic and at worst adversarial to their hopes and aspirations. The political roadblocks erected by the state compel these individuals to form civil society organizations of their own in an attempt both to replace some of the specific functions of the state and to provide themselves with channels of democratic expression.

Who exactly are these individuals who come together and form civil society organizations? And what social and cultural imperatives prompt them to do so? The answers lie in the particular formation of social forces that the state is seeking to subdue. The pivotal role of intellectuals in the flowering of civil society has already been discussed at great length elsewhere.[12] Intellectuals alone are not enough, however, as every society has its own literati elite no matter how minuscule and socially vacuous they may be. If civil society is to develop, the intellectual elite must have three particular characteristics.

First and foremost, it must be committed to the principles and practices of democracy to the point of having internalized them. Simple rhetoric and heroism do not a democratic intellectual make; he or she must be both a believer and a practitioner of democracy in every facet of life, including in relationships with work colleagues, family members, and others with different viewpoints. Equally important is the social resonance of intellectuals, in terms of both the message they propound and their accessibility to the rest of society. Elite intellectuals, in other words, can no longer be so *elite* in their social standing and the learned plains on which they dwell. They must have drawn themselves close enough to the population to be heard and understood by them, even if not necessarily followed. Lastly, these intellectuals must give themselves an institutional forum, no matter how informal, through which they can meet and circulate ideas, consolidate their links with one or more social classes, and apply direct or indirect pressures on the state. These institutional forums may range from ad hoc clubs and syndicates (e.g. a writers' association or the Civic Forum) to full-blown grass-roots organizations (e.g. Base Ecclesiastical Communities (CEBs)) and political parties (e.g. Solidarity).

The resonance of civil society's intellectual progenitors itself requires certain necessary social pre-conditions, chief among which are the existence of a nationally uniform cultural milieu and a spirit of tolerance. To begin with, there must be a national culture that is homogeneous and not composed of smaller cultural sub-units that may at best overlap but continue to retain distinctive qualities in such core areas as communication, rituals, status, and the like. There is in such a society a "standardization of idiom", where "communication occurs, if not with man as such, then at any rate with man-as-standard-specimen-of-a-codified-culture".[13] Civil society requires cultural uniformity on a national level, where people are bound not by segmentary, exclusivist institutions that differentiate, but by associations that are unsanctified, instrumental, revocable, and yet effective.[14]

Uniform national cultural homogeneity is important, but again not enough. In addition, civil society requires a near-total psychological trans-formation, both of the individual on a personal level and of the larger collective whole—be it a syndicate, a political party, or an entire nation—to which he or she belongs. Communicating through the same idiom that is free of ritualized sub-contexts is an essential prerequisite of forming voluntary associations and groups. Thus members of the same national entity who come from different parts of the country, have different accents, and prefer particular kinds of food may join together to form an association in which the goals of the association are far more binding on them than any of their specific idiosyncrasies. In countries with at least a semblance of a national culture, this is how most workers', teachers', merchants', writers', and other types of syndicate organizations are formed and operate.

But taking part in a syndicate organization alone, while quite important, is an insufficient indication of a burgeoning civil society. What must take place is an internalization of democratic norms and mores on an emotional, personal level. What must happen is first a democratization of the self, and then of selves, and from there on and on to the larger community, until a critical mass of like-minded, democratic aspirants begin to exert pressure on the state. If a syndicate, or a group of syndicates, were simply to press their own narrowly defined demands upon the state, the state might easily co-opt them into itself or placate their demands with minor adjustments to its policies. At most, it might re-orient its agendas and institutions to better fit an emerging corporatist arrangement.[16] But if there is an element of corporatism in civil society, it must be decidedly democratic: groups and organizations that are self-democratizing and democratizing of the larger polity, if successful, force the state to become democratic also.

Here the contest becomes political. Civil society presses democratic demands on the state and its various institutions, and much of the outcome of the transition depends on the precise manner in which these state institutions react to pressures from below. In this respect, the politically grounded analyses of Huntington and Di Palma have much to offer, especially in so far as the role of the military is concerned.[16] The state and its various institutional arms must be vulnerable enough to democratic pressures from below for a viable democratic transition to take place. The specific political actors who are in official positions at the time of democratization must have already been weakened and thus eager to compromise with the opposition—the actual reasons for their weakness and vulnerability may differ from case to case.[17] Moreover, the different auxiliary institutions on which the office-holders' powers are directly or indirectly based (the military, the official political party, the bureaucracy, etc.) must also be willing to negotiate away some of their present privileges.

The paralysis of the state need not necessarily be complete for a viable democratic transition to occur, but it must be sufficiently extensive to compel those in official positions to come to the bargaining table. The situation in pseudo-democratic transitions is often quite different, as seldom are all state institutions sufficiently weakened to go along with a fully open democratization process. In some instances, state institutions, and especially the military, demand extensive guarantees in the post-transition era and exert considerable influence afterwards (as in Turkey, Peru, Venezuela, and the Philippines).[18] But transition processes do not always succeed, even partially, and in these cases the powers and intentions of state actors have proven critical. In such instances, elements within the state are unwilling to yield to any democratic opening and thus seek to abort the democratization process altogether.

Examples from successful, partial, and aborted democratic transitions illustrate the point better. In most of the former communist states of eastern Europe, in the mid- and late 1980s such crucial arms of the state as the communist party and the bureaucracy were in a state of near paralysis, if not fully paralyzed already, but the army still maintained much of its coercive capabilities and had not undergone the extensive atrophy of the other two institutions. Nevertheless, when the democratic transition process gathered steam and began threatening the very existence of the communist state, the army did not, and in some instances could not, intervene in the political process.[19]

This sequence of events is markedly different from what took place in Algeria in the early 1990s, when the country witnessed a bloody reversal of a democratization process that had started in the late 1980s.[20] As President Chadli Bendjedid inaugurated the country's ostensibly liberal democratic constitution of 1989 and promised open parliamentary elections, the military begrudgingly looked on as its once-extensive powers were greatly reduced and the Islamic Salvation Front (FIS), whom the military considered "anti-democratic", gained in strength. When the FIS won a majority of seats in the 1992 parliamentary elections, the military duly stepped it, removed Bendjedid from power, annulled the elections, and reasserted itself as the dominant institution of the state. The military either had not been weakened enough or was somehow unwilling to face the uncertain possibilities of a fully democratic transition.

Between these two extremes, one a viable transition and the other an aborted one, falls the Turkish case.[21] The Turkish army has always considered itself the ultimate guardian of the Turkish Republic and the protector of the legacy of the country's modern founder, Kemal Ataturk. Consistent with this self-ascribed mission, the army launched a coup in 1980 in reaction to what it saw as the inability of politicians to maintain domestic order, in turn handing power over to elected civilians in 1983. As this was a controlled transition, initiated and directed from above, in today's Turkey the military retains extensive powers and there are severe limits imposed on the country's democratic system. The overall flavor and nature of Turkey's political system, at best a pseudo-democracy, is very different from the viable democratic systems of Poland and Hungary, both of which were largely the results of pressure from below.

Does civil society ever end or die out? Developments in post-communist Poland, where civil society was at one point on the most solid footing, are most instructive. Within three to five years of the democratic transition there, some of the civil society organizations that were once the primary engines of the country's new democracy had begun a steady decline in popular legitimacy and social resonance. Solidarity and the Catholic Church were especially affected, having lost much of the unparalleled popularity that they had acquired at the height of the democratization process in 1989 and 1990. By December 1995, Poles had elected an ex-communist as their new president.[22]

What does this say about civil society's resonance and its relationship with democratization? These events demonstrate not necessarily the demise of civil society but rather the institutionalization and routinization of civil society organizations. In today's Poland as in most other post-communist countries, no longer do civil society organizations operate in a non-democratic environment, where they have constantly to guard against possible state encroachment. They can now take their operations and their very existence for granted, gradually, therefore, losing the defensive zeal which marked their earlier years. In fact, once the democratic polity has been established and the threat of authoritarian reversal appears remote, most civil society organizations (the church, intellectual groups, etc.) begin to look like any other social institution.

Poland is a classic case of a country in which *civil society* has ceased to exist but *civil society organizations* continue to operate. Unlike in the heyday of the communist collapse, Polish society today is neither actively nor self-consciously democratizing itself—as Anthony Giddens would maintain, most Poles would these days consider themselves to have gone beyond the phase of "emancipatory politics" and to have entered the era of "life politics".[23] But the institutional residues of civil society are still there, and, although not as feverishly active now as they once were, could again kick into action if need be (i.e. if their individual members deem their political activism and defense of representative democracy to be necessary). In fact, given that such organizations once served as powerful vehicles for the establishment and institutionalization of a democratic polity by incorporating social actors into themselves, they now have an easier time in mobilizing the population in defense of specific corporate interests or larger democratic goals.

Thus the relationship between civil society organizations and civil society is cyclical: civil society organizations may combine to give rise to civil society; given the right political environment, civil society may usher in a democratic polity; once a democracy is established, civil society tends to peter out although civil society organizations continue to operate, albeit in a more routinized and less feverishly defensive form; if the newly established democratic system faces serious threats to its existence, the existing civil society organizations, conceivably reinforced by new ones, could once again mobilize social actors in defense of the political system and reactivate the civil society that had become dormant. So long as the political system is democratic and allows autonomous self-organization on the part of society, the cycle could repeat itself indefinitely.

Democratic Transitions

Most of the recent English language literature on democratization has focused on the political variables involved both before and after the actual process of democratic transformation takes place. This is particularly true of American political scientists writing on the topic, for most European and especially British scholars tend to be more receptive to the idea of conducting social and cultural analysis along with their political analysis.[24] Nevertheless, few if any of the published works on the subject have yet drawn a systemic parallel between the sociocultural emergence of civil society and the political institutionalization of democratic states. Examining the two phenomena of democracy and democratization needs to have a sharper cultural and sociological focus. Concurrent with political analysis, attention must be paid to the exact point at which civil society appears and the precise role that it plays. In some democratization processes, civil society either does not initially play a determining role and emerges only later on, or does not appear at all, even well into the life of the supposedly democratic country.

Examples from southern Europe are most instructive in this respect. In Greece, Portugal, and Spain during the mid-1970s, when each country witnessed a democratic transition, civil society was only nascent at the time of the changeover and was caught largely off guard by the collapse of the old order and its reconstitution into a democratic one.[25] Today, however, by most accounts democracy appears to be on a solid social and cultural footing in each of these countries and is built on a strong foundation of civil society.[26] Turkey, on the other hand, is an exception, for while the political transformation there into a democratic system has long been completed, a similar, compatible social and cultural change has not yet taken place.[27] Civil society, in other words, has not evolved yet and does not appear likely to do so soon.[28] Thus the Turkish political system is at best quasi-democratic and is, in fact, highly susceptible to populist and demagogic movements from below.[29] This is not, however, what has happened in most of the democratic transitions of eastern Europe and South America.

There are instances where civil society appears first and eventually leads to democratic political change. In such countries as Poland, Hungary, former Czechoslovakia, and South Africa (and one may even include Argentina and Brazil), civil society organizations preceded, sometimes by a good many years, the actual political transformation of authoritarian structures into democratic ones. From the start, therefore, the ensuing political system in each of these countries started out as a viable democracy, sustained not just by democratic institutions but by a democratized and democratizing society as well.

As mentioned earlier, democratic transitions that result in viable democracies must necessarily have a social component and are often brought about as a result of pressures exerted on the state by various autonomously organized social groups. In such instances, the pre-democratic state and its society have very few or absolutely no cultural links to bind them together, their inter-relations being based largely or exclusively on coercion on the part of the state and submission by society. The state, therefore, is praetorian par excellence, having practically no popular ideological legitimacy, instead relying overwhelmingly on a mammoth bureaucracy and a brutal police force to stay in power. This was particularly the case in the former fascist or neo-fascist states of southern Europe, the bureaucratic-authoritarian states of Latin America, and communist ones in east and central Europe.[30] Most contemporary African and Middle Eastern states, however, have managed to devise a variety of cultural, uninstitutionalized means to both consolidate and complement their institutional ties with their respective societies. In Africa, most nominally democratic states, and even some overtly authoritarian ones, have allowed just enough political space to contending social forces to blunt their potentially disruptive nature, although not always successfully.[31] A vast majority of Middle Eastern states have, however, been highly astute at placating social opposition by playing up (and into) whatever culturally resonant forces happen to dictate popular norms and values: they adopt religion and make it official (hence *Islam rasmi*, "official Islam"), the leader becomes a father to the nation and relies on a patriarchical cult of personality, government nepotism becomes a normal method of co-option into the system, etc.[32]

In addition to political dynamics, society also experiences its own nuances in transitions to democracy. Lack of viable cultural and functional links with the state prompts social actors to look to themselves for providing organizational alternatives to those official agencies of the government which they perceive as useless, corrupt, coercive, and manipulated. These are, most frequently, members of the middle classes who, although a direct product of praetorian economic policies, cannot nevertheless be absorbed or co-opted by the state. Through social change and economic development, these middle-class professionals have achieved a comparatively high level of education and affluence. But this very elevated social status makes them all the more alienated from the state, which they can only view in an adversarial light. Thus they form politically autonomous groups and organizations that not only are independent of the state but also, even if only indirectly, are meant to replace some of the specific cultural and functional operations of the state.

Whereas the state does not allow open expression of political thought, for example, these organizations provide a forum for exactly that (e.g. the Civic Forum in Czechoslovakia).[33] While the state may ridicule or suppress religion, some of these organizations may be devoted to spreading a religious gospel and other teachings (e.g. Base Ecclesiastical Communities in Latin America).[34] While the state's glorification of the workers may be hollow propaganda, such groups may be trying actually to do something to enhance working conditions and wages (as was the case with Solidarity in Poland).[35] These organizations are the building-blocks of civil society: they are autonomous, self-organized, and political in consequence if not in original intent. But they must also have an additional characteristic, one which is of great significance: they must be democratic in their internal workings as well as in their larger political goals.

In itself, forming a politically autonomous syndicate organization is no indication of a burgeoning democratic civil society. Most states can easily dismantle or co-opt such organizations through repression or corporatist modifications. A civil society organization must have overtly democratic goals, no matter how specific or narrowly defined those goals might be, and must press the state for a general opening up of the political process rather than simply ask that particular demands be met. Civil society formations may come perilously close to becoming corporatist ones; but they cannot do so, having at all times to retain subtle as well as overt taints of democracy. This is not a minor feat, for it involves not only democratically committed intellectuals but, more importantly, an internal, psychic transformation of the authoritarian self into a democratic one.[36] Democratic intellectuals must establish links of their own with the larger population to give popular purchase to their ideals—they must sell the idea of democracy to the people—and that is neither easy nor, under authoritarian circumstances, always possible.

How a democratic political culture comes about and civil society flourishes varies from case to case. There are some universals, however. To begin with, there must be a democratically committed core of intellectuals. Not every university student or professor is an intellectual, and not every intellectual is a democrat.[37] In the developing world, in fact, it is only recently that a number of intellectuals have become dismayed with the more prevalent ideological strands of communism, socialism, nationalism, or some other "ism" and have embraced the tenets of democracy.[38] It is also one thing to call one's self democratic; it is quite another to be a true democrat. Additionally, democratic intellectuals must sell the idea of democracy to the popular classes and there needs to be a genuine, popular imperative for a democratic political system.

Ironically, the most brutal authoritarian dictatorships are often the best catalysts for the growth of popular democratic yearnings among the masses. The insanity of Nazism in Germany, the horrors of fascism in southern Europe and of bureaucratic-authoritarianism in South America, and the fallacies of life under communism in eastern Europe were all instrumental in instilling in the average person in each place a fundamental yearning for democracy. Democracy becomes culturally popular when all the other "isms", especially those with a penchant for bombastic self-glorification, exhaust themselves and fail to provide the salvation they promise.

Again, not every authoritarian system drives its citizens to the opposite extreme and makes democrats out of them. Few systems, in fact, exhaust all of their legitimacy in the way those mentioned above did. Most of the non-democratic political systems found around the world today are successful in at least one or two of the functions that give them some legitimacy. Some effectively manipulate certain popular sentiments (nationalism is a favorite); others are economically successful enough to keep the middle classes pre-occupied or content; and still others make just enough concessions to placate potential opposition activists. Most, meanwhile, retain enough of their powers and capabilities not to take seriously pressures for democratization.

It is only logical that a transition to democratic rule involves different phases, and that in each phase a different set of factors and dynamics is at work. Transition phases do, of course, often overlap and the nuances involved in one phase often spill over into the next. Nevertheless, especially given the determining influence played by the timing of civil society's emergence, it is important to distinguish between the characteristics of one transition phase and those of another.

In cases where the democratic impulse emanates from below, social actors begin to agitate, not just for political space but specifically for democratic liberties. They either begin to organize themselves into previously non-existent organizations which are specifically set up to further their demands (e.g. Solidarity in Poland), or begin to re-orient the nature and the message of existing organizations to formulate and express their agendas (e.g. the church in both Latin America and eastern Europe). As with most spontaneous revolutions,[39] their demands, meeting with increasingly more receptive ears in society, begin to snowball and the state is gradually confronted with a serious political crisis it cannot easily contain. Soon negotiations are the only option left open to the political elite, resulting in an actual transfer of power through elections, followed by the institutional consolidation of the new order via the inauguration of a constitution, appointment of new policy-makers and bureaucrats, and the like.

The important point to keep in mind is that this type of society-initiated democratization was brought about as a result of the workings of civil society, which in turn set in motion a host of political dynamics that culminated in the replacement of the old order with a new, democratic one. Thus social actors, the politically most important of whom are the primary components of civil society, have a vested interest in maintaining the essence and integrity of the new system. It is precisely for this reason that the incoming democratic state is a genuinely democratic, viable one.

But the phases involved in democratic transitions from above, and the precise chronology of when each event occurs, is quite different (see Table 9.1). In such instances, state actors are first faced with some unsettling development that is often of their own doing, an indigenously initiated turmoil with which they cannot effectively deal. Their inability to deal with their difficulties is compounded by the untenable institutional and structural predicaments that such states often force themselves into, so much so that soon a situation of paralysis and dysfunctionality, at first quite internal to the state, evolves. The structural weaknesses of the state are in turn exploited by various social actors who seize the opportunity to press their specific demands on the state, demands that may or may not be democratic. Negotiations ensue, and a *controlled* process of transition is set in motion.[40] The controlled nature of the transition assures the involved parties that the incoming order will not be too severe in its prosecution of those formerly in power. But the negotiations have always had an air of democracy about them, and all the parties gathered around the negotiating table with claims of acting in the interests of democracy.

Thus the outcome of the negotiations is ostensibly democratic, complete with elections, a liberal democratic constitution, and all the other necessary trappings. But there was no popular, mass element involved in these negotiations (no electrician-as-national hero), no struggle per se, no grand re-thinking of

Table 9.1 Phases in democratic transitions

	Transition from below	*Transition from above*
Catalyst	Civil society	Internal political turmoil
Process	Shake-up	Crisis
	Crisis	Negotiation and transition
	Negotiation and transition	Institutional consolidation
	Institutional consolidation	
Most likely outcome	Viable democracy	Pseudo-democracy

national priorities and cultural dispositions. It was the elite who negotiated, and it was the elite who won, both those belonging to the government's side and those claiming to represent the masses. The system they usher in as a result of their efforts cannot help but be elitist, even if it is democratic. Such a system is in reality a quasi-democracy, a quintessentially elitist political system wrapped in a thin democratic layer.

Slight differences and/or overlapping notwithstanding, four general sets of actors are involved in practically every democratic transition. What differs from one case to another, and what eventually determines the nature and overall direction of the transition, is the exact point in the transition process at which each actor becomes involved, and the cultural as well as institutional ties each has with a larger constituency it claims to represent. The four actors are: intellectuals, who at first act as representatives of the larger society; specific political actors from the state; various other state institutions, whose influence may not be direct but nevertheless is consequential; and social institutions, on behalf of which intellectuals claim to be acting. In one form or another, each of these actors is found in almost every transition process (see Table 9.2).

The ties that intellectuals have with the rest of society are an important determinant of the precise nature of a democratic transition. In transitions that are brought about as a result of pressure from below, where intellectuals have spearheaded an increasingly popular social movement to overturn the dictatorial state, intellectuals possess incredibly strong ties to the rest of society. These ties, more than anything else, are cultural and valuative: the intellectuals' call for political democracy has real and tangible meaning for the rest of the social classes they address. The intellectuals are, to put it differently, operating within a civil society, where their calls for democracy are occurring simultaneously with a democratically hospitable social and cultural transformation of society. Ad hoc, unofficial groups spring up at the grass-roots level—the New Forum in the former East Germany, Solidarity in Poland, Mothers of Plaza de Mayo in Argentina, CEBs throughout Latin America—and make the abstract ideal of democracy a

Table 9.2 Nature and chronological involvement of transition actors

Viable democratic transitions

Intellectuals	Grass-roots movements and political parties
Political actors	Weakened, eager to compromise
State institutions	(Military, political parties, etc.) willing to negotiate
Social institutions	(Religion, family, etc.) democratizing and/or democratized

Pseudo-democratic transitions

Political actors	Compelled to reform
Intellectuals	Seeking democracy; weak ties to the masses
State institutions	Retain many privileges and non-democratic traits
Social institutions	Not always fully democratized

tangible, or at least reachable, reality at the local level. As Solidarity and the "Beer Drinkers Party" in Poland show, some of these grass-roots movements go on to become actual political parties in the democratic era.

It is this crucial axiom of civil society that turns successful democratic transitions initiated from below into viable democracies. At a time when intellectuals are pressing for democratic openings, society is also undergoing its own democratic transformation of sorts, and the two complement and reinforce one another. The emerging democratic system cannot help but have a strong social and cultural component.

If widespread democratic ideals are important before and during the transition process, they are all the more so after democracy has been politically institutionalized, especially in cases where the non-democratic state itself took the lead in handing over power. The tenets of political culture, democratic or otherwise, do not emerge on their own and independently, and are contingent on several variables.

These variables include political economy, the choices and capabilities of the new political elite, political history and degree of past experience with democracy, and such other contingent factors as political geography and transnational cultural forces. A political system acquires widespread and resonant popular legitimacy when it delivers on the promises for which it stands and keeps pace with the political and economic expectations of the politically relevant classes. The pursuit of neo-liberal market reforms— necessitated by the ruinous results of years of import-substitution industrialization or state-led capitalist policies—often greatly jeopardizes the legitimacy of newly democratic states.[41]

Many of the new democracies of South America have brought with them real declines in standards of living for most members of the lower and middle classes, have removed former protectionist barriers that helped insulate small and medium-sized industries from international competition, and have completely washed their hands of any policies aimed at helping the burgeoning armies of the poor and the indigent.[42] In the long run, the successful implementation of anti-inflationary measures and steady improvements in economic output and growth may restore popular confidence in the system and help expedite the popularization of democratic ideals. This has evidently happened in Brazil and Argentina, where the overall economic picture has improved and the democratic state has withstood several challenges from within and without. In the short run, however, the "Fujimorismo" phenomenon is a real possibility not only in Peru (where it is an actual reality) but also in places like Colombia, Venezuela, Ecuador, and most countries of Central America.[43]

The fragile economies of Estonia, Latvia, Lithuania, and Ukraine pose similar fundamental challenges to the cultural consolidation of democratic norms in the post-Soviet era in each of these new republics.[44] But further west, in Poland, Hungary, the Czech Republic, and to a lesser extent Bulgaria, the steady influx of Western investments and financial assistance has reinforced popular desires not only to be anti-communist but also to become more like the west European cousins.

This relates directly to the transnational influence of political norms and values. In today's world, or at least in the non-Muslim world where religion is not being politically used as an all-encompassing source of identity, most people consider it fashionable to be called democrats. East Europeans and Latin Americans want to be known simply as *European* and *American* respectively (meaning affluent and democratic); Estonians, Latvians, Lithuanians, Ukrainians, and Turks want to be known as West European, and so on. Soft power seems to have had its most compelling effect in the global currency of democratic norms and ideals.[45] This is frequently reinforced by romantic images of an indigenous democratic golden age once in existence and by the living memories of an authoritarian nightmare that was reality only a few years ago.

Domestic political performance is an equally consequential legitimizing agent, as corruption and nepotism can not only threaten the legitimacy of the new holders of power but make the public question the wisdom of the entire political system. Similarly, the strategic choices that elites make in the post-transition era, about how responsive to remain to grass-roots pressures from below, and to what extent they should present themselves as a democratic role model to the rest of society, are crucially important in the overall perceptions of the population toward the larger, democratic system. Are the elites more interested in maintaining power or in upholding democratic principles if the two come into conflict? Are they willing to abide by the rules of the democratic game or are they not above resorting to some of the dirty tricks for which the old elite was infamous? All of these are areas from which the larger population can takes its cue and in turn internalize, or at least be influenced by, the norms that seem to govern the political behavior of those in power.

Conclusion

The cultural consolidation of democracy in post-transition democracies is one of the major areas in which future research is needed. Although few of the structural, political, and economic aspects of democratic transitions remain unexplored, the social and cultural dynamics at work in pre- and post-transition democratic polities have been largely overlooked by the major theorists in the field. Examining the choices that elites and actors make, or systemic economic successes and failures, or class and international forces, all tell us much about some of the most important aspects of the possibilities for democratic opening and/or reversal. But such perspectives overlook the equally significant contributions that norms and cultural values make in compelling social actors to seek and act on their democratic ideals, and, if they succeed in getting rid of the non-democratic state, either to hold on to those ideals and popularize them or to abandon them altogether.

Cultural forces are an important component of the transition to democracy, either before the actual transition process is set in motion, or after the transition is complete, or in both phases. A successful democratic transition does not simply end with careful and non-violent negotiations, even if state institutions are genuine in their intent to relinquish power to groups that have emerged from grass-roots movements. That merely signals the end of the *transition* process. It does not signify the continued operation and integrity of a representative, democratic polity. It is fully conceivable for a democratic transition to take place and for previously authoritarian political structures to become democratic. But such a transition process in itself does not give currency to the spirit of democracy among all social actors or even only among those who are charged with articulating society's larger demands (intellectuals). A democratic political culture—conditioned by the political and economic performance of the new elite, historical considerations, and elite choices—must evolve and complement the political and institutional characteristics of the new system. Without such a popular, cultural base for the legitimacy of the new state, the incoming system is likely to be pseudo-democratic at best. A true, viable democracy is as culturally grounded as it is politically free and representative.

10 Conclusion

The study of comparative politics has come a long way since its inception more than a century ago. The initial focus on the nature and characteristics of the state and its constituent institutions remained resilient for a number of decades and has never been fully cast aside, its latter-day theoretical refurbishing and resurrection the subject of much scholarly excitement and debate since the 1980s. The "behavioralists" and other proponents of systems theory have lost much ground since the 1960s and 1970s, when their theories of social input and political output closely resembled the revolutionary air of most Western societies at the time. To this day, nevertheless, such ardent proponents of the functionalist perspective as Gabriel Almond remain convinced of the paradigm's superior merits. Drawing on some of the insights and contributions of each of these differing paradigms, in the preceding chapters I have sought to bring into sharper focus a recurring theme in much of the recent literature in the discipline, namely attention to the separate phenomena of state and society as well as their interactions.

Comparative analysis must begin by highlighting the crucial systemic and functional differences between state and society as separate phenomena. Even in democratic polities, where gaps between state and society are frequently bridged through electoral and other institutional means, there are still distinct groups who hold "official" state power and those who do not. But the distinction between state and society does not mean the two operate in isolation from one another. For, in fact, while politics does entail the "goings-on" within the state, it also involves, especially at the national level, the exchange of power and influence between the state and society. This exchange occurs through the institutions that both states and societies have, institutions which, depending on national context, are bound to have different names or even different levels of significance but function as conveyor belts of influence in either direction. The comparativist must thus go beyond concentrating on the comparative exercise of power within and by states. The degree and effectiveness of political institutionalization in enabling the state to penetrate and influence society, the strength and political potential of various existing social institutions, and the political culture which provides the formulating context for the whole set of state-society interactions must all be taken into account. Only then can a thorough understanding of politics be attained.

It may be worth repeating that emphasis on state and society is not a new paradigm and that it has been implicit in many analyses of comparative phenomena. What this work has done is to give cohesion and consistency to a trend that can be found in much of the recent literature of the discipline. It has presented an abstract framework for many of the empirical studies in the discipline and sketched the broad outlines of an emerging comparative paradigm.

Through a dual focus on state and society, a host of previous and contemporary political phenomena may be explained, and even future projections may be made with a degree of certainty. Revolutionary eruptions around the world, for example, may be conceptualized as successful societal movements that overthrow and reconstitute the state and which, in turn, establish a new pattern of relationships between state and society. The waves of democratization across southern Europe in the 1970s and eastern Europe in the 1980s may be similarly explained. Can the dramatic events surrounding the collapse of communism be attributed to anything other than a radical restructuring of state-society relations and their normative contexts (i.e. political culture)? The exclusionary, communist states proved incapable of effectively weakening societal pressures for political participation, especially as exerted by such outgrowths of civil society as the Solidarity movement in Poland, the New Forum in East Germany, the Civic Forum in Czechoslovakia, and others. Again, the new states that emerged out of the transformations of the 1980s re-established their links to society under different, this time democratic, auspices. It was the political culture of the region, itself radically transformed under the crushing weight of communist authoritarianism, that accounted for much of the success of democracy there.

But the same series of analytical concepts may also be used to explain the failures of democracy or the strains it experiences, the perseverance of authoritarianism, or the near-complete internal disintegration of entire national entities. Authoritarian states may remain in power indefinitely so long as the institutional mechanisms through which the masses are kept at bay and prevented from political participation continue to function effectively and properly. For such regimes, the bureaucracy, the military, the police, and even the judiciary serve as tools that ensure the exclusion of the masses from the political process.

The precise reasons that underlie the longevity of dictatorships vary from one case to another. Some authoritarian regimes may rely on the economic preoccupations of the population in order to maintain themselves in power, while others may lengthen their tenure by successfully cultivating the less democratic aspects of the popular culture. But there is always an imbalance in the powers of state and society in favor of the former, making it a relationship between socially impenetrable states and politically incapacitated societies. This is the type of state-society relationship that—with such exceptions as South Africa, Turkey, and Israel—marks the political landscapes of the Middle East and much of Africa.

There are also instances where neither the state nor society can effectively penetrate the other, nor can they decide on a regularized pattern of interaction within and between themselves. Dysfunctionality and paralysis mark both state and society, as was the unhappy predicament first of Ethiopia and later Somalia in recent years, of Lebanon in the 1970s, and of former Yugoslavia since the late 1980s. A viable state-society relationship cannot re-emerge until one has established its dominance over the other.

Throughout this work, I have taken great care to avoid the trap of ethnocentricity, which, as a recent book has pointed out, is almost second nature to the comparativist. "Every researcher", the book's authors caution, "even a comparativist researcher, belongs to a culture, and that can limit his or her capacity to perceive. These blinkers have not been easily recognized."[1] This tendency has been reinforced by the overwhelmingly Western and specifically American character of comparative politics. From the very beginnings, comparative politics has been a product of Western rationalists' efforts to conceptualize the politics of other nations. Under these broad auspices, the influence of American scholars and of American views towards comparative politics has been particularly dominant, as represented, for example, by the preponderance of scholarly American journals and other publications focusing on the subject.[2] It is more than simply coincidental that the cautionary statement above comes from two French comparativists, Dogan and Pelassy.

With this warning in mind, I have tried to formulate an approach that accounts for differing national, institutional, cultural, and social contexts. Viewing states and societies in terms of their constituent institutions, and pointing to their varying interactions as the key to political analysis, does not smack of ethnocentrism.

After all the time and effort that went into the writing of this book, it is with a measure of irony that I must admit to the transitory and impermanent nature of the approach I have surmised out of recent trends in the scholarship. However we define and perceive *politics*, it remains by nature a changeable phenomenon, its norms continually molded to our time-specific interests, its parameters altered by the scope of institutional and technological forces that continually challenge and reshape the face of human existence. However analytically sound, the details of an approach to the study of comparative politics that is put forward in the early twenty-first century may be no more valid a hundred years from now than are the late nineteenth-century approaches valid today.

If past historical trends are any indicator of the changes to come in the future, then national and international political arenas around the globe are bound to undergo fundamental changes in both substance and direction. Even within the past decade, awesome political revolutions around the world have shattered some of the basic premises that were once accepted as given within the discipline of comparative politics. Where national and global trends will take politics in the future cannot be predicted with any measure of certainty. What is certain, however, is that our present perceptions of politics will most definitely need to be changed accordingly. Only an unrealistic idealist would strive to put forward an approach to comparative politics with supposed eternal validity. I have no such pretensions. Instead, I am counting on the hope that neither states, nor societies, nor their mutual interactions will become obsolete any time in the near future and that at least the broad outlines of this emerging approach will withstand the inevitable political, institutional, and technological changes of the coming generations.

Notes

1 Introduction

1 David Easton. "Political Science". In David Sills (ed.). *International Encyclopedia of the Social Sciences*, Vol. 12. (New York, NY: Crowell Collier & Macmillan, 1968), p. 282.

2 Theories of comparative politics: a brief overview

1 John Dearlove. "Bringing the Constitution Back In: Political Science and the State". *Political Science*. Vol. 37, (1989), p. 521.
2 Op. cit., p. 522. See, for example, A.V. Dicey. *The Law of the Constitution*. (London: Macmillan, 1885).
3 Jesse S. Reeves. "Perspectives in Political Science, 1903–28". *American Political Science Review*. Vol. 23, No. 1, (February 1929), p. 1.
4 James Bryce. "The Relations of Political Science to History and to Practice". *American Political Science Review*. Vol. 3, No. 1, (February 1909), p. 6.
5 George Sioussat. "Notes on Works in Political Science". *The Sewanee Review Quarterly*. Vol. 15, No. 3, (July 1907), p. 372.
6 Raymond G. Gettell. "Nature and Scope of Present Political Theory". *American Political Science Review*. Vol. 18, Supplement, (February 1914), p. 48.
7 W. W. Willoughby. *An Examination of the Nature of the State*. (London: Macmillan, 1922), p. 14.
8 Raymond Gettell. "The Nature of Political Thought". *American Political Science Review*. Vol. 17, No. 2, (May 1923), p. 206.
9 See also George Sioussat. "Notes on Works in Political Science" for a discussion of other works published at the time, most of which dealt with the state.
10 W. W. Willoughby. *An Examination of the Nature of the State*, p. 134.
11 James Quayle Dealey. *The Development of the State: Its Government Organization and Its Activities*. (New York, NY: Silver, Burdett, & Co., 1909), p. 26.
12 Jesse Reeves. "Perspectives in Political Science, 1903–28". p. 10.
13 Raymond Gettell. "Nature and Scope of Present Political Theory", p. 49.
14 See John Dickinson. "Social Order and Political Authority", (Parts 1 and 2). *American Political Science Review*. Vol. 23, No. 2, (May 1929), pp. 293–328 and Vol. 23, No. 3, (August 1929), pp. 593–632.
15 James A. Bill and Robert L. Hardgrave. *Comparative Politics: The Quest for Theory*. (Washington, DC: University Press of America, 1981), p. 2.
16 Sigmund Neumann. "Comparative Politics: A Half-Century Appraisal". *Journal of Politics*. Vol. 19, (August 1957), pp. 374–75.

17 See George Sioussat. "Notes on Works in Political Science", pp. 374–75. For a discussion of the role of the "vote" in the United States see Munroe Smith. "The Consent of the Governed". *Proceedings of the Academy of Political Science.* Vol. 15, No. 1, (October 1914), pp. 82–88. For an examination of the government of the United States see Henry L. Stimson. "The Principle of Responsibility in the Government". Vol. 15, No. 1, (October 1914), pp. 20–26.

18 James Bill and Robert Hardgrave. *Comparative Politics*, p. 5.

19 George H. Sabine, "Pluralism: A Point of View". *American Journal of Political Science.* Vol. 17, No. 1, (February 1923), p. 49. See also Ellen Deborah Ellis. "The Pluralist State". *American Political Science Review.* Vol. 14, No. 3, (August 1920), pp. 393–407.

20 George Sioussat. "Notes on Works in Political Science", pp. 373–75.

21 James Bill and Robert Hardgrave. *Comparative Politics*, p. 7.

22 Op. cit., p. 6.

23 Sigmund Neumann. "Comparative Politics: A Half-Century Appraisal", p. 381.

24 Op. cit., p. 377.

25 See, for example, Karl Lowenstein. "Autocracy Versus Democracy in Contemporary Europe", (Parts I and II). *American Political Science Review.* Vol. 29, No. 4, (August 1935), pp. 571–93, and Vol. 29, No. 5, (October 1935), pp. 755–84.

26 Leslie Lipson. "The Comparative Method in Political Studies". *The Political Quarterly.* Vol. 28, No. 4, (October–December 1957), pp. 374–76.

27 John H. Herz. "Rise and Demise of the Territorial State". *World Politics.* Vol. 9, No. 4, (July 1957), p. 457.

28 Sigmund Neumann. "Comparative Politics: A Half-Century Appraisal", pp. 379–80.

29 John H. Herz. "The Rise and Demise of the Territorial State", especially pp. 489–93.

30 James Bill and Robert Hardgrave. *Comparative Politics*, pp. 13–15.

31 Op. cit., p. 10.

32 Sigmund Neumann. "Comparative Politics: A Half-Century Appraisal", p. 383.

33 Ervin Laszlo. *The Systems View of the World.* (New York, NY: George Braziller, 1972), p. 14.

34 Ronald Chilcote. *Theories of Comparative Politics: The Search for a Paradigm.* (Boulder, CO: Westview, 1981), p. 153.

35 David Easton. *A Framework for Political Analysis.* (Chicago, IL: University of Chicago Press, 1965), pp. 24–25.

36 Op. cit., p. 49.

37 Ibid.

38 Ronald Chilcote. *Theories of Comparative Politics*, p. 169.

39 Gabriel Almond and G. Bingham Powell. "Introduction". Gabriel Almond and G. Bingham Powell (eds). *Comparative Politics Today: A World View.* 5th edition, (New York, NY: HarperCollins, 1992), p. 4.

40 Gabriel Almond and G. Bingham Powell. *Comparative Politics: System, Process, and Policy.* (Boston, MA: Little, Brown, & Co., 1978), p. 9.

41 Gabriel Almond. "Introduction: A Functional Approach to Comparative Politics". In Gabriel Almond and James Coleman (eds). *The Politics of Developing Areas.* (Princeton, NJ: Princeton University Press, 1960), p. 17.

42 Gabriel Almond and G. Bingham Powell. "Introduction", pp. 11–12.

43 Gabriel Almond. "Comparative Political Systems". *Journal of Politics.* Vol 18, (August 1956), p. 396.

44 Gabriel Almond and G. Bingham Powell. *Comparative Politics*, p. 25.

45 Gabriel Almond. "Introduction: A Functional Approach to Comparative Politics", p. 11.

46 Gabriel Almond and G. Bingham Powell. "Introduction", p. 17.

47 See, for example, the seven volumes on political development published in the 1960s on the basis of research done under the auspices of the Committee on

Comparative Politics of the Social Sciences Research Council. They include Lucian Pye, (ed.). *Communications and Political Development.* (Princeton, NJ: Princeton University Press, 1963); Joseph LaPalombra (ed.). *Bureaucracy and Political Development.* (Princeton, NJ: Princeton University Press, 1963); Lucian Pye and Sidney Verba (eds). *Political Culture and Political Development.* (Princeton, NJ: Princeton University Press, 1965); James S.Coleman (ed.). *Education and Political Development.* (Princeton, NJ: Princeton University Press, 1965); Joseph LaPalombra and Myron Weiner (eds). *Political Parties and Political Development.* (Princeton, NJ: Princeton University Press, 1966); and Leonard Binder, et al. *Crises and Sequences in Political Development.* (Princeton, NJ: Princeton University Press, 1971).

48 Samuel Huntington. *Political Order in Changing Societies.* (New Haven, CT: Yale University Press, 1968), pp. 360–62.

49 Samuel Huntington. "Political Development and Political Decay". *World Politics.* Vol. 17, No. 3, (April 1965), p. 383.

50 Op. cit., p. 407. See also Samuel Huntington. *Political Order in Changing Societies*, pp. 78–92.

51 Samuel Huntington. "Political Development and Political Decay", p. 393.

52 Leonard Binder. "Crises of Political Development". In Leonard Binder, et al. *Crises and Sequences in Political Development*, p. 66. Emphasis added.

53 Op. cit., p. 65.

54 Ronald Chilcote. *Theories of Comparative Politics*, p. 179.

55 Op. cit., p. 180.

56 Op. cit., p. 181.

57 Quoted ibid.

58 Gabriel Almond. "Introduction: A Functional Approach to Comparative Politics", p. 17.

59 Gabriel Almond and Sidney Verba. *The Civic Culture.* (Princeton, NJ: Princeton University Press, 1963), especially p. 37. Although Mexican politics cannot be characterized as democratic, it is far less authoritarian, especially at the time when the study was prepared, than most other similar polities.

60 Sigmund Neumann. "Comparative Politics: A Half-Century Appraisal", p. 382.

61 Theodore J. Lowi. "The Return of the State: Critiques". *American Political Science Review.* Vol. 82, No. 3, (September 1988), p. 888.

62 Sergio Fabbrini. "The Return to the State: Critiques". *American Political Science Review.* Vol. 82, No. 3, (September 1988), p. 894.

63 John Dearlove. "Bringing the Constitution Back In: Political Science and the State", p. 527.

64 Ibid.

65 See, for example, John Dunn. *Modern Revolutions: An Introduction to the Analysis of a Political Phenomenon.* 2nd edition (Cambridge: Cambridge University Press, 1988); Theda Skocpol. *States and Social Revolutions.* (Cambridge: Cambridge University Press, 1979); and Alfred Stepan. *State and Society: Peru in Comparative Perspective.* (Princeton, NJ: Princeton University Press, 1978).

66 Peter Evans, Dietrich Rueschemeyer, and Theda Skocpol (eds). *Bringing the State Back In.* (Cambridge: Cambridge University Press, 1985).

67 Peter Evans, Dietrich Rueschemeyer, and Theda Skocpol. "Preface". In *Bringing the State Back In.* p. vii.

68 Sergio Fabbrini. "The Return to the State: Critiques", p. 896.

69 See Eric Nordlinger. *On the Autonomy of the Democratic State.* (Cambridge, MA: Harvard University Press, 1981); Theda Skocpol. "Bringing the State Back In: Strategies of Analysis in Current Research". In. *Bringing the State Back In.* pp. 3–37.

70 John Dearlove. "Bringing the Constitution Back In: Political Science and the State", p. 527.

71 For a review of the debate between proponents of the modernization school and the dependency approach, see Mehran Kamrava. *Politics and Society in the Third World*. (London: Routledge, 1993), pp. 35–41.

72 See especially Andre Gunder Frank. *Capitalism and Underdevelopment in Latin America: Historical Studies of Chile and Brazil*. (New York, NY: Monthly Review Press, 1967).

73 See, for example, Michael Bratton. "Patterns of Development and Under-development". *International Studies Quarterly*. Vol. 26, No. 3, (September 1982), pp. 333–72.

74 Immanuel Wallerstein. *The Politics of the World Economy: the States, the Movements and the Civilizations*. (Cambridge: Cambridge University Press, 1984).

75 Op. cit., p. 29.

76 Op. cit., p. 37.

77 Op. cit., p. 29.

78 Op. cit., p. 30.

79 See, for example, Michael Bratton. "Patterns of Development and Under-development", and David Collier (ed.). *The New Authoritarianism in Latin America*. (Princeton, NJ: Princeton University Press, 1979).

80 Guillermo O'Donnell and Philippe Schmitter are two of the more notable of this group of scholars. See especially Phillippe C. Schmitter (ed.). *Military Rule in Latin America: Functions, Consequences and Perspectives*. (London: Sage, 1973), and Guillermo O'Donnell, Philippe Schmitter, and Laurence Whitehead (eds). *Transitions From Authoritarian Rule: Comparative Perspectives*. (Baltimore, MD: Johns Hopkins University Press, 1986).

81 Sergio Fabbrini. "The Return to the State: Critiques", p. 896; Eric Nordlinger. "The Return to the State: Critiques". *American Political Science Review*. Vol. 82, No. 3, (September 1988), p. 879.

82 Eric Nordlinger. "The Return to the State: Critiques", p. 897.

83 John Dearlove. "Bringing the Constitution In: Political Science and the State", p. 528.

84 Eric Nordlinger. *On the Autonomy of the Democratic State*. (Cambridge, MA: Harvard University Press, 1981) p. 7.

85 Op. cit., p. 9.

86 Op. cit., p. 7.

87 Eric Nordlinger. "The Return to the State: Critiques", p. 884.

88 See, for example, Theda Skocpol. "Bringing the State Back In: Strategies of Analysis in Current Research", p. 19.

89 Op. cit., p. 8.

90 Op. cit., p. 9.

91 Op. cit., p. 14.

92 Op. cit., p. 16.

93 Ibid.

94 Op. cit., p. 21.

95 Ibid.

96 Theodore Lowi. "The Return to the State: Critiques", p. 887.

97 John Dearlove. "Bringing the Constitution Back In: Political Science and the State", p. 528.

98 Op. cit., p. 529.

99 Sergio Fabbrini. "The Return to the State: Critiques", pp. 896–97.

100 John Dearlove. "Bringing the Constitution Back In: Political Science and the State", p. 529.

101 See Gabriel Almond. "The Return to the State". *American Political Science Review*. Vol. 82, No. 3, (September 1988), pp. 853–74, as well as the articles by

Theodore Lowi and Sergio Fabbrini entitled "The Return to the State: Critiques" in the same volume, pp. 885–91 and 891–98 respectively.
102 Gabriel Almond. "The Return to the State", pp. 855–56.
103 Op. cit., p. 869.
104 Ibid.
105 Theodore Lowi. "The Return to the State: Critiques", p. 891.
106 Ibid.
107 Sergio Fabbrini. "The Return to the State: Critiques", p. 897.

3 A synthesis

1 Michael Bratton. "Patterns of Development and Underdevelopment". *International Studies Quarterly.* Vol. 26, No. 3, (September 1982), p. 333.
2 Anthony Giddens. *Sociology: A Brief but Critical Introduction.* (London: Macmillan, 1982), p. 10.
3 Almond discusses the "universality of the political functions" in "Introduction: A Functional Approach to Comparative Politics". Gabriel Almond and James Coleman (eds). *The Politics of Developing Areas.* (Princeton, NJ: Princeton University Press), pp. 12–25.
4 Gabriel Almond and G. Bingham Powell. *Comparative Politics: System, Process, and Policy.* (Boston, MA: Little, Brown, 1978), p. 12.
5 Put differently, the state is made up of "a set of institutions invested with the authority to make binding decisions for people and organizations juridically located in a particular territory and to implement these decisions using, if necessary, force". Dietrich Rueschemeyer and Peter Evans. "The State and Economic Transformation: Toward an Analysis of the Conditions Underlying Effective Intervention". In Peter Evans, Dietrich Rueschemeyer, and Theda Skocpol (eds). *Bringing the State Back In.* (Cambridge: Cambridge University Press, 1985), pp. 46–47.
6 For a treatment of the role of state in a revolutionary situation see Mehran Kamrava. *Revolutionary Politics.* (Westport, CT: Praeger, 1992), pp. 11–26
7 Stephen Chilton. "Defining Political Culture". *Western Political Quarterly.* Vol. 41, No. 3, (September 1988), p. 427.
8 For more on political culture see chapter 6.

4 States and social institutions

1 See, for example, Samuel Huntington. "Political Development and Political Decay." *World Politics.* Vol. 17, No. 3, (April 1965), p. 393, in which Huntington equates political development with the "institutionalization of political organizations and procedures".
2 Mehran Kamrava. *Politics and Society in the Third World.* (London: Routledge, 1993), p. 2.
3 Samuel Huntington. "Political Development and Political Decay", p. 394.
4 Mehran Kamrava. *Politics and Society in the Third World*, pp. 2–3. Original emphasis.
5 Leonard Binder. "The Crisis of Political Development." In Leonard Binder, et al. *Crises and Sequences in Political Development.* (Princeton, NJ: Princeton University Press, 1971), pp. 3–72.
6 James S. Coleman. "The Development Syndrome: Differentiation-Equality-Capacity". In Leonard Binder, et al. *Crises and Sequences in Political Development*, pp. 73–100.
7 Samuel Huntington. "Political Development and Political Decay", pp. 386–430.
8 Op. cit., p. 388.

9 Leonard Binder. "The Crisis of Political Development", p. 68. Emphasis added.
10 James Coleman. "The Development Syndrome: Differentiation-Equality-Capacity", p. 75.
11 Ibid.
12 Vernon W. Rutton. "What Happened to Political Development?" *Economic Development and Cultural Change.* Vol. 39, No. 2, (January 1991), p. 279.
13 See, for example, Talcott Parsons. *The Social System.* (New York, NY: The Free Press, 1951); S. N. Eisenstadt. "Social Institutions." In David Sills (ed.). *International Encyclopedia of the Social Sciences.* Vol. 14. (New York, NY: Crowell Collier & Macmillan, 1968), pp. 409–29; Anthony Giddens. *The Constitution of Society.* (Cambridge: Polity Press, 1984); and Anthony Giddens. *Social Theory and Modern Sociology.* (Stanford, CA: Stanford University Press, 1987).
14 Anthony Giddens. *The Constitution of Society*, p. 24.
15 S. N. Eisenstadt. "Social Institutions", p. 409.
16 Op. cit., p. 410.
17 W. Richard Scott. *Social Processes and Social Structures: An Introduction to Sociology.* (New York, NY: Holt, Rinehart, & Winston, 1970), p. 199.
18 Candace Clark and Howard Robboy. *Social Interaction: Readings in Sociology.* (New York, NY: St. Martin's, 1988), p. 347. Original emphasis.
19 Jack P. Gibbs. *Control: Sociology's Central Notion.* (Chicago, IL: University of Illinois Press, 1989), p. 422.
20 Talcott Parsons. *The Social System*, p. 39.
21 Peter Blau. *Approaches to the Study of the Social Structure.* (New York, NY: The Free Press, 1975), p. 96.
22 W. Richard Scott. *Social Processes and Social Structures*, p. 527.
23 Peter Blau. *Approaches to the Study of the Social Structure*, p. 12.
24 Jerry D. Rose. *Introduction to Sociology.* (Chicago, IL: Rand McNally, 1974), p. 222.
25 Op. cit., p. 223.
26 Anthony Giddens. *The Constitution of Society*, pp. 164–65.
27 Most scholars tend to discuss political and governmental institutions alongside social institutions. See, for example, Jerry Rose. *Introduction to Sociology*, p. 15. In S. N. Eisenstadt. "Social Institutions", p. 410, the author speaks of "institutional spheres", identifying such spheres as family and kinship, education, economics, politics, cultural institutions, and social stratification. See also W. Richard Scott. *Social Processes and Social Structures*, p. 529.
28 Anthony Giddens. *Social Theory and Modern Sociology*, pp. 221–22.
29 Peter Blau. *Approaches to the Study of the Social Structure*, pp. 8–9; Candace Clark and Howard Robboy. *Social Interaction*, p. 348; Robert K.Merton. *Social Theory and Social Structure.* (New York, NY: The Free Press, 1968), p. 176; Jerry Rose. *Introduction to Sociology*, pp. 281–82.
30 Jerry Rose. *Introduction to Sociology*, pp. 281–82.
31 Anthony Giddens. *The Constitution of Society*, p. 171.

5 A framework for analysis

1 Samuel Huntington introduced his interpretations of cultural geography in "The Goals of Development". In Myron Weiner and Samuel Huntington (eds). *Understanding Political Development.* (New York: Harper Collins, 1987), pp. 3–32. He later elaborated on these views in the much more provocative, celebrated article "The Clash of Civilizations". *Foreign Affairs.* Vol. 72, No. 3, (Summer 1993), pp. 22–49, later expanded into the book *The Clash of Civilizations and the Remaking of World Order.* (New York: Simon & Schuster, 1996).

2 Joel Migdal, Atul Kohli, and Vivienne Shue. "Introduction: Developing a State-in-Society Perspective". In Joel Migdal, Atul Kohli, and Vivienne Shue (eds). *State Power and Social Forces: Domination and Transformation in the Third World.* (Cambridge: Cambridge University Press, 1994), p. 1.

3 Although the approach informs the underlying premise of a number of case studies dealing with comparative politics, its theoretical parameters have been explicitly outlined in only a few publications. See, for example, Joel Migdal. *Strong Societies and Weak States: State-Society Relations and State Capabilities in the Third World.* (Princeton, NJ: Princeton University Press, 1988); Joel Migdal, Atul Kohli, and Vivienne Shue (eds). *State Power and Social Forces: Domination and Transformation in the Third World.*

4 For a brief critique of *States Power and Social Forces* see Robert Jackson's review in *American Political Science Review.* Vol. 89, No. 2, (June 1995), pp. 520–21.

5 Joel Migdal. *Strong Societies and Weak States*, pp. 28–29.

6 Joel Migdal, Atul Kohli, and Vivienne Shue. "Introduction: Developing a State-in-Society Perspective". In Joel Migdal et al. (eds). *State Power and Social Forces*, p. 3.

7 Ibid.

8 Atul Kohli and Vivienne Shue. "State Power and Social Forces: On Political Contention and Accommodation in the Third World". In Joel Migdal et al. (eds). *State Power and Social Forces*, p. 319.

9 Joel Migdal, Atul Kohli, and Vivienne Shue. "Introduction: Developing a State-in-Society Perspective", p. 3.

10 Joel Migdal. "The State in Society: An Approach to Struggles for Domination". Joel Migdal et al. (eds). *State Power and Social Forces*, p. 30.

11 The dependency-modernization debate has been extensively treated in a number of publications. See, for example, Kevin Clements. *From Left to Right in Development Theory: An Analysis of the Political Implications of Different Models of Development.* (Singapore: The Institute of Southeast Asian Studies, 1980); Ronald Chilcote and Dale Johnson (eds). *Theories of Development: Mode of Production or Dependency?* (London: Sage, 1983); and Richard Higgot. *Political Development Theory: The Contemporary Debate.* (London: Croom Helm, 1983).

12 Joel Migdal, Atul Kohli, and Vivienne Shue. "Introduction: Developing a State-in-Society Perspective", p. 9.

13 Joel Migdal. *Strong Societies and Weak States*, p. 40.

14 Joel Migdal, Atul Kohli, and Vivienne Shue. "Introduction: Developing a State-in-Society Perspective". p. 3.

15 John Dearlove. "Bringing the Constitution Back In: Political Science and the State". *Political Science.* Vol. 37, (1989), p. 521.

16 Theda Skocpol. "Bringing the State Back In: Strategies of Analysis in Current Analysis". In Peter Evans, Dietrich Rueschemeyer, and Theda Skocpol (eds). *Bringing the State Back In.* (Cambridge: Cambridge University Press, 1985), pp. 3–37.

17 Anthony Giddens. *Capitalism and Modern Social Theory: An Analysis of the Writings of Marx, Durkheim and Max Weber.* (Cambridge: Cambridge University Press, 1991), p. 156.

18 See, for example, Gabriel Almond and G. Bingham Powell. "The Study of Comparative Politics". In Gabriel Almond and G. Bingham Powell (eds). *Comparative Politics Today: A World View*, 5th edition (New York: Harper Collins, 1992), pp. 4–6.

19 Stephen White, John Gardner, and George Schopflin. *Communist Political Systems*, 2nd edition (New York: St. Martin's, 1987), p. 20.

20 B. Guy Peters. *European Politics Reconsidered.* (New York: Holmes & Meier, 1991), pp. 171–72.

21 Gerhard Loewenberg and Samuel Patterson. "Legislatures and Political Systems". In Louis Cantori and Andrew Ziegler (eds). *Comparative Politics in the Post-Behavioral Era*. (Boulder, CO: Lynne Rienner, 1988), p. 280.

22 Samuel Huntington. *Political Order in Changing Societies*. (New Haven, CT: Yale University Press, 1968), p. 196.

23 Ibid.

24 These instances arise when there are multiple and competing centers of authority in both the state and society which cannot effectively establish their dominance over one another. Consequently, a broken state tries to govern a deeply fractured society, with a multi-authority polity being the outcome. For more on this see Mehran Kamrava. "Conceptualising Third World Politics: the state-society see-saw", *Third World Quarterly*. Vol. 13, No. 4 (December 1993), pp. 703–16.

25 In Egypt, for example, there is fairly overt competition among religious and secular professors over which group becomes more dominant on university campuses and in particular departments. Personal interview, Professor Kamal El-Menouphi, Associate Dean of the College of Politics and Economics, Cairo University, Cairo, June 2, 1996.

26 Iliya Harik. "The Origins of the Arab State System". In Ghassan Salame (ed.). *The Foundations of the Arab State System*. (London: Croom Helm, 1987), p. 24.

27 David Easton. *A Framework for Political Analysis*. (Chicago, IL: University of Chicago Press, 1965), pp. 24–25.

28 A discussion of social divisions, both in themselves and in terms of their cultural consequences, is more elaborate than the scope of this chapter allows.

29 Migdal alludes to political culture when discussing civil society, which he claims to assume "the existence of a normative consensus or hegemony of fundamental ideas among social forces ...; this consensus represents a prevailing moral or social order." Joel Migdal. "The State in Society", p. 28.

30 Gradually, many scholars have come to believe that there was indeed some merit in cultural factors and that they can potentially serve as important forces in politics. Theda Skocpol, for example, who was once one of the main figures among the neo-statists, later modified some of her original arguments to make room for culture. See Theda Skocpol. "Rentier State and Shi'a Islam in the Iranian Revolution". *Theory and Society*. Vol. 11, No. 3, (May 1982), pp. 265–83. Huntington has also slowly but surely moved from a non-cultural extreme to an opposing extreme in which he sees the globe as a collection of distinct cultural entities divided along various "civilizational fault lines".

31 This is not to say that examinations of Latin American culture and its political significance do not exist. For two sample studies looking at the significance of political culture in Latin America see John Booth and Mitchell Seligson. "Paths to Democracy and the Political Culture of Costa Rica, Mexico, and Peru." In Larry Diamond (ed.). *Political Culture and Democracy in Developing Countries*. (Boulder, CO: Lynne Rienner, 1994), pp. 99–130; and Howard Wiarda. "Introduction: Social Change, Political Development, and the Latin American Tradition." In Howard Wiarda (ed.). *Politics and Social Change in Latin America*. (Boulder, CO: Westview, 1992), pp. 1–22.

32 Mehran Kamrava and Frank Mora. "Civil Society in Comparative Perspective: Lessons from Latin America and the Middle East". *Third World Quarterly*. Vol. 19, No. 5, (1998).

33 Mehran Kamrava. *Politics and Society in the Third World*. (London: Routledge, 1993), pp. 144–45.

34 Gabriel Almond and Sidney Verba. *The Civic Culture*. (Princeton, NJ: Princeton University Press, 1963).

35 Ezra Vogel. *The Four Little Dragons*. (Cambridge, MA: Harvard University Press, 1991). pp. 92–93.

36 James Bill and Robert Springborg. *Politics in the Middle East.* 4th edition. (New York: Harper Collins, 1994), pp. 160–62.

37 Hisham Sharabi. *Neopatriarchy: A Theory of Distorted Change in the Arab World.* (Oxford: Oxford University Press, 1988), p. 9.

38 Jean-François Bayart. *The State in Africa: The Politics of the Belly.* (London: Longman, 1993), pp. 174–75.

39 S. E. Finer. *The Man on Horseback: The Role of the Military in Politics.* (Boulder, CO: Westview, 1988), pp. 214–15.

40 Economy is not given any systematic treatment in Joel Migdal et al. (eds). *State Power and Social Forces,* although the concluding chapter touches upon it in passing (pp. 300–301). Other relevant discussions are found in Dietrich Rueschemeyer and Peter Evans. "The State and Economic Transformation: Toward an Analysis of the Conditions Underlying Effective Intervention". In Peter Evans, Dietrich Rueschemeyer, and Theda Skocpol (eds). *Bringing the State Back In.* (Cambridge: Cambridge University Press, 1984).

41 Dietrich Rueschemeyer and Peter Evans. "The State and Economic Transformation". p. 68.

42 Dietrich Rueschemeyer, Evelyne Huber Stephens, and John Stephens. *Capitalist Development and Democracy.* (Chicago, IL: University of Chicago Press, 1992), p. 269.

43 Barrington Moore. *The Social Origins of Democracy and Dictatorship: Lord and Peasant in the Making of the Modern World.* (New York: Penguin, 1966), p. 415.

44 For a discussion of the natures of and relationship between corporatism and fascism in inter-war Europe see H. R. Kedward. *Fascism in Western Europe 1900–45.* (New York, NY: New York University Press, 1971), pp. 207–19.

45 Keith Laybourn. *The Evolution of British Social Policy and the Welfare State.* (Keele: Keele University Press, 1995), p. 222; Susan Pedersen. *Family, Dependence, and the Origins of the Welfare State: Britain and France, 1914–1945.* (Cambridge: Cambridge University Press, 1993), pp. 290–91.

46 Guillermo O'Donnell. *Bureaucratic Authoritarianism: Argentina, 1966–1973, in Comparative Perspective.* (Berkeley, CA: University of California Press, 1988), p. 32.

47 Michael Foley. "Debt, Democracy, and Neoliberalism in Latin America: Losses and Gains of the 'Lost Decade'". In Manochehr Dorraj (ed.). *The Changing Political Economy of the Third World.* (Boulder, CO: Lynne Rienner, 1995), p. 20.

48 J. G. Valdés. *La Escuela de Chicago: Operación Chile* (The Chicago School: Operation Chile). (Buenos Aires: Ediciones Grupo Zeta, 1989).

49 Michael Foley. "Debt, Democracy, and Neoliberalism in Latin America: Losses and Gains of the 'Lost Decade'", p. 21.

50 Luiz Carlos Bresser Pereira, Jose Maria Maravall, and Adam Przewoski. *Economic Reform in New Democracies: A Social-Democratic Approach.* (Cambridge: Cambridge University Press, 1993), pp. 132–33.

51 Michael Todaro. *Economic Development.* 5th edition. (New York: Longman, 1997), pp. 34–35. The mixed (or statist) economies found in parts of the developing world today are not very different from the mercantilism that Europe witnessed from the seventeenth to the nineteenth century.

52 Howard Wiarda. *Latin American Politics.* (Belmont, CA: Wadsworth, 1995), pp. 112–16.

53 Clifford Geertz, Hildred Geertz, and Lawrence Rosen. *Meaning and Order in Moroccan Society: Three Essays in Cultural Analysis.* (Cambridge: Cambridge University Press, 1979), pp. 123–264.

54 Crawford Young. "Patterns of Social Conflict: State, Class, and Ethnicity". *Daedalus.* Vol. 111, No. 2, (Spring 1982), p. 86.

55 Antony Gadzey. "The Political Economy of Centralization and Delayed Capitalism in Sub-Saharan Africa". In Manochehr Dorraj (ed.). *The Changing Political*

Economy of the Third World. (Boulder, CO: Lynne Rienner, 1995), p. 89. Gadzey attributes Africa's semicapitalism to two factors: the colonial commodity export trade; and the fact that "the total external focus of the trade deprived it of the normal forward and backward linkages necessary to make commodity trade an adequate lead-off sector for the complete capitalization of the larger subsistence economy".

56 Stephen Lewis. *The Economics of Apartheid.* (New York: Council on Foreign Relations Press, 1990), pp. 17–18.

57 Anthony Giddens. *Beyond Left and Right: The Future of Radical Politics.* (Stanford, CA: Stanford University Press, 1994), p. 4.

58 Op. cit., p. 5.

59 Giddens calls this "social reflexivity". Globalization, he claims, transforms tradition. Individuals must therefore "become used to filtering all sorts of information relevant to their life situations and routinely act on the basis of that filtering process". Op. cit., p. 6.

60 Michael Todaro. *Economic Development*, p. 524.

61 Adam Przeworski. *Democracy and the Market: Political and Economic Reforms in Eastern Europe and Latin America.* (Cambridge: Cambridge University Press, 1991), p. 165.

62 In the Middle East, a favorite national pastime is to blame a neighboring country for domestic political difficulties. In Turkey and Algeria, for example, most secularists are convinced that the activities of the (now banned) Welfare Party and the FIS are financed by Iran and Saudi Arabia. In Egypt, Sudan is seen as the main culprit behind the rise of domestic terrorism. And so on. When another Muslim country does not fit into the conspiracy theory, Israel is always a sure bet. In Iran, meanwhile, pro-monarchists are convinced that the United States installed Ayatollah Khomeini and the Islamic Republic in power.

63 See Nazih Ayubi. *Political Islam: Religion and Politics in the Arab World.* (London: Routledge, 1991).

64 Basil Davidson. *The Black Man's Burden: Africa and the Curse of the Nation-State.* (New York: Times Books, 1992), pp. 185–86.

65 Joel Migdal, Atul Kohli, and Vivienne Shue. "Introduction: Developing a State-in-Society Perspective". p. 3.

66 Stephen Hawking. *A Brief History of Time: From the Big Bang to Black Holes.* (London: Bantam Books, 1988), pp. 55–56.

67 The argument that the responsibility for the Holocaust rests primarily with Hitler is not universally accepted. For more on this debate see Michael Marrus. *The Holocaust in History.* (Hanover, MA: The University Press of New England, 1987), especially pp.1–30.

68 See the arguments made in Joseph Needham. *Science and Civilisation in China*, Volume 5, Part 3. (Cambridge: Cambridge University Press, 1976), pp. xxv–xxvi. A brief overview of the historical roots of the differences between China and the West may be found in Liu Xiaojun. "Politics, Law and Culture: Historical Differences Between China and West". *Beijing Review.* No. 28, (July 10–16, 1989), pp. 34–37.

69 Henry Steele Commager. *The Study of History.* (Columbus, OH: Charles Merrill, 1966), p. 86.

70 Ibid.

71 Op. cit., p. 87.

72 Ibid.

73 Mohammad Reza Pahlavi. *Answer to History.* (New York: Stein and Day, 1980), p. 19; Samuel Schmucker. *A History of the Four Georges.* (New York: D. Appleton & Co., 1865), pp. 204–205.

6 Democratic states

1 See, for example, James Bill and Robert Hardgrave. *Comparative Politics: Quest for Theory.* (Washington, DC: University Press of America, 1981); Jean Blondel. *Comparing Political Systems.* (New York, NY: Praeger, 1972); Roy Macridis and Steven Burg. *Introduction to Comparative Politics: Regimes and Change.* (New York, NY: Harper Collins, 1991); Roy Macridis. *Modern Political Regimes: Patterns and Institutions.* (Boston, MA: Little, Brown, 1986); Geir Lundestad. *East, West, North, South: Major Developments in International Politics.* Gail Adams Kvam, trans. (Oslo: Norwegian University Press, 1986); Dirk Berg-Schlosser. "African Political Systems: Typology and Performance". *Comparative Political Studies.* Vol. 17, No. 1, (April 1984), pp. 121–51; Hans Mouritzen. "Tensions Between the Strong, and the Strategies of the Weak". *Journal of Peace Research.* Vol. 28, No. 2, (1991), pp. 217–30; and Iliya Harik. "The Origins of the Arab State System". In Ghassan Salame (ed.). *The Foundations of the Arab State.* (London: Croom Helm, 1987), pp. 19–46. For a discussion of the role of leadership see Stanley Hoffman. "The Case for Leadership". *Foreign Policy.* No. 81, (Winter 1990–91), pp. 20–39; Lewis J. Eddinger. "Approaches to the Comparative Analysis of Political Leadership". *Review of Politics.* Vol. 52, No. 4, (Fall 1990), pp. 509–23; James Schubert. "Age and Active-Passive Leadership Style". *American Political Science Review.* Vol. 82, No. 3, (September 1988), pp. 763–72; H. G. Peter Wallach. "Political Leadership". *Journal of Politics.* Vol 50, No. 4, (November 1988), pp. 1090–95.
2 Harry Redner. "Beyond Marx-Weber: A Diversified and International Approach to the State". *Political Studies.* Vol 38, (1990), pp. 648–49.
3 Op. cit., p. 648.
4 Op. cit., p. 649.
5 Latin American countries, for example, are often dependent on, or at least extremely sensitive to, policies and initiatives by multi-national (non-state) lending agencies such as the World Bank and the International Monetary Fund.
6 See *World Press Review.* Vol. 39, No. 7, (July 1992), pp. 9–14.
7 Harry Redner. "Beyond Marx-Weber: A Diversified and International Approach to the State", p. 649.
8 Michael Bratton. "Patterns of Development and Underdevelopment". *International Studies Quarterly.* Vol. 26, No. 3, (September 1982), pp. 361–62. Bratton concentrates on "patterns of (economic) development" of non-Western countries.
9 Irving Louis Horowitz. *Three Worlds of Development: The Theory and Practice of International Stratification.* (New York: Oxford University Press, 1966), p. 39.
10 Jean-Pierre Lehmann. "Dictatorship and Development in Pacific Asia: Wider Implications". *International Affairs.* Vol. 61, No. 4, (Autumn 1985), p. 591.
11 Michael Bratton. "Patterns of Development and Underdevelopment", p. 362.
12 Ibid.
13 Op. cit., pp. 360–61.
14 In one form or another, the states of Germany and Italy had records which were marred by spurts of militaristic authoritarianism in the 1920s and the 1930s. The sovereign, democratic states of Austria, the Netherlands, Norway, Denmark, France, and Belgium were all subsumed under foreign occupation during World War II. Spain, Portugal, and Greece were all under military rule until the 1970s and are even more recent democracies. Japan's democratic state also does not pre-date the end of World War II. See also Dennis Kavanagh. "Western Europe". In Robert Wesson (ed.). *Democracy: A Worldwide Survey.* (New York, NY: Praeger, 1987), pp. 11–12.

15 Alan Ball. *Modern Politics and Government*. (Chatham, NJ: Chatham House, 1988), p. 136.

16 Gerhard Loewenberg and Samuel Patterson. "Legislatures and Political Systems". In Louis Cantori and Andrew Ziegler (eds). *Comparative Politics in the Post-Behavioralist Era*. (Boulder, CO: Lynne Rienner, 1988), p. 280.

17 Michael Curtis. *Introduction to Comparative Government*. (New York, NY: Harper Collins, 1990), p. 21. For an interesting analysis of parliaments in Denmark, Iceland, Norway, Sweden, and Finland see David Apter. *The Nordic Parliament*. (New York, NY: St. Martin's Press, 1984).

18 Rod Hague and Martin Harrop. *Comparative Government and Politics: An Introduction*. (Atlantic Heights, NJ: Humanities Press, 1989), p. 188.

19 For a detailed and concise account of events in China in April and May 1989 see John Cooper and Ta-Ling Lee. *Failure of Democracy Movement: Human Rights in the People's Republic of China, 1988/1989*. (Baltimore, MD: University of Maryland School of Law, 1991), especially pp. 25–27 and 123–26.

20 Alan Ball. *Modern Politics and Government*, p. 194.

21 Rod Hague and Martin Harrop. *Comparative Government and Politics: An Introduction*, p. 179.

22 Roy Macridis. *Modern Political Regimes: Patterns and Institutions*, p. 51.

23 Alan Ball. *Modern Politics and Government*, pp. 150–51.

24 Roy Macridis and Steven L. Burg. *Introduction to Comparative Politics: Regimes and Change*, p. 25.

25 Alan Ball. *Modern Politics and Government*, p. 153.

26 Eva Etzioni-Halevy. *Bureaucracy and Democracy: A Political Dilemma*. (London: Routledge, 1983), p. 131.

27 John Creighton Campbell. "Democracy and Bureaucracy in Japan". In Takeshi Ishida and Ellis S. Krauss (eds). *Democracy in Japan*. (Pittsburgh, PA: University of Pittsburgh Press, 1989), pp. 133–34.

28 Eva Etzioni-Halevy. *Bureaucracy and Democracy: A Political Dilemma*, p. 133.

29 Roy Macridis. *Modern Political Regimes: Patterns and Institutions*, p. 108.

30 Mark Kesselman and Joel Krieger (eds). *European Politics in Transition*. (Lexington, MA: D. C. Heath, 1986), p. 8. There are, it is important to note, some scholars who disagrees with this assertion. Blondel, for example, argues that "there is indeed a correlation between liberal democracy and socio-economic development, in that the richest polities are most inclined to be stable liberal democracies, while Latin American polities and other Third World countries can be expected to shift periodically between liberal democracy and some other form of regime". Jean Blondel. *Comparing Political Systems*, p. 169.

31 Arend Lijphart and Markus M. L. Crepaz. "Corporatism and Consensus Democracy in Eighteen Countries: Conceptual and Empirical Linkages". *British Journal of Political Science*. Vol. 21, (1991), p. 245.

32 S. E. Finer. *Five Constitutions: Contrasts and Comparisons*. (New York, NY: Penguin, 1979), p. 15.

33 Rod Hague and Martin Harrop. *Comparative Politics and Government: An Introduction*, pp. 163–64.

34 S. E. Finer. *Five Constitutions: Contrasts and Comparisons*, p. 17.

35 Leslie Lipson. *The Democratic Civilization*. (Oxford: Oxford University Press, 1964), p. 406.

36 W. W. Rostow. *Politics and the Stages of Growth*. (Cambridge: Cambridge University Press, 1971), p. 269.

37 J. Lloyd Mecham. "Latin American Constitutions: Nominal and Real." In Harvey Kebschull (ed.). *Politics in Transitional Societies*. (New York, NY: Appleton-Century-Crofts, 1973), p. 224.

38 W. W. Rostow. *Politics and the Stages of Growth*, p. 270.

39 For a discussion of the breakdown of previous democracies, see Juan Linz and Alfred Stepan (eds). *The Breakdown of Democratic Regimes*. (Baltimore, MD: Johns Hopkins University Press, 1978).

40 See Larry Diamond, Juan Linz, and Seymour Martin Lipset (eds). *Democracy in Developing Countries*. (Boulder, CO: Lynne Rienner, 1988). In subsequent years, three additional volumes dealing with Africa, Asia, and Latin America respectively were also published as part of a series.

41 Larry Diamond, Juan J. Linz, and Seymour Martin Lipset. *Politics in Developing Countries: Comparing Experiences with Democracy*. (Boulder, CO: Lynne Rienner, 1990), pp. 18–21.

42 Juan J. Linz. "The Breakdown of Democratic Regimes: Elements of a Breakdown". In Juan J.Linz and Alfred Stepan (eds). *The Breakdown of Democratic Regimes*, p. 40.

43 Larry Diamond, Juan J. Linz, and Seymour Martin Lipset. *Politics in Developing Countries: Comparing Experiences with Democracy*, p. 23

44 Juan J. Linz. "The Breakdown of Democratic Regimes: Elements of a Breakdown", p. 41.

45 Some of the more notable examples of pseudo-democracies in the Third World include the Philippines, India, Pakistan, and Turkey in Asia, Kenya and Tanzania in Africa, and Jamaica, the Dominican Republic, Colombia, Costa Rica, Honduras, Venezuela, and Ecuador in Latin America. Diamond, Linz, and Lipset use the same title of pseudo-democratic for a quite different type of regime. Such a political system, they argue, is a "subset of authoritarian regimes … because the existence of formally democratic institutions, such as multiparty electoral competition, masks (often in part to legitimate) the reality of authoritarian domination. Central America has long lived under such regimes. While this regime type overlaps in some way with the hegemonic regime, it is less institutionalized and typically more personalized, coercive, and unstable." Larry Diamond, Juan Linz, and Seymour Martin Lipset. "Introduction: Comparing Experiences with Democracy". In Larry Diamond, Juan Linz, and Seymour Martin Lipset. *Politics in Developing Countries: Comparing Experiences with Democracy*, p. 8.

46 See below, chapter 8.

47 See, for example, Arend Lijphart (ed.). *Parliamentary Versus Presidential Government*. (Oxford: Oxford University Press, 1992). See also Arend Lijphart. "Democratic Political Systems". In Anton Bebler and Jim Seroka (eds). *Contemporary Political Systems: Classifications and Typologies*. (Boulder, CO: Lynne Rienner, 1990), pp. 71–87.

48 Georg Sorensen. *Democracy and Democratization*. (Boulder, CO: Westview, 1993), pp. 80–85.

49 Barrington Moore. *Social Origins of Dictatorship and Democracy*. (New York, NY: Penguin, 1966).

7 Non-democratic states

1 Samuel Huntington. *The Third Wave: Democratization in the Late Twentieth Century*. (Norman, OK: University of Oklahoma Press, 1991).

2 For more on power and its relationship with the political system, especially in the international system, see John Rothgeb, Jr. *Defining Power: Influence and Force in the Contemporary International System*. (New York, NY: St. Martin's Press, 1993), especially pp. 17–50.

3 Lucian W. Pye. "The NonWestern Political Process". In Harvey G. Kebschull (ed.). *Politics in Transitional Societies: The Challenge of Change in Asia, Africa, and Latin America*. (New York, NY: Appleton-Century-Crofts, 1973), p. 30.

4 See Mehran Kamrava. *Politics and Society in the Third World*. (London: Routledge, 1993), chapter 1.

5 Ann Ruth Willner and Dorothy Willner. "The Rise and Role of Charismatic Leaders". In Harvey Kebschull (ed.). *Politics in Transitional Societies.*, p. 233.

6 Douglas Madsen and Peter G. Snow. "Recruitment Contrasts in a Divided Charismatic Movement". *American Political Science Review*. Vol. 81, No. 1, (March 1987), p. 233.

7 Dankwart Rustow. "Ataturk's Political Leadership." In R. Bayly Winder (ed.). *Near Eastern Round Table, 1967–1968*. (New York, NY: New York University, 1969), p. 145.

8 E. B. Portis. "Charismatic Leadership and Cultural Democracy". *Review of Politics*, Vol. 41, No. 2, (Spring 1987), p. 241.

9 Op. cit., p. 237.

10 Ann Ruth Willner and Dorothy Willner. "The Rise and Role of Charismatic Leaders", p. 235.

11 E. B. Portis. "Charismatic Leadership and Cultural Democracy", pp. 230–31.

12 Douglas Madsen and Peter G. Snow. "Recruitment Contrasts in a Divided Charismatic Movement", p. 238.

13 For more on the efforts of post-revolutionary regimes to keep the flames of revolution burning, see Mehran Kamrava. *Revolutionary Politics*. (Westport, CT: Praeger), chapter 2.

14 Douglas Madsen and Peter G. Snow. "Recruitment Contrasts in a Divided Charismatic Movement", p. 238.

15 David Apter. "Political Religion in the New Nations". In Clifford Geertz (ed.). *Old Societies and New States*. (New York, NY: Free Press, 1963), p. 59.

16 Kenneth Lieberthal and Michael Oksenburg. *Policy Making in China: Leaders, Structures, Processes*. (Princeton, NJ: Princeton University Press, 1988), p. 58.

17 Jan Pakulski. "Legitimacy and Mass Compliancy: Reflections on Max Weber and Soviet-type Societies". *British Journal of Political Science*. Vol. 16, (January 1986), p. 36.

18 Eric Hoffer. *The True Believer: Thoughts on the Nature of Mass Movements*. (New York, NY: Harper & Row, 1951), p. 94.

19 Giovanni Sartori. "The Party as Part." In Louis Cantori and Andrew Ziegler (eds). *Comparative Politics in the Post-Behavioral Era*. (Boulder, CO: Lynne Rienner, 1988), p. 254.

20 Jean Blondel. *Comparing Political Systems*. (New York, NY: Praeger, 1972), pp. 206–207.

21 Op. cit., p. 207.

22 Samuel Huntington. "Social and Institutional Dynamics of One Party Systems". In Samuel Huntington and Clement Moore (eds). *Authoritarian Politics and Modern Society*. (London: Basic Books, 1970), p. 12.

23 Roy Macridis. *Modern Political Regimes: Patterns and Institutions*. (Boston, MA: Little, Brown, 1986), pp. 126–27.

24 John L. Stanley. "Is Totalitarianism a New Phenomenon? Reflections on Hannah Arendt's Origins of Totalitarianism". *Review of Politics*. Vol. 49, (Spring 1987), p. 180–81.

25 Guillermo O'Donnell. "Corporatism and the Question of the State". In James Malloy (ed.). *Authoritarianism and Corporatism in Latin America*. (Pittsburgh, PA: University of Pittsburgh Press, 1977), p. 69.

26 Vernon W. Ruttan. "What Happened to Political Development?" *Economic Development and Cultural Change*. Vol. 39, No. 2, (January 1991), p. 277.

27 Samuel Huntington. "Political Development and Political Decay." *World Politics*. Vol. 17, No. 3, (April 1965), p. 407.

28 Joel S. Migdal. *Strong Societies and Weak States: State-Society Relations and State Capabilities in the Third World.* (Princeton, NJ: Princeton University Press, 1988), p. 213.

29 Op. cit., p. 214.

30 Op. cit., pp. 214–23.

31 Eric Nordlinger. *Soldiers in Politics: Military Coups and Governments.* (Englewood Cliffs, NJ: Prentice-Hall, 1977), pp. 22–23.

32 Frank Tachau and Metin Heper. "The State, Politics, and the Military in Turkey". *Comparative Politics.* Vol. 16, No. 1, (October 1983), p. 28.

33 Eric Nordlinger. *Soldiers in Politics*, p. 25.

34 Op. cit., pp. 26–27.

35 Samuel Decalo. "Modalities of Civil-Military Stability in Africa". *Journal of Modern African Studies.* Vol. 27, No. 4, (1989), p. 548.

36 Edward Feit. *The Armed Bureaucrats: Military Administrative Regimes and Political Development.* (Boston, MA: Houghton Mifflin, 1973), p. 164.

37 Rosemary O'Kane. "A Probabilistic Approach to the Causes of Coups d'Etat". *British Journal of Political Science.* Vol. 11, (1981), p. 293.

38 Robert Bianchi. "Interest Group Politics in the Third World". In Louis Cantori and Andrew Ziegler (eds). *Comparative Politics in the Post-Behavioral Era.*, p. 205.

39 Guillermo O'Donnell. "Corporatism and the Question of the State". James Malloy, ed. *Authoritarianism and Corporatism in Latin America,* p. 48.

40 Robert Bianchi. "Interest Group Politics in the Third World". In Louis Cantori and Andrew Ziegler (eds). *Comparative Politics in the Post-Behavioral Era.*, pp. 207–208.

41 North Korea remains an exception, where the cult of personality of the late Kim Ill Sung, officially referred to as the "Great Leader", and of his son, the "Dear Leader", remain in full force.

42 Leslie Holmes. *Politics in the Communist World.* (Oxford: Clarendon, 1986), p. 130.

43 Stephen White, John Gardner, and George Schopflin. *Communist Political Systems: An Introduction.* (New York, NY: St. Martin's Press, 1987), p. 84.

44 Kenneth Lieberthal and Michael Oksenburg. *Policy Making in China*, p. 35.

45 Leslie Holmes. *Politics in the Communist World.* (Oxford: Clarendon, 1986), p. 203.

8 Revolutions

1 For an examination of the concept of revolution see James Farr. "Historical Concepts in Political Science: The Case of 'Revolution'". *American Journal of Political Science.* Vol. 26, No. 4, (November 1982), pp. 688–708, and John Dunn. "Revolution", in T. Ball, J. Farr, and R. Hanson (eds). *Political Innovation and Conceptual Change.* (Cambridge: Cambridge University Press, 1988), pp. 133–56.

2 John Dunn. *Modern Revolutions: An Introduction to the Analysis of a Political Phenomenon.* 2nd edition. (Cambridge: Cambridge University Press, 1989), p. xvi.

3 Ibid.

4 Peter Calvert. *Politics, Power, and Revolution: An Introduction to Comparative Politics.* (London: Wheatsheaf, 1983), p. 163.

5 See, for example, Laszlo Bruszt. "1989: The Negotiated Revolution in Hungary". *Social Research.* Vol. 57, No. 2, (Summer 1990), pp. 365–87.

6 Op.cit., p. 386.

7 Mehran Kamrava. "Causes and Leaders of Revolution". *Journal of Social, Political, and Economic Studies.* Vol. 15, No. 1, (Spring 1990), p. 84.

8 A few examples of works on revolutions include: Michael Freeman. "Review Article: Theories of Revolution". *British Journal of Political Science.* Vol. 2, (1972), pp. 339–59; Rod Aya. "Theories of Revolution: Contrasting Models of Collective Violence". *Theory and Society.* Vol. 8, No. 1, (July 1979), pp. 39–99; Perez Zagorin. "Theories of Revolution in Contemporary Historiography". *Political Science Quarterly.* Vol. LXXXVIII, No. 1, (March 1973), pp. 23–52; Theda Skocpol. *States and Social Revolutions.* (Cambridge: Cambridge University Press, 1979), chapter 1; Issac Kromnick. "Reflections on Revolution: Definition and Explanation in Recent Scholarship". *History and Theory.* Vol. Xl, No. 1, (1972), pp. 22–63; J. M. Maravall. "Subjective Conditions and Revolutionary Conflicts: Some Remarks". *British Journal of Sociology.* Vol. 27, No. 1, (March 1976), pp. 21–34; and, L. Stone. "Theories of Revolution". *World Politics.* Vol. 18. (1966), pp. 159–76.

9 For a look at the merits of some of the more dominant theories of revolutions see, especially, Barbara Salert. *Revolutions and Revolutionaries.* (New York: Elsevier, 1976); Rod Aya. "Theories of Revolution: Contrasting Models of Collective Violence"; Farrokh Moshiri. "Revolutionary Conflict Theory in an Evolutionary Perspective". In Jack Goldstone, Ted Robert Gurr, and Farrokh Moshiri (eds). *Revolutions of the Late Twentieth Century.* (Boulder, CO: Westview, 1991), pp. 4–36.

10 James Farr. "Historical Concepts in Political Science: The Case of 'Revolution'", p. 706.

11 Ibid.

12 John Dunn. *Rethinking Modern Political Theory.* (Cambridge: Cambridge University Press, 1985), p. 77.

13 Mehran Kamrava. "Causes and Leaders of Revolutions", p. 84.

14 The developing world is inundated with examples of movements which embrace foreign ideologies and import them with little alteration to fit local conditions. "Maoist" groups across the Middle East and Latin America, especially the Shining Path in Peru, are a prime example.

15 Chalmers Johnson. *Revolutionary Change.* (London: Longman, 1983).

16 James Davies. "Toward a Theory of Revolution". *American Sociological Review.* Vol. 27, No. 1, (February 1962), pp. 7–19; and Ted Gurr. *Why Men Rebel.* (Princeton, NJ: Princeton University Press, 1970).

17 Samuel Huntington. *Political Order in Changing Societies.* (New Haven, CT: Yale University Press, 1968).

18 Jerrold Green. "Countermobilization as a Revolutionary Form". *Comparative Politics.* Vol. 16, No. 2, (January 1984), pp. 153–69.

19 Theda Skocpol. *States and Social Revolutions.*

20 Mehran Kamrava. "Causes and Leaders of Revolutions". pp. 80–81.

21 See, for example, Theda Skocpol. "Rentier State and Shi'a Islam in the Iranian Revolution". *Theory and Society.* Vol. 11, No. 3, (May 1982), pp. 265–83.

22 Diplomatic pressures and conditional relations with the United States were highly instrumental in the direction and success of revolutions in Iran and the Philippines, as were relations between the Soviet Union and those governments which fell to revolutions in eastern Europe in the late 1980s.

23 Samuel Huntington. *Political Order in Changing Societies,* pp. 4–5.

24 Huntington calls these states "praetorian". Op. cit., p. 168.

25 Edmond Keller. "Revolution and the Collapse of Traditional Monarchies: Ethiopia". In Barry Schutz and Robert Slater (eds). *Revolution and Political Change in the Third World.* (Boulder, CO: Lynne Rienner, 1990), p. 87.

26 Lucian Pye. "Legitimacy Crisis". In Lucian Pye et al. *Crises and Sequences in Political Development.* (Princeton, NJ: Princeton University Press, 1971), p. 183.

27 Chalmers Johnson. *Revolutionary Change,* p. 65.

28 Lucian Pye. "Legitimacy Crisis", p. 138.
29 Samuel Huntington. *Political Order in Changing Societies*, p. 31.
30 Lucian Pye. "Legitimacy Crisis", p. 141.
31 Barry Schultz and Robert Slater. "A Framework for Analysis". In Barry Schultz and Robert Slater (eds). *Revolution and Political Change in the Third World*, p. 5.
32 Lucian Pye. "Legitimacy Crisis", p. 150.
33 Samuel Huntington. *Political Order in Changing Societies*, p. 275.
34 Jeff Goodwin and Theda Skocpol. "Explaining Revolutions in the Contemporary Third World". *Politics and Society*. Vol. 17, No. 4, (December 1989), p. 498.
35 Jeff Goodwin and Theda Skocpol. "Explaining Revolutions in the Contemporary Third World", pp. 498–99.
36 Op.cit., p. 500.
37 Barry Schultz and Robert Slater. "A Framework for Analysis", p. 7.
38 Barry Schultz and Robert Slater. "Patterns of Legitimacy and Future Revolutions in the Third World". In Barry Schultz and Robert Slater (eds). *Revolution and Political Change in the Third World*, p. 248.
39 See Mehran Kamrava. *Politics and Society in the Developing World*, 2nd edition. (London: Routledge, 2000), chapter 2.
40 Theda Skocpol. *States and Social Revolutions*, p. 286.
41 Barry Schultz and Robert Slater. "A Framework for Analysis", p. 5.
42 James Davies. "Toward a Theory of Revolution", p. 17.
43 Ted Gurr. *Why Men Rebel*, pp. 121–22.
44 R. Ben Jones. *The French Revolution*. (London: Hodder & Stoughton, 1967), p. 16.
45 Richard Charques. *The Twilight of the Russian Empire*. (Oxford: Oxford University Press, 1965), p. 204.
46 Pedro Perez Sarduy. "Culture and the Cuban Revolution". *The Black Scholar*. Vol. 20, nos. 5–6, (Winter 1989), p. 18.
47 Mehran Kamrava. *Revolution in Iran: Roots of Turmoil*. (London: Routledge, 1990), p. 68.
48 Laszo Bruszt. "1989: The Negotiated Revolution in Hungary", p. 386.
49 R. Ben Jones. *The French Revolution*, p. 15.
50 Pedro Perez Sarduy. "Culture and the Cuban Revolution", p. 19.
51 Mehran Kamrava. *Revolution in Iran*, p. 66.
52 Theda Skocpol. *States and Social Revolutions*, p. 17.
53 John Dunn. *Modern Revolutions*, p. xxi.
54 Theda Skocpol. States and Social Revolutions, p. 31.
55 Op.cit., p. 47.
56 See, especially, Samuel Huntington. *Political Order in Changing Societies*, chapter 4, and Jeff Goodwin and Theda Skocpol. "Explaining Revolutions in the Contemporary Third World", pp. 498–99.
57 Jeff Goodwin and Theda Skocpol. "Explaining Revolutions in the Contemporary Third World", p. 504.
58 Op.cit., p. 496.
59 T. David Mason. "Indigenous Factors". In Barry Schultz and Robert Slater (eds). *Revolution and Political Change in the Third World*, p. 40.
60 Jeff Goodwin and Theda Skocpol. "Explaining Revolutions in the Contemporary Third World", p. 500.
61 David Mason. "Indigenous Factors", p. 33.
62 Mehran Kamrava. "Causes and Leaders of Revolutions", pp. 83–84.
63 See Mehran Kamrava. *Revolution in Iran*, pp. 30–32 and 40–45; and Laszlo Bruszt. "1989: The Negotiated Revolution In Hungary", pp. 381–82.
64 Jeff Goodwin and Theda Skocpol. "Explaining Revolutions in the Contemporary Third World", p. 501.

65 Barry Schultz and Robert Slater. "Patterns of Legitimacy and Future Revolutions in the Third World", p. 248.

66 Jeff Goodwin and Theda Skocpol. "Explaining Revolutions in the Contemporary Third World", p. 502.

67 William Foltz. "External Causes". In Barry Schultz and Robert Slater (eds). *Revolution and Political Change in the Third World*, pp. 54–59.

68 Girard Chaliand. *Revolution in the Third World: Myths and Prospects.* (New York: Viking Press, 1977), p. 40.

69 William Foltz. "External Causes", p. 63.

70 See Bruce Miroff. *Pragmatic Illusions: The Presidential Politics of John F. Kennedy.* (New York: David McKay, 1976), especially pp. 110–66. A more up-to-date discussion of US foreign policy toward Latin America can be found in Thomas Paterson, J. G. Clifford, and Kenneth Hagan. *American Foreign Policy: A History.* (Lexington, MA: D.C. Heath & Co., 1991), pp. 588–90, 627–32.

71 Quoted in Clifford Krauss. "Revolution in Central America?" *Foreign Affairs.* Vol. 65, No. 3, (1987), p. 564.

72 Op.cit., pp. 564–65.

73 Thomas Paterson, J. G. Clifford, and Kenneth Hagen. *American Foreign Policy*, p. 588.

74 Samuel Huntington. *Political Order in Changing Societies*, p. 34.

75 See Kamrava. *Politics and Society in the Developing World*, chapter 1.

76 Samuel Huntington. *Political Order in Changing Societies*, p. 37.

77 Op.cit., p. 56.

78 Op.cit., p. 403.

79 Op.cit., p. 21.

80 Irma Adelman and Janus Hihn. "Crisis Politics in Developing Countries". *Economic Development and Cultural Change.* Vol. 33, No. 1, (October 1984), p. 20.

81 Elbaki Hermassi. *The Third World Reassessed.* (Berkeley, CA: University of California Press, 1980), pp. 59–60.

82 Op.cit., p. 44.

83 See Kamrava. *Politics and Society in the Developing World*, chapter 1.

84 For a discussion of "corporatism" see Rod Hague and Martin Harrop. *Comparative Politics and Government: An Introduction.* (Atlantic Highlands, NJ: Humanities Press, 1987), pp. 134–37.

85 Jeff Goodwin and Theda Skocpol. "Explaining Revolutions in the Contemporary Third World", p. 500.

86 John Dunn. *Rethinking Modern Political Theory*, p. 77.

87 John Dunn. *Modern Revolutions*, p. 236.

88 In *Political Order in Changing Societies*, Samuel Huntington classifies revolutions into "Eastern" and "Western" ones (p. 266).

89 Planned revolutions correspond closely to the variety Robert Dix calls "Latin American". Such revolutions occur, he writes, "in regimes that have been narrow, modernizing, military-based dictatorships rather than, say, weak monarchies. They have not simply collapsed, almost of their own weight, as in the Western style of revolution. Instead, they have had to be overthrown and their supporting armed forces defeated or demoralized in combat with those bent on revolution". Robert Dix. "Varieties of Revolution". *Comparative Politics.* Vol. 15, No. 3, (April 1983), p. 283.

90 Jeff Goodwin and Theda Skocpol. "Explaining Revolutions in the Contemporary Third World", p. 492.

91 Carlos Vilas. "Popular Insurgency and Social Revolution in Central America". *Latin American Perspectives.* Vol. 15, No. 1, (Winter 1988), p. 69.

92 Op.cit., p. 70.

93 James Scott. "Hegemony and the Peasantry". *Politics and Society*. Vol. 17, No. 3, (1977), p. 294.

94 Theda Skocpol. "What Makes Peasants Revolutionary?" *Comparative Politics*. Vol. 14, No. 3, (April 1982), p. 364.

95 James Scott. "Hegemony and the Peasantry", p. 295.

96 Girard Chaliand. *Revolution in the Third World*, p. 48.

97 Op.cit., pp. 42–43.

98 Samuel Huntington. *Political Order in Changing Societies*, p. 290.

99 Jeff Goodwin and Theda Skocpol. "Explaining Revolutions in the Contemporary Third World", p. 496.

100 Girard Chaliand. *Revolution in the Third World*, p. 35.

101 Stuart Schram. *The Political Thought of Mao Tse Tung*. (New York: Praeger, 1972), p. 253. See also op. cit., pp. 236–64.

102 James Scott. "Hegemony and the Peasantry", p. 289.

103 Eric Wolf. *Peasant Wars of the Twentieth Century* (New York, NY: Harper & Row, 1969), p. 276.

104 Op. cit., p. 279. Also see Theda Skocpol. "What Makes Peasants Revolutionary?"

105 Jeff Goodwin and Theda Skocpol. "Explaining Revolutions in the Contemporary Third World", p. 497.

106 T. David Mason. "Indigenous Factors", p. 42.

107 Jeff Goodwin and Theda Skocpol. "Explaining Revolutions in the Contemporary Third World", p. 493.

108 Ibid. There are, of course, instances (especially in Central America and in Africa) where guerrilla armies levy heavy "revolutionary taxes" on local peasants, disrupt village lives by raping women or forcibly recruiting children into their armies, and ransack and pillage villages which refuse to support their cause.

109 Jerrold Green. "Countermobilization as a Revolutionary Form", p. 147.

110 Op. cit., pp. 160–61.

111 Chalmers Johnson. *Revolutionary Change*, p. 101.

112 This was precisely the case in the revolutions that occurred in France and Iran, and in eastern Europe in the end of the 1980s. In the Russian revolution, however, the soviets played an important organizational role.

113 Girard Chaliand. *Revolution in the Third World*, p. 40.

114 See Mehran Kamrava. *Revolution in Iran*, chapter 5, esp. pp. 128–30; for eastern Europe, see the special edition on eastern European revolutions in *Social Research*. Vol. 57, No. 2, (Summer 1990).

115 Gerald Greene. *Comparative Revolutionary Movements* (Englewood Cliffs, NJ: Prentice-Hall, 1974), p. 57.

116 This was particularly the case in the Cuban and Ethiopian revolutions, where the ideological orientations of post-revolutionary political leaders did not fully become apparent until some time after their success.

117 Jeff Goodwin and Theda Skocpol. "Explaining Revolutions in the Contemporary Third World", p. 494.

118 Samuel Huntington. *Political Order in Changing Societies*, pp. 300–301.

119 Gerald Greene. *Comparative Revolutionary Movements*, p. 63.

120 T. David Mason. "Indigenous Factors", p. 48.

121 Op. cit. p. 44.

122 Barrington Moore. *Injustice: The Social Base of Obedience and Revolt*. (London: Macmillan, 1978), p. 459.

123 Peter Calvert. *Politics, Power, and Revolution*, p. 168.

124 Ted Gurr. *Why Men Rebel*, pp. 121–22.

125 James Davies. "Toward a Theory of Revolution", p. 8.

126 Ted Gurr. *Why Men Rebel*, p. 46. For a full analysis of relative deprivation see op. cit., pp. 46–56.

127 Op. cit., p. 37.
128 Op. cit., p. 205.
129 Manus Midlarsky. "Rulers and the Ruled: Patterned Inequality and the Onset of Mass Political Violence". *American Political Science Review.* Vol. 82, No. 2, (June 1988), p. 492.
130 Op. cit., p. 493.
131 See Jack Goldstone. "State Breakdown in the English Revolution: A New Synthesis". *American Journal of Sociology* Vol. 92, No. 2, (September 1986), pp. 257–322.
132 Op. cit., pp. 310–11.
133 Manus Midlarsky. "Scarcity and Inequality: Prologue to the Onset of Mass Revolution". *Journal of Conflict Resolution.* Vol. 26, No. 1, (March 1982), p. 34.
134 Manus Midlarsky. "Rulers and the Ruled: Patterned Inequality and the Onset of Mass Political Violence", pp. 493–94.
135 Jerome Himmelstein and Michael Kimmel. "Review Essay: States and Revolutions: The Implications and Limits of Skocpol's Structural Model". *American Journal of Sociology* Vol. 86, No. 5, (March 1981), p. 1147. Also see Theda Skocpol. "What makes Peasants Revolutionary?"
136 Jeffrey Paige. *Agrarian Revolution: Social Movements and Export Agriculture in the Underdeveloped World* (New York, NY: Free Press, 1975), p. 41.
137 Val Moghadam. "Industrial Development, Culture, and Working Class Politics: A Case Study of Tabriz Industrial Workers in the Iranian Revolution". *International Sociology.* Vol. 2, No. 2, (June 1987), pp. 164–65.
138 Chalmers Johnson. *Revolutionary Change*, p. 62.
139 Samuel Huntington. *Political Order in Changing Societies*, p. 290.
140 See John Dunn. *Modern Revolutions.*

9 Democratization

1 Samuel Huntington. *The Third Wave: Democratization in the Late Twentieth Century.* (Norman, OK: University of Oklahoma Press, 1991).
2 See, for example, Larry Diamond, Juan Linz, and Seymour Martin Lipset. "Introduction: Comparing Experiences with Democracy." In Larry Diamond, Juan Linz, and Seymour Martin Lipset (eds). *Politics in Developing Countries: Comparing Experiences with Democracy.* (Boulder, CO: Lynne Rienner, 1990), pp. 1–37; Doh Chull Shin. "On the Third Wave of Democratization." *World Politics.* Vol. 47, No. 3, (October 1994), pp. 135–70; and Larry Diamond. "Introduction: Political Culture and Democracy." In Larry Diamond (ed.). *Political Culture and Democracy in Developing Countries.* (Boulder, CO: Lynne Rienner, 1993), pp. 1–33.
3 Bouhui Zhang. "Corporatism, Totalitarianism, and Transitions to Democracy." *Comparative Political Studies.* Vol. 27, No. 1, (April 1994), pp. 108–109.
4 Giuseppe Di Palma. *To Craft Democracies: An Essay on Democratic Transitions.* (Berkeley, CA: University of California Press, 1990), p. 35.
5 Adam Przeworski. *Democracy and the Market: Political and Economic Reforms in Eastern Europe and Latin America.* (Cambridge: Cambridge University Press, 1991), p. 136.
6 Stephen Haggard and Robert Kaufman. *The Political Economy of Democratic Transitions.* (Princeton, NJ: Princeton University Press, 1995), pp. 158–59.
7 Claude Ake. "Rethinking African Democracy." In Larry Diamond and Marc Plattner (eds). *The Global Resurgence of Democracy.* (Baltimore, MD: Johns Hopkins University Press, 1993), p. 75.
8 Victor Pérez-Diaz. "The Possibility of Civil Society: Traditions, Character and Challenges." In John Hall (ed.). *Civil Society: Theory, History, Comparison.* (Cambridge: Polity Press, 1995), p. 103.

9 See, for example, Ernest Gellner. *Conditions of Liberty: Civil Society and its Critics.* (New York, NY: Penguin, 1994); John Hall (ed.). *Civil Society: Theory, History, Comparison.* (Cambridge: Polity, 1995); Ian Budge and David McKay (eds). *Developing Democracy.* (London: Sage, 1994); and Keith Tester. *Civil Society.* (London: Routledge, 1992), to mention only a few books on the topic.

10 Victor Pérez-Diaz. "The Possibility of Civil Society", p. 83.

11 Ernest Gellner. *Conditions of Liberty: Civil Society and its Critics,* p. 103.

12 Op. cit., p. 164.

13 Ernest Gellner. *Conditions of Liberty: Civil Society and its Critics,* p. 105.

14 Op. cit., p. 101. Gellner's arguments in this regard are much more thorough and complex than can be done justice to in the context of the present chapter. Briefly, Gellner considers the development of a modern, homogeneous culture as a natural by-product of the emergence of "the modular man", someone who is changeable, unbound to uncompromising, non-rationalized rituals and traditions, adaptable in outlook and social functions to the changing realities of social desires and political roadblocks. For more see op. cit., pp. 97–108, esp. 99–101.

15 Fascist Italy and bureaucratic-authoritarian Latin America remind us that, unlike present-day Germany, corporatism is not always democratic.

16 See especially Samuel Huntington. *The Third Wave,* pp. 110–74; and Giuseppe Di Palma. *To Craft Democracies,* pp. 103–104.

17 Samuel Huntington. *The Third Wave,* p. 124.

18 Claude Welch. "Changing Civil-Military Relations." In Robert Slater, Barry Schutz, and Steve Dorr (eds). *Global Transformation and the Third World.* (Boulder, CO: Lynne Rienner, 1993), p. 85.

19 For a brief survey of the revolutions of 1989 see David Mason. *Revolution in East-Central Europe: The Rise and Fall of Communism and the Cold War.* (Boulder, CO: Westview Press, 1992), pp. 54–67.

20 When this passage was written, in early 1996, Algeria was in the throes of a costly civil war, with scores having been killed by FIS commandos and in clashes between government soldier and FIS supporters.

21 J. Brown. "The Military and Society: The Turkish Case." *Middle Eastern Studies.* Vol. 21, (July 1989), pp. 387–404.

22 "President Elect Aleksander Kwasniewksi." *Donosy.* No. 1707, (Monday, November 20, 1995), p. 1.

23 Anthony Giddens. *Modernity and Self-Identity: Self and the Society in the Late Modern Age.* (Stanford, CA: Stanford University Press, 1991), pp. 209–10.

24 Compare, for example, such books by British authors as Ernest Gellner. *Conditions of Liberty*; John Hall (ed.). *Civil Society*; and Ian Budge and David McKay (eds). *Developing Democracy,* with those by Americans like Di Palma. *To Craft Democracies*; Samuel Huntington. *The Third Wave.* (Norman, OK: University of Oklahoma Press, 1991); and Robert Dahl. *Democracy and its Critics.* (New Haven, CT: Yale University Press, 1989), to name only a few.

25 See Guillermo O'Donnell, Philippe Schmitter, and Laurence Whitehead (eds). *Transitions from Authoritarian Rule: Southern Europe.* (Baltimore, MD: Johns Hopkins University Press, 1986).

26 Philippe Schmitter. "An Introduction to Southern European Transition for Authoritarian Rule: Italy, Greece, Portugal, Spain, and Turkey." In Guillermo O'Donnell, Philippe Schmitter, and Laurence Whitehead (eds). *Transitions from Authoritarian Rule: Southern Europe,* p. 9.

27 Ilkay Sunar and Sabri Sayari. "Democracy in Turkey: Problems and Prospects." In Guillermo O'Donnell, Philippe Schmitter, and Laurence Whitehead (eds). *Transitions from Authoritarian Rule: Southern Europe,* p. 186.

28 In Eastern Europe, Romania and Albania are also in the same predicament after their respective democratic transitions. See J. F. Brown. *Surge to Freedom: The End of Communist Rule in Eastern Europe.* (Durham, NC: Duke University Press, 1991), pp. 199–220 and 221–45.

29 For more on this point see Rusen Cakir. *Ne Seriat, Ne Democrasi: Refah Partisini Anlamak.* (Neither Shariat, Nor Democracy: Understanding the Refah Party). (Istanbul: Siyahbeyaz, 1994).

30 Stephen White, John Gardner, and George Schopflin. *Communist Political Systems: An Introduction.* 2nd edition. (New York, NY: St. Martin's Press, 1987), pp. 20–21.

31 See Jean Francois Bayart. *The State in Africa: The Politics of the Belly.* (London: Longman, 1993), pp. 242–52.

32 Iliya Harik. "The Origins of the Arab State System." In Ghassan Salame (ed.). *The Foundations of the Arab State.* (London: Croom Helm, 1987), pp. 22–23.

33 David Mason. *Revolution in East-Central Europe,* p. 37.

34 Daniel Levine. "Assessing the Impact of Liberation Theology in Latin America." *Review of Politics.* Vol. 50, No. 2, (Spring 1988), p. 253.

35 Andrew Michta. *The Government and Politics of Postcommunist Europe.* (Westport, CT: Praeger, 1994), p. 12.

36 Victor Pérez-Diaz. "The Possibility of Civil Society", p. 82.

37 Mehran Kamrava. *Politics and Society in the Third World.* (London: Routledge, 1993), pp. 160–63.

38 Op. cit., p. 162.

39 Mehran Kamrava. *Revolutionary Politics.* (Westport, CT: Praeger, 1992), pp. 27–28.

40 Samuel Huntington. *The Third Wave,* pp. 124–25.

41 Adam Przeworski. *Democracy and the Market,* p. 136.

42 Scott Mainwaring. "Democracy in Brazil and the Southern Cone: Achievements and Problems." *Journal of Interamerican Studies and World Affairs.* Vol. 37, No. 1, (Spring 1995), p. 145.

43 Karen Remmer argues the opposite, maintaining that "Latin America is not merely experiencing another episode in a cycle of democratic and authoritarian alterations, but has instead entered a distinctive historical phase in which broad electoral participation and respect for oppositional rights have become widespread and relatively durable features of the political landscape." See Karen Remmer. "Democratization in Latin America." In Robert Slater, Barry Schutz, and Steven Dorr (eds). *Global Transformation and the Third World,* p. 107. Mainwaring disagrees, maintaining that "democratic institutions are not only weak in Brazil, but, though to a lesser degree, in Argentina as well. So long as this situation remains, the prospects for the further consolidation of democracy are in doubt." Scott Mainwaring. "Democracy in Brazil and the Southern Cone: Achievements and Problems", pp. 114–15.

44 Alexander Motyl. *Dilemmas of Independence: Ukraine after Totalitarianism.* (New York, NY: Council on Foreign Relations Press, 1993), pp. 63–64.

45 Joseph Nye. *Bound to Lead: The Changing Nature of American Power.* (New York, NY: Basic Books, 1990), pp. 190–91.

10 Conclusion

1 Mattei Dogan and Dominique Pelassy. *How to Compare Nations: Strategies in Comparative Politics.* 2nd edition. (Chatham, NJ: Chatham House, 1990), p. 9.

2 Research on earlier journal articles in non-American publications in comparative politics is especially difficult. As a case in point, whereas the *American Political Science Review* was first published in 1903, the *Revue française de science politique* was not published until 1964 and the *British Journal of Political Science* started only in 1971.

Bibliography

Aberbach, Joel D., et al. *Bureaucrats and Politicians in Western Democracies*. Cambridge, MA: Harvard University Press, 1981.

Adelman, Irma, and Jairus M. Hihn. "Crisis Politics in Developing Countries". *Economic Development and Cultural Change*. Vol. 33, No. 1, (October 1984), pp. 1–22.

Adelman, Jonathan. *Revolution, Armies, and War: A Political History*. Boulder, CO: Lynne Rienner, 1985.

Adomeit, Hannes. "Soviet Ideology, Risk-Taking, and Crisis Behavior". In Robbin Laird and Erik Hoffman (eds). *Soviet Foreign Policy in a Changing World*. New York, NY: Aldine, 1986, pp. 99–108.

Aguirre, B. E. "The Conventionalization of Collective Behavior in Cuba". *American Journal of Sociology*. Vol. 90, No. 3, (1984), pp. 541–66.

Ahmad, Zakaria Haji. "Evolution and Development of the Political System in Malaysia". In Robert Scalapino, Seizaburo Sato, and Jusuf Wanandi (eds). *Asian Political Institutionalization*. Berkeley, CA: Institute of East Asian Studies, 1986, pp. 221–40.

Al-e Ahmad, Jalal. *Gharbzadegi*. [Westoxication]. Tehran: Ravvaq, 1341/1962.

Alatas, Syed Hussein. *Modernization and Social Change*. London: Angus and Robertson, 1972.

—— *Intellectuals in Developing Societies*. London: Frank Cass, 1977.

Almond, Gabriel, "Comparative Political Systems". *Journal of Politics*. Vol. 18, (August 1956).

—— "Introduction: A Functional Approach to Comparative Politics". In Gabriel Almond and James Coleman (eds). *The Politics of the Developing Areas*. Princeton, NJ: Princeton University Press, 1960, pp. 1–64.

——"Politics, Comparative." In David L. Sills (ed.). *International Encyclopedia of the Social Sciences*. Vol. 12. New York, NY: Crowell Collier & Macmillan, 1968. pp. 331–36.

—— "The Return to the State". *American Political Science Review*. Vol. 82, No. 3, (September 1988), pp. 853–74.

Almond, Gabriel, and James Coleman (eds). *The Politics of Developing Areas*. Princeton, NJ: Princeton University Press, 1960.

Almond, Gabriel, and G. Bingham Powell. *Comparative Politics: System, Process, and Policy*. Boston, MA: Little, Brown, & Co., 1978.

—— (eds). *Comparative Politics Today: A World View*. 5th edition, New York, NJ: HarperCollins, 1992.

Almond, Gabriel, and Sidney Verba. *The Civic Culture*. Princeton, NJ: Princeton University Press, 1963.

—— (eds). *The Civic Culture Revisited*. Boston, MA: Little, Brown, 1980.

Alsalam, Nabeel. "Interpreting Conditions in the Job Market for College Graduates". *Monthly Labor Review*. Vol. 116, No. 8, (February 1993), p. 54.

Alter, Peter. *Nationalism*. London: Routledge, 1989.

Amin, Samir. *Unequal Development*. New York, NY: Monthly Review Press, 1976.

Anderson, Lisa. "Lawless Government and Illegal Opposition: Reflections on the Middle East". *Journal of International Affairs*. Vol. 42, No. 2, (Winter/ Spring 1987), pp. 219–32.

Andrain, Charles. *Political Change in the Third World*. Winchester, MA: Unwin Hyman, 1988.

Apter, David. "Political Religion in the New Nations". In Clifford Geertz (ed.). *Old Societies and New States*. New York, NY: Free Press, 1963, pp. 57–104.

——*The Politics of Modernization*. Chicago, IL: The University of Chicago Press, 1965.

—— *Some Conceptual Approaches to the Study of Modernization*. Englewood Cliffs, NJ: Prentice-Hall, 1968.

—— *The Nordic Parliament*. New York, NY: St. Martin's, 1984.

—— *Rethinking Development*. Beverly Hills, CA: Sage, 1987.

Arato, Andrew. "Civil Society Against the State: Poland 1980–81". *Telos*. Vol. 47, 1981, pp. 23–47.

(1) "Empire vs. Civil Society: Poland 1981–82". *Telos*. Vol. 15, 1982. pp. 19–48.

Ashford, Douglas. "Attitudinal Change and Modernization". In Chandler Morse et al. *Modernization by Design: Social Change in the Twentieth Century*. Ithaca, NY: Cornell University Press, 1969, pp. 147–88.

Aya, Rod. "Theories of Revolution Reconsidered: Contrasting Models of Collective Violence". *Theory and Society*. vol. 8, no. 1, (1979), pp. 39–99.

Badie, Bertrand, and Pierre Birnbaum. *The Sociology of the State*. Arthur Goldhammer, trans. Chicago, IL: University of Chicago Press, 1983.

Ball, Alan. *Modern Politics and Government*. Chatham, NJ: Chatham House, 1988.

Banuazizi, Ali. "Social-Psychological Approaches to Political Development". In Myron Weiner and Samuel P. Huntington (eds). *Understanding Political Development*. New York, NY: HarperCollins, 1987, pp. 281–316.

Barbalet, J. M. "Power and Resistance". *British Journal of Sociology*. Vol. 35, No. 4, (December 1985), pp. 531–48.

Barghoorn, F. C., and T. F. Remington. *Politics in the USSR*. 3rd edition, Boston, MA: Little, Brown, 1986.

Barnes, Samuel H., and Max Kaase. *Political Action: Mass Participation in Five Western Democracies*. Beverly Hills, CA: Sage, 1979.

Barry, D. D., and Carol Barner-Barry. *Contemporary Soviet Politics: An Introduction*. 3rd edition, Englewood Cliffs, NJ: Prentice-Hall, 1987.

Baxter, Craig. "Democracy and Authoritarianism in South Asia". *Journal of International Affairs*. Vol. 38, No. 2, (Winter 1985), pp. 307–19.

Beauchamp, Edward. "Education". In Takeshi Ishida and Ellis Krauss (eds). *Democracy in Japan*. Pittsburgh, PA: University of Pittsburgh Press, 1989, pp. 225–51.

Bebler, Anton, and Jim Seroka (eds). *Contemporary Political Systems: Classifications and Typologies*. Boulder, CO: Lynne Rienner, 1990.

Beer, Lawrence. "Law and Liberty". In Takeshi Ishida and Ellis Krauss (eds). *Democracy in Japan*. Pittsburgh, PA: University of Pittsburgh Press, 1989, pp. 67–87.

Bell, Daniel. *The Coming of Post-Industrial Society*. New York, NY: Basic Books, 1973.

—— *The End of Ideology*. Cambridge, MA: Harvard University Press, 1988.

Ben-Porat, Amir. "Proletarian Immigrants in Israel". *Sociological Inquiry*. Vol. 60, No. 4, (November 1990), pp. 393–403.

Bent, Frederick. "A Comparative Analysis of Public Administration in Modern, Traditional, and Modernizing Societies". In Chandler Morse et al. *Modernization by Design: Social Change in the Twentieth Century*. London: Cornell Unversity Press, 1969, pp. 189–237.

Berg-Schlosser, Dirk. "African Political Systems: Typology and Performance". *Comparative Political Studies*. Vol. 17, No. 1, (April 1984), pp. 121–51.

Bertsch, Gary, Robert P. Clark, and David M. Wood. *Comparing Political Systems: Power and Policy in Three Worlds*. 4th edition, New York, NY: Macmillan, 1991

Bianchi, Robert. "Interest Group Politics in the Third World". In Louis Cantori and Andrew Ziegler, Jr. (eds). *Comparative Politics in the Post-Behavioral Era*. Boulder, CO: Lynne Rienner, 1988, pp. 203–30.

Bigo, Pierre. *The Church and Third World Revolution*. Jeanne Marie Lyons, trans. New York, NY: Orbis, 1977.

Bill, James A., and Robert L. Hardgrave. *Comparative Politics: The Quest for Theory*. Washington, DC: University Press of America, 1981.

Binder, Leonard. "The Crisis of Political Development". In Leonard Binder et al. *Crises and Sequences in Political Development*. Princeton, NJ: Princeton University Press, 1971, pp. 3–72.

Blanchard, William. *Revolutionary Morality: A Psychosexual Analysis of Twelve Revolutionists*. Oxford: Clio, 1984.

Blau, Peter M. *Approaches to the Study of Social Structure*. New York, NY: Free Press, 1975.

Blondel, Jean. *Comparing Political Systems*. New York, NY: Praeger, 1972.

Bobbio, Norberto. *The Future of Democracy: A Defense of the Rules of the Game*. Roger Friffin, trans. Minneapolis, MN: University of Minnesota Press, 1987.

—— "Gramsci and the Concept of Civil Society". In John Keane et al. *Civil Society and the State: New European Perspectives*. New York, NY: Verso, 1988, pp. 73–99.

—— *Democracy and Dictatorship: Elements for a General Theory of Politics*. Peter Kennealy, trans. Minneapolis, MN: University of Minnesota Press, 1989.

Boggs, Carl. *Social Movements and Political Power: Emerging Forms of Radicalism in the West*. Philadelphia, PA: Temple University Press, 1986.

Bollinger, Lee C. *The Tolerant Society*. Oxford: Oxford University Press, 1983.

Bottomore, Tom (ed.). *A Dictionary of Marxist Thought*. London: Basil Blackwell, 1983.

Bozorgmehr, Mehdi, and Georges Sabagh. "High States Immigrants: A Statistical Profile of Iranians in the United States". *Iranian Studies*. Vol. 21, Nos. 3–4, (1988), pp. 5–35.

Bratton, Michael. "Patterns of Development and Underdevelopment". *International Studies Quarterly*. Vol. 26, No. 3, (September 1982), pp. 333–72.

Breuilly, John. *Nationalism and the State*. Chicago, IL: University of Chicago Press 1982.

Bright, Charles, and Susan Harding (eds). *Statemaking and Social Movements*. Ann Arbor, MI: University of Michigan Press, 1984.

Brinton, Carne. *The Anatomy of Revolution*. New York, NY: Prentice-Hall, 1952.

Bruneau, Thomas, and Alex Macleod. *Politics in Contemporary Portugal: Parties and the Consolidation of Democracy*. Boulder, CO: Lynne Rienner, 1986.

Bruszt, Laszlo. "1989: The Negotiated Revolution in Hungary". *Social Research*. Vol. 57, No. 2, (Summer 1990), pp. 365–87.

Bryce, James. "The Relations of Political Science to History and to Practice". *American Political Science Review*. Vol. 3, No. 1, (February 1909), pp. 1–19.

Buckley, Roger. *Japan Today*. 2nd edition, Cambridge: Cambridge University Press, 1990.

Buckley, William. *Up from Liberalism*. New York, NY: Madison, 1988.

Buckley, Willam, and Charles Kesler (eds). *Keeping the Tablets: Modern American Conservative Thought*. New York, NY: HarperCollins, 1988.

Bumpess, Larry L. "What's Happening to the Family? Interactions Between Demographic and Institutional Change". *Demography*. Vol. 27, No. 4, (Nov. 1990), pp. 483–98.

Calvert, Peter. *Politics, Power, and Revolution: An Introduction to Comparative Politics*. London: Wheatsheaf, 1983.

Calvez, Jean-Yves. *Politics and Society in the Third World*. M. J. O'Connell, trans. Maryknoll, NY: Orbis, 1973.

Cammack, Paul, David Pool, and William Tordoff. *Third World Politics: A Comparative Introduction*. Baltimore, MD: Johns Hopkins University Press, 1988.

Campbell, John Creighton. "Democracy and Bureaucracy in Japan". In Takeshi Ishida and Ellis Krauss (eds). *Democracy in Japan*. Pittsburgh, PA: University of Pittsburgh Press, 1989.

Cantori, Louis J., and Andrew H. Ziegler, Jr. (eds). *Comparative Politics in the Post-Behavioral Era*. Boulder, CO: Lynne Rienner, 1988.

Caporaso, James A., and Stephen Haggard. "Power in International Political Economy". In Richard J. Stoll and Michael D. Ward (eds). *Power in World Politics*. Boulder, CO: Lynne Rienner, 1989, pp. 99–120.

Capps, Walter. *The New Religious Right: Piety, Patriotism, and Politics*. Columbia, SC: University of South Carolina Press, 1990.

Cardosa, F. H., and E. Faletto. *Dependency and Development in Latin America*. Berkeley, CA: University of California Press, 1979.

Carpenter, Ted Galen. "The New World Disorder". *Foreign Policy*. No. 84, (Fall 1991), pp. 24–39.

Chaliand, Gerard. *Revolution in the Third World: Myths and Prospects*. New York, NY: Viking, 1977.

Chalmers, Douglas. "The Politicized State in Latin America". In James Malloy (ed.). *Authoritarianism and Corporatism in Latin America*. Pittsburgh, PA: University of Pittsburgh Press, 1977, pp. 23–45.

Charlton, Roger. *Comparative Government*. New York, NY: Longman, 1986.

Charques, Richard. *The Twilight of the Russian Empire*. Oxford: Oxford University Press, 1965.

Chazan, Naomi. "The New Politics of Participation in Tropical Africa". *Comparative Politics*. Vol. 14, No. 2, (January 1982), pp. 169–90.

Chazan, Naomi, Robert Mortimer, John Ravenhill, and Donald Rothchild. *Politics and Society in Contemporary Africa*. Boulder, CO: Lynne Rienner, 1988.

Chilcote, Ronald. *Theories of Comparative Politics: The Search for a Paradigm.* Boulder, CO: Westview, 1981.

Chilton, Stephen. "Defining Political Culture". *Western Political Quarterly.* Vol. 41, No. 3, (September 1988), pp. 419–45.

—— *Defining Political Development.* Boulder, CO: Lynne Rienner, 1988.

Chung, Chin-Wee. "The Evolution of Political Institutions in North Korea". In Robert Scalapino, Seizaburo Sato, and Jusuf Wanadi (eds). *Asian Political Institutionalization.* Berkeley, CA: Institute for East Asian Studies, 1986, pp. 18–41.

Claessen, Henry. "Changing Legitimacy". In Ronald Cohen and Judith Toland (eds). *State Formation and Political Legitimacy.* New Brunswick, NJ: Transaction, 1988, pp. 23–44.

Clapham, Christopher. *Third World Politics: An Introduction.* Madison, WI: University of Wisconsin Press, 1985.

Clapham, Christopher, and George Philip (eds). *The Political Dilemmas of Military Regimes.* Savage, MD: Rowman and Littlefield, 1985.

Clark, Candace, and Howard Robboy. *Social Interaction: Readings in Sociology.* New York, NY: St. Martin's Press, 1988.

Cohen, Youssef, and Franco Pavoncello. "Corporatism and Pluralism: A Critique of Schmitter's Typology". *British Journal of Political Science.* Vol. 17, (January 1987), pp. 117–22.

Colburn, Forrest. *Post-Revolutionary Nicaragua: State, Class, and the Dilemmas of Agrarian Policy.* Berkeley, CA: University of California Press, 1986.

Coleman, David, and Frederick Nixson. *Economics of Change in Less Developed Countries.* Savage, MD: Rowman and Littlefield, 1986.

Coleman, James S. (ed.). *Education and Political Development.* Princeton, NJ: Princeton University Press, 1965.

—— "The Development Syndrome: Differentiation-Equality-Capacity". In Leonard Binder et al. (eds). *Crisis and Sequences in Political Development.* Princeton, NJ: Princeton University Press, 1971, pp. 73–100.

Collier, David (ed.). *The New Authoritarianism in Latin America.* Princeton, NJ: Princeton University Press, 1979.

Collier, Ruth Berins, and David Collier. *Shaping the Political Arena.* Princeton, NJ: Princeton University Press, 1991.

Colton, Timothy J. *The Dilemma of Reform in the Soviet Union.* New York, NY: Council of Foreign Relations, 1986.

Conradt, David P. *The German Polity.* 4th edition, White Plains, NY: Longman, 1991.

Conway, M. Margaret. "The Political Context of Political Behavior". *Journal of Politics.* Vol. 15, No. 1, (February 1989), pp. 3–10.

Cooper, John, and Ta-Ling Lee. *Failure of Democracy Movement: Human Rights in the People's Republic of China, 1988/1989.* Baltimore, MD: University of Maryland School of Law, 1991.

Cox, Andrew. "The Old and New Testaments of Corporatism: Is it a Political Form or a Method of Policy-making?" *Political Studies.* Vol. 36, (1988), pp. 294–308.

Curtis, Michael (ed.). *Introduction to Comparative Government*, 2nd edition, New York: Harper & Row, 1990.

Dahl, Robert A. *Who Governs? Democracy and Power in an American City.* New Haven, CT: Yale University Press, 1961.

—— *Pluralist Democracy in the United States: Conflict and Consent.* Chicago, IL: Rand McNally, 1967.

—— "Power". In David L. Sills (ed.). *International Encyclopedia of the Social Sciences.* Vol. 12, New York: Crowell Collier & Macmillan, 1968, pp. 405–13.

—— *Democracy and Its Critics.* New Haven, CT: Yale University Press, 1989.

Dahrendorf, Ralph. *A New World Order: Problems and Prospects of International Relations in the 1980s.* Accra: University of Ghana Press, 1979.

Dalton, Russell J. "Generational Change in Elite Political Beliefs: The Growth of Ideological Polarization". *Journal of Politics.* Vol. 49, (August–November 1987), pp. 976–97.

—— *Citizen Politics in Western Democracies.* Chatham, NJ: Chatham House, 1988.

Dalton, Russell J., Scott Flanagann, and Paul Beck (eds). *Electoral Change: Realignment and Dealignment in Advanced Industrial Democracies.* Princeton, NJ: Princeton University Press, 1984.

Daniels, Robert. "Russian Political Culture and the Post-Revolutionary Impasse". *Russian Review.* Vol. 46, (1987), pp. 165–76.

David, Paul, and David Everson (eds). *The Presidential Election and Transition 1980–81.* Carbondale, IL: Southern Illinois University, 1983.

Davidheiser, Evenly B. "Strong States, Weak States: The Role of the State in Revolution". *Comparative Politics.* Vol. 24, No. 4, (July 1992) pp. 463–75.

Davis, Harold E. *Revolutionaries, Traditionalists, and Dictators in Latin America.* Savage, MD: Rowland and Littlefield, 1973.

Davis, James C. "Maslow and Theory of Political Development: Getting to Fundamentals". *Political Psychology.* Vol. 12, No. 3, (1991), pp. 389–420.

Dealey, James Quayle. *The Development of the State: Its Government Organization and Its Activities.* New York: Silver, Burdett, & Co., 1909.

Dearlove, John. "Bringing the Constitution Back In: Political Science and the State". *Political Studies.* Vol. 37, (1989), pp. 521–39.

Decalo, Samuel. "African Personal Dictatorships". *Journal of Modern African Studies.* Vol. 23, No. 2, (1985), pp. 209–37.

—— "Modalities of Civil-Military Stability in Africa". *Journal of Modern African Studies.* Vol. 27, No. 4, (1989), pp. 547–78.

—— *Coups and Army Rule in Africa.* New Haven, CT: Yale University Press, 1990.

DeFronzo, James. *Revolutions and Revolutionary Movements.* Boulder, CO: Westview, 1991.

Denyer, Tom. "The Ethics of Struggle". *Political Theory.* Vol. 17, No. 4, (November 1989), pp. 535–49.

Di Palma, Giuseppe. *To Craft Democracies: An Essay on Democratic Transitions.* Berkeley, CA: University of California Press, 1990.

Diamond, Larry. "Introduction: Persistence, Erosion, Breakdown, and Renewal". In Larry Diamond, Jaun J. Linz, and Seymour Martin Lipset (eds). *Democracy in Developing Countries: Asia.* Boulder, CO: Lynne Rienner Publishers, 1989, pp. 1–52.

—— "Introduction: Roots of Failure, Seeds of Hope". In Larry Diamond, Jaun J. Linz, and Seymour Martin Lipset (eds). *Democracy in Developing Countries: Africa.* Boulder, Colorado: Lynne Rienner Publishers, 1988, pp. 1–52.

—— *Political Culture and Democracy in Developing Countries.* Boulder, CO: Lynne Rienner, 1992.

Diamond, Larry, Juan J. Linz, and Seymour Martin Lipset, *Democracy in Developing Countries.* Boulder, CO: Lynne Rienner, 1988.

—— *Democracy in Developing Countries: Africa.* Boulder, CO: Lynne Rienner, 1988.

—— *Democracy in Developing Countries: Asia.* Boulder, CO: Lynne Rienner, 1989.

—— *Democracy in Developing Countries: Latin America*. Boulder, CO: Lynne Rienner, 1989.

—— (eds) *Politics in Developing Countries: Comparing Experiences with Democracy*. Boulder, CO: Lynne Rienner, 1990.

Dicey, A. V. *The Law of the Constitution*. London: Macmillan, 1885.

Dickinson, John. "Social Order and Political Authority". *American Political Science Review*. Vol. 23, No. 2, (May 1929), pp. 293–328.

—— "Social Order and Political Authority". (Part 2). *American Political Science Review*. Vol. 23, No. 3, (August 1929), pp. 593–632

Dittmer, Lowell. "Mao and the Politics of Revolutionary Morality". *Asian Survey*. Vol. XXVII, No. 3, (March 1987), pp. 316–39.

Dix, Robert. "The Varieties of Revolution". *Comparative Politics*. Vol. 15, No. 3, (April 1983), pp. 281–94.

diZerega, Gus. "Elites and Democratic Theory: Insights from the Self-organizing Model". *Review of Politics*. Vol. 53, No. 2, (Spring 1991), pp. 340–72.

Djilas, Milovan. *The New Class*. London: Unwin, 1966.

Dogan, Mattei, and Dominique Pelassey. *How to Compare Nations: Strategies in Comparative Politics*. 2nd edition, Chatham, NJ: Chatham House, 1990.

Domes, Jurgen. *The Government and the Politics of the PRC: A Time of Transition*. Boulder, CO: Westview, 1985.

Dominguez, Jorge I. "Political Change: Central America, South America, and the Caribbean". In Myron Weiner and Samuel P. Huntington (eds). *Understanding Political Development*. New York: HarperCollins, 1987, pp. 65–99.

Dougherty, James, and Robert Pfaltzgraff. *American Foreign Policy: FDR to Reagan*. New York, NY: Harper & Row, 1986.

Downing, Brian M. *The Military Revolution and Political Change*. Princeton, NJ: Princeton University Press, 1992.

Dragnich, Alex, Lawrence S. Graham, Jorgen Rasmussen, and Taketsugu Tsurutani. *Politics and Government*. Chatham, NJ: Chatham House, 1987.

Dragnich, Alex, Jorgen Rasmussen, and Joel Moses. *Major European Governments*. 8th edition, Pacific Grove, CA: Brooks/Cole, 1991.

Dror, Yehezkel. "Public-Policy-Making in Avant-Garde Developing States". In Harvey Kebschull (ed.). *Poliltics in Transitional Societies*. New York, NY: Appleton-Century-Crofts, 1973, pp. 278–86.

Dube, S.C. *Modernization and Development: The Search for Alternative Paradigms*. Tokyo: United Nations University, 1988.

Dunn, John. *Rethinking Modern Political Theory*. Cambridge: Cambridge University Press, 1985.

—— *Modern Revolutions: An Introduction to the Analysis of a Political Phenomenon*. 2nd edition, Cambridge: Cambridge University Press, 1988.

—— "Revolution". In T. Ball, J. Farr, and R. Hanson (eds). *Political Innovation and Conceptual Change*. Cambridge: Cambridge University Press, 1988.

Easton, David. "Political Science". In David L. Sills (ed.). *International Encyclopedia of the Social Sciences*. Vol. 12, New York, NY: Crowell Collier & Macmillan, 1968, pp. 282–97.

—— *A Framework for Political Analysis*. Chicago, IL: University of Chicago Press, 1965.

Ebenstein, William. *Great Political Thinkers: Plato to the Present*. 4th edition, New York, NY: Holt, Rinehart and Winston, 1969.

Eckhardt, William. "Authoritarianism". *Political Psychology*. Vol. 12, No. 1, (1991), pp. 97–124.

Eckstein, Harry. "A Culturalist Theory of Political Change". *American Political Science Review*. Vol. 82, No. 3, (September 1988), pp. 789–804.

Eddinger, Lewis J. "Approaches to the Comparative Analysis of Political Leadership". *Review of Politics*. Vol. 52, No. 4, (Fall 1990), pp. 509–23.

Eisenstadt, S. N. "Social Institutions". In David Sills (ed.). *International Encyclopedia of the Social Sciences*. Vol. 14. New York, NY: Crowell, Collier & Macmillan, 1968, pp. 409–29.

—— "Problems of Emerging Bureaucracies in Developing Areas and New States". In Harvey Kebschull (ed.). *Politics in Transitional Societies*. New York, NY: Appleton-Century-Crofts, 1973, pp. 286–93.

—— *Revolution and the Transformation of Societies*. New York, NY: Free Press, 1978.

Eisenstadt, S. N., and R. Lemarchand. *Political Clientelism, Patronage, and Development*. Beverly Hills, CA: Sage, 1981.

Ellis, Ellen Deborah. "The Pluralistic State". *American Political Science Review*. Vol. 14, No. 3, (August 1920), pp. 393–407.

Enders, Thomas O., and Mattione, Richard P. *Latin America: The Crisis of Debt and Growth*. Washington, D.C.: The Brookings Institution, 1984.

Epstein, Edward. "Legitimacy, Institutionalization, and Opposition in Exclusive Bureaucratic Authoritarian Regimes: The Situation in the 1980s". *Comparative Politics*. Vol. 17, No. 1, (October 1984), pp. 37–54.

Etzioni-Halevy, Eva. *Bureaucracy and Democracy: A Political Dilemma*. London: Routledge, 1983.

Evans, Graham, and Jeffrey Newnham. *Dictionary of World Politics*. New York, NY: Simon and Schuster, 1990.

Evans, Peter, Dietrich Rueschemeyer, and Theda Skocpol (eds). *Bringing the State Back In*. Cambridge: Cambridge University Press, 1985.

Fabbrini, Sergio. "The Return to the State: Critiques". *American Political Science Review*. Vol. 82, No. 3, (September 1988), pp. 891–98.

Fairlie, John A. "Political Developments and Tendencies". *American Political Science Review*. Vol. 24, No. 1, (February 1930), pp. 1–15.

Falola, Tonin, and Julius O. Ihonvbere (eds). *Nigeria and the International Capitalist System*. Boulder, CO: Lynne Rienner, 1987.

Farr, James. "Historical Concepts in Political Science: The Case of Revolution". *American Journal of Political Science*. Vol. 26, No. 4, (November 1982), pp. 688–708.

Featherstone, Mike. *Global Culture: Nationalism, Globalization and Modernity*. Newbury Park, CA: Sage, 1990.

Feit, Edward. *The Armed Bureaucrats: Military Administrative Regimes and Political Development*. Boston, MA: Houghton Mifflin, 1973.

Finer, S. E. *Five Constitutions: Contrasts and Comparisons*. New York, NY: Penguin, 1979.

Finkle, J. A., and R.W. Gable (eds). *Political Development and Social Change*. New York, NY: Wiley, 1971.

Fleet, Michael. *The Rise and Fall of Chilean Christian Democracy*. Princeton, NJ: Princeton University Press, 1985.

Flekkoy, Mallfrid Crude. "Child Advocacy in Norway: The Ombudsman". *Child Welfare*. Vol. LXVIII, No. 2, (March-April 1989), pp. 113–22.

Foltz, William. "External Causes". In Barry Shutz and Robert Slater (eds). *Revolution and Political Change in the Third World*. Boulder, CO: Lynne Rienner, 1990, pp. 54–68.

Ford, Henry J. *Representative Government*. New York, NY: Henry Holt, 1924.

Frank, Andre Gunder. *Capitalism and Underdevelopment in Latin America: Historical Studies of Chile and Brazil*. New York, NY: Monthly Review Press, 1967.

Freedman, Robert. *The Marxist System; Economic, Political, and Social Perspectives*. Chatham, NJ: Chatham House, 1981.

Freeman, Michael. "Review, Article: Theories of Revolution". *British Journal of Political Science*. vol. 2, 1972, pp. 339–59.

Friedland, William. "A Sociological Approach to Modernization". In Chandler Morse (ed.). *Modernization by Design: Social Change in the Twentieth Century*. London: Cornell University Press, 1969, pp. 34–84.

Friedman, Milton, and Rose Friedman. *Free to Choose: A Personal Statement*. New York, NY: Avon, 1981.

Fukushima, Glen. "Corporate Power". In Ellis Krauss and Takeshi Ishida (eds). *Democracy in Japan*. Pittsburgh, PA: University of Pittsburgh Press, 1989, pp. 255–79.

Fukuyama, Francis. *The End of History and the Last Man*. New York, NY: Free Press, 1992.

Gallup, George Jr., and Jim Castelli. *The People's Religion: America's Faith in the 90's*. New York, NY: Macmillan, 1989.

Gamson, William. "Commitment and Agency in Social Movement". *Sociological Forum*. Vol. 6, No. 1, (1991), pp. 27–50.

Gardner, David. *The California Oath Controversy*. Berkeley, CA: University of California Press, 1967.

Geddes, Barbara, and John Zaller. "Sources of Popular Support for Authoritarian Regimes". *American Journal of Political Science*. Vol. 33, No. 2, (May 1989), pp. 319–47.

Geertz, Clifford. "The Integrative Revolution: Primordial Sentiments and Civil Policies in the New States". In Clifford Geertz (ed.). *Old Societies and New States: The Quest for Modernity in Asia and Africa*. New York, NY: The Free Press, 1963, pp. 109–29.

Gellner, Ernest. *Nations and Nationalism*. Ithaca, NY: Cornell University Press, 1983.

—— *Plough, Sword and Book: the Structure of Human History*. Chicago, IL: University of Chicago Press, 1988.

—— "Islam and Marxism: Some Comparisons". *International Affairs*. Vol. 67, No. l, (1991) pp. 1–6.

Gerlich, Peter, Edgar Grande, and Wolfgang C. Muller. "Corporatism in Crisis: Stability and Change of Social Partnership in Austria". *Political Studies*. Vol. 36, (1988), pp. 209–23.

Gettell, Raymond G. "The Nature and the Scope of Present Political Theory". *American Political Science Review*. Vol. 8, Supplement (February 1914), pp. 47–60.

—— "The Nature of Political Thought". *American Political Science Review*. Vol. 17, No. 2, (May 1923), pp. 204–15.

Gibbs, Jack P. *Control: Sociology's Central Nation*. Chicago, IL: University of Illinois Press, 1989.

Giddens, Anthony. *Sociology: A Brief But Critical Introduction*. London: Macmillan, 1982.

—— *The Constitution of Society.* Cambridge: Polity Press, 1984.

—— *The Nation-State and Violence.* Berkeley, CA: University of California Press, 1985.

—— *Modernity and Self-Identity: Self and Society in the Late Modern Age.* Stanford, CA: Stanford University Press, 1991.

—— *Social Theory and Modern Sociology.* Stanford, CA: Stanford University Press, 1987.

Gill, Graeme. *The Origins of the Stalinist Political System.* Cambridge: Cambridge University Press, 1990.

Ginger, Ray. *Six Days or Forever? Tennessee vs. John Thomas Scopes.* Oxford: Oxford University Press, 1958.

Goldstein, Joshua S., and John R. Freeman. *Three Way Street: Strategic Reciprocity in World Politics.* Chicago, IL: University of Chicago Press, 1990.

Goldstone, Jack. "State Breakdown in the English Revolution: A New Synthesis". *American Journal of Sociology.* Vol. 92, No. 2, (Sept. 1986), pp. 257–322.

—— *Revolution and Rebellion in the Early Modern World.* Berkeley, CA: University of California Press, 1991.

Goldthorpe, J. E. *The Sociology of the Third World: Disparity and Development.* Cambridge: Cambridge University Press, 1984.

Goodwin, Jeff, and Theda Skocpol. "Explaining Revolutions in the Contemporary World". *Politics and Society.* Vol. 17, No. 4, (Dec. 1989), pp. 489–509.

Gordon, April, and Donald L. Gordon (eds). *Understanding Contemporary Africa.* Boulder, CO: Lynne Rienner, 1992.

Gordon, David. *Images of the West: Third World Perspectives.* Savage, MD: Rowman and Littlefield, 1989.

Gottlieb, S. E. "In the Name of Patriotism: The Constitutionality of 'Bending' History in Public Secondary Schools". *The History Teacher.* Vol. 22, (August 1989), pp. 158–60.

Grady, Robert C. "Reindustrialization, Liberal Democracy, and Corporatist Representation". *Political Science Quarterly.* Vol. 101, No. 3, (1986), pp. 415–32.

Green, Jerrold. "Counter Mobilization as a Revolutionary Form". *Comparative Politics.* Vol. 16, No. 2, (January 1984), pp. 153–69.

Greenfeld, Liah. "Reflections on Two Charismas". *The British Journal of Sociology.* Vol. 36, No. 1, (March 1985), pp. 117–32.

Greenstein, Fred. "Political Socialization". In David Sills (ed.). *International Encyclopedia of the Social Sciences,* Vol. 14. New York, NY: Crowell Collier & Macmillan, 1968, pp. 551–55.

Gregg, Phillip, and Arthur S. Banks. "Dimensions of Political Systems: Factor Analysis of a Cross-Polity Survey". *American Political Science Review.* Vol. 59, No. 3, (September 1965), pp. 602–14.

Griffiths, John. "The Cuban Communist Party". In Vicky Randall (ed.). *Political Parties in the Third World.* London: Sage, 1988, pp. 153–73.

Gripp, Richard C. *The Political System of Communism.* New York, NY: Harper and Row, 1973.

Gurevitch, Michael, and Jay G. Blumler. "Political Communication Systems and Democratic Values". In Judith Lichtenberg (ed.). *Democracy and the Mass Media.* Cambridge: Cambridge University Press, 1990, pp. 269–89.

Gurr, Ted Robert. "War, Revolution, and the Growth of the Coercive State". *Comparative Political Studies.* Vol. 21, No. 1, (April 1988), pp. 45–65.

Haferkamp, Hans, and Neil Smelser (eds). *Social Change and Modernity.* Berkeley, CA: University of California Press, 1990.

Hagan, Joe D. *Political Opposition and Foreign Policy in Comparative Perspective.* Boulder, CO: Lynne Rienner, 1992.

Haggard, Stephan. *Pathways From the Periphery: The Politics of Growth in the Newly Industrializing Countries.* Ithaca, NY: Cornell University Press, 1992.

Haggard, Stephan, and Robert Kaufman. *The Political Economy of Democratic Transitions.* Princeton, NJ: Princeton University Press, 1995.

Hague, Rod, and Martin Harrop. *Comparative Government and Politics: An Introduction.* Atlantic Highlands, NJ: Humanities Press, 1989.

Hamrin, Carol. *China and the Challenge of the Future: Changing Political Patterns.* Boulder, CO: Westview, 1990.

Hancock, M. Donald. *Politics of Democratic Corporatism.* Chatham, NJ: Chatham House, 1989.

Hancock, M. Donald, David P. Conradt, Guy B. Peters, William Safran, and Raphael Zariski. *Politics in Western Europe: France, Germany, Italy, Sweden, and the United Kingdom.* Chatham, NJ: Chatham House, 1989.

Hanrieder, Wolfram F. *Germany, America, Europe: Forty Years of German Foreign Policy.* New Haven, CT: Yale University Press, 1989.

Harik, Iliya. "The Origins of the Arab State System". In Ghassan Salame (ed.). *The Foundations of the Arab State.* London: Croom Helm, 1987, pp. 19–46.

Havel, Vaclav. "The Power of the Powerless". In Vaclav Havel et al. *The Power of the Powerless.* Armonk, NY: M. E. Sharp, 1985, pp. 23–96.

—— "Anti-Political Politics". In John Keane et al. *Civil Society and the State: New European Perspectives.* New York, NY: Verso, 1988, pp. 381–98.

Hedjanek, Ladislav. "Prospects for Democracy and Socialism in Eastern Europe". In Vaclav Havel et al. *The Power of the Powerless.* Armonk, NY: M. E. Sharp, 1985, pp. 141–51.

Held, David. *Political Theory and the Modern State: Essays on State, Power, and Democracy.* Stanford, CA: Stanford University Press, 1989.

—— (ed.) *Political Theory Today.* Stanford, CA: Stanford University Press, 1991.

Heller, Agnes. "On Formal Democracy". In John Keane et al. *Civil Society and the State: New European Perspectives.* New York, NY: Verso, 1988, pp. 129–45.

Hendel, Samuel (ed.). *The Soviet Crucible: The Soviet System in Theory and Practice.* 5th edition, Pacific Grove, CA: Brooks/Cole, 1991.

Hermassi, Elbaki. *The Third World Reassessed.* Berkeley, CA: University of California Press, 1990.

Hernandez, Gloria. "Political Institution Building in the Philippines". In Robert Scalapino, Seizaburo Sato, and Jusuf Wanandi (eds). *Asian Political Institutionalization.* Berkeley, CA: Institute of East Asian Studies, 1986. pp. 261–87.

Hernandez, Rafael, and Haroldo Dilla. "Political Culture and Popular Participation in Cuba". *Latin American Perspectives.* Issue 69, Vol. 18, No. 2, (Spring 1991), pp. 38–54.

Herz, John H. "Rise and Demise of the Territorial State". *World Politics.* Vol. 9, No. 4, (July 1957), pp. 473–93.

Hibbs, Douglas. *The Political Economy of Industrial Democracies.* Cambridge, MA: Harvard University Press, 1987.

Hobsbawm, Eric J. *Age of Revolution, 1789–1884.* New York, NY: World, 1962.

—— *Nations and Nationalism Since 1780: Programme, Myth, Reality.* Cambridge: Cambridge University Press, 1990.

Hoffer, Eric. *The True Believer: Thoughts on the Nature of Mass Movements.* New York, NY: Harper & Row, 1951.

Hoffman, Stanley. "The Case for Leadership". *Foreign Policy.* No. 81, (Winter 1990–91), pp. 20–39.

Holmes, Leslie. *Politics in the Communist World.* Oxford: Clarendon, 1986.

Hong, Yung Lee. *From Revolutionary Cadres to Party Technocrats in Socialist China.* Berkeley, CA: University of California Press, 1990.

Hood, Christopher C. *The Tools of Government.* Chatham, NJ: Chatham House, 1986.

Horowitz, Dan. "Dual Authority Polities". *Comparative Politics.* Vol. 14, No. 3, (April 1982), pp. 329–49.

Horowitz, Donald. *Coup Theories and Officers' Motives: Sri Lanka in Comparative Perspective.* Princeton, NJ: Princeton University Press, 1980.

Horowitz, Irving Louis. *Three Worlds of Development: The Theory and Practice of International Stratification.* Oxford: Oxford University Press, 1966.

Hough, Jerry F. *The Soviet Union and Soviet Science Theory.* Cambridge, MA: Harvard University Press, 1977.

Hough, Jerry F, and Merle Fainsod. *How the Soviet Union is Governed.* Cambridge, MA: Harvard University Press, 1979.

Hourani, Albert. *The Emergence of the New Modern Middle East.* Berkeley, CA: University of California Press, 1981.

Howard, M. "A European Perspective on the Reagan Years". *Foreign Affairs.* Vol. 66, No. 3, (1988), pp. 478–93.

Howe, Irving. "Totalitarianism Reconsidered". *Dissent.* Vol. 38, No. 1, (Winter 1991), pp. 63–71.

Huntington, Samuel. *Political Order in Changing Societies.* New Haven, CT: Yale University Press, 1968.

—— "Political Development and Political Decay". *World Politics.* Vol. 17, No. 3, (April 1965), pp. 386–430.

—— "Social and Institutional Dynamics of One-Party Systems". In Samuel Huntington and Clement Moore (eds). *Authoritarian Politics in Modern Society.* London: Basic Books, 1970, pp. 3–47.

—— *The Third Wave: Democratization in the Late Twentieth Century.* Norman, OK: University of Oklahoma Press, 1991.

Huntington, Samuel, and Joan Nelson. *No Easy Choice: Political Participation in Developing Countries.* Cambridge, MA: Harvard University Press, 1976.

Im, Hyug Baeg. "The Rise of Bureaucratic Authoritarianism in South Korea". *World Politics.* Vol. 39, No. 2, (January 1987), pp. 231–57.

Inglehart, Ronald. *The Silent Revolution: Changing Values and Political Styles Among Western Publics.* Princeton, NJ: Princeton University Press, 1977.

—— "The Renaissance of Political Culture". *American Political Science Review.* Vol. 82, No. 4, (December 1988), pp. 1203–30.

—— *Culture Shift in Advanced Industrial Society.* Princeton, NJ: Princeton University Press, 1990.

Ishida, Takeshi, and Ellis Krauss. "Democracy in Japan: Issues and Questions". In Takeshi Ishida and Ellis Krauss (eds). *Democracy in Japan.* Pittsburgh, PA: University of Pittsburgh Press, 1989, pp. 3–16.

Jackson, Robert. *Quasi-States: Sovereignty, International Relations, and the Third World.* Cambridge: Cambridge University Press, 1990.

Jackson, Robert, and Carl Rosberg. "Personal Rule: Theory and Practice in Africa". *Comparative Politics.* Vol. 16, No. 4, (July 1984), pp. 421–22.

Jacobs, Dan N., David P. Conradt, B. Guy Peters, and William Safran. *Comparative Politics.* Chatham, NJ: Chatham House, 1983.

Jacobs, Struan. "Popper, Weber and the Rationalist Approach to Social Explananation". *British Journal of Sociology.* Vol. 41, No. 4, (December 1990), pp. 559–70.

Jenkins, Peter. *Mrs. Thatcher's Revolution: The Ending of the Socialist Era.* Cambridge, MA: Harvard University Press, 1988.

Jervis, Robert. "The Future of World Politics: Will it Resemble the Past?". *International Security.* Vol. 16, No. 3, (1991/1992), pp. 39–73.

Johnson, Chalmers. *Revolutionary Change.* London: Longman, 1983.

Johnson, Kenneth. "Causal Factors in Latin American Political Instability". In Harvey Kebschull (ed.). *Politics in Transitional Societies.* New York, NY: Appleton-Century-Crofts, 1973, pp. 311–17.

Jones, R. Ben. *The French Revolution.* London: Hodder & Stoughton, 1967.

Kamrava, Mehran. "Intellectuals and Democracy in the Third World". *Journal of Social, Political, and Economic Studies.* Vol. 14, No. 2, (Summer 1989), pp. 227–34.

—— "Causes and Leaders of Revolutions". *Journal of Social, Political, and Economic Studies.* Vol. 15, No. 1, (Spring 1990), pp. 79–89.

—— *Revolution in Iran: The Roots of Turmoil.* London: Routledge, 1990.

—— *Revolutionary Politics.* Westport, CT: Praeger, 1992.

—— *Politics and Society in the Third World.* London: Routledge, 1993.

—— "Conceptualising Third World Politics". *Third World Quarterly.* Vol. 13, No. 4, (December 1993), pp. 703–16.

Kavanagh, Dennis. *Political Culture.* London: Macmillan, 1972.

—— "Western Europe". In Robert Wesson (ed.). *Democracy: A Worldwide Survey.* New York, NY: Praeger, 1987, pp. 11–24.

Kay, Cristobal. *Latin American Theories of Development and Underdevelopment.* New York, NY: Routledge, 1989.

Keane, John, et al. *Civil Society and the State: New European Perspectives.* New York, NY: Verso, 1988.

Keller, Edmund. "Revolution and the Collapse of Traditional Monarchies: Ethiopia". In Barry Schutz and Robert Slater (eds). *Revolution and Political Change in the Third World.* Boulder, CO: Lynne Rienner, 1990, pp. 81–98.

Keller, Suzanne. "Elites". In David L. Sills (ed.). *International Encyclopedia of the Social Sciences.* Vol. 5. New York, NY: Crowell Collier & Macmillan, 1968, pp. 26–29.

Kennedy, Paul. *The Rise and Fall of the Great Powers.* New York, NY: Random House, 1987.

Keohane, Robert. *After Hegemony: Cooperation and Discord in the World Political Economy.* Princeton, NJ: Princeton University Press, 1984.

Keohane, Robert, and Joseph Nye. *Power and Independence.* Boston, MA: Little Brown, 1977.

Kesselman, Mark, and Joel Krieger (eds). *European Politics in Transition.* Lexington, MA: D. C. Heath, 1986.

King, Roger. *The State in Modern Society: New Directions in Political Sociology.* Chatham, NJ: Chatham House, 1987.

Kingdom, John. *No Such Thing as Society? Individualism and Community.* London: Open University Press, 1992.

Kishima, Takako. *Political Life in Japan*. Princeton, NJ: Princeton University Press, 1992.

Kitchins, G. N. *Development and Underdevelopment in Historical Perspective*. New York, NY: Methuen, 1982.

Kittrie, Nicholas N., and Ivan Volgyes (eds). *The Uncertain Future: Gorbachev's Eastern Bloc*. New York, NY: PWPA, 1992.

Klitgaard, Robert. *Controlling Corruption*. Berkeley, CA: University of California Press, 1988.

Knight, Caroline. "Traditional Influences Upon Lebanese Politics". *Journal of Social, Political, and Economic Studies*. Vol. 17, Nos. 3–4, (Fall/ Winter 1992), pp. 327–43.

Kolankiewicz, George, and Ray Taras. "Poland: Socialism for Everyman?". In Archie Brown and Jack Gray (eds). *Political Culture and Political Change in Communist States*. New York, NY: Holmes and Meier, 1979, pp. 101–30.

Krauss, Clifford. "Revolution in Central America?". *Foreign Affairs*. Vol. 65, No. 3, (1987), pp. 564–81.

Krauss, Ellis S., and Takeshi Ishida. "Japanese Democracy in Perspective". In Takeshi Ishida and Ellis Krauss (eds). *Democracy in Japan*. Pittsburgh, PA: University of Pittsburgh Press, 1989, pp. 327–39.

Kromnick, Issac. "Reflections on Revolution: Definition and Explanation in Recent Scholarship". *History and Theory*. vol. XI, no. 1, 1972, pp. 22–63.

Lancaster, Roger. *Thanks to God and the Revolution: Popular Religious and Class Consciousness in the New Nicaragua*. New York, NY: Columbia University Press, 1988.

Landau, Saul. "A New World to Exploit: The East Joins the South". *Monthly Review*. Vol. 42, No. 5, (October 1990), pp. 29–37.

Landim, Leilah. "Non-governmental Organizations in Latin America". *World Development*. Vol. 15, (1987), Supplement, pp. 29–38.

Lane, Jan-Erik, and Svante O. Ersson. *Politics and Society in Western Europe*. 2nd edition, London: Sage, 1987.

LaPalombara, Joseph (ed.). *Bureaucracy and Political Development*. Princeton, NJ: Princeton University Press, 1963.

—— *Democracy, Italian Style*. New Haven, CT: Yale University Press, 1987.

LaPalombara, Joseph, and Myron Weiner (eds). *Political Parties and Political Development*. Princeton, NJ: Princeton University Press, 1966.

Laszlo, Ervin. *The Systems View of the World*. New York, NY: George Braziller, 1972.

Lehmann, Jean-Pierre, "Dictatorship and Development in Pacific Asia: Wider Implications". *International Affairs*. Vol. 61, No. 4, (Autumn 1985), pp. 591–606.

Lehoucq, Fabrice Edouard. "Class Conflict, Political Crisis, and the Breakdown of Democratic Practices in Costa Rica: Reassessing the Origins of the 1948 Civil War". *Journal of Latin American Studies*. Vol. 23, No. 1, (February 1991), pp. 37–60.

Leighley, Jane. "Participation as a Stimulus of Political Conceptualization". *Journal of Politics*. Vol. 53, No. 1, (February 1991), pp. 198–212.

LeoGrande, William. "Central America". In Barry Schutz and Robert Slater (eds). *Revolution and Political Change in the Third World*. Boulder, CO: Lynne Rienner, 1990, pp. 142–60.

Levy, Daniel. "Comparing Authoritarian Regimes in Latin America: Insights from Higher Education Policy". *Comparative Politics*. Vol. 14, No. 1, (October 1981), pp. 31–52.

Lichtenberg, Judith. "Foundation and Limits of Freedom of the Press". In Judith Lichtenberg (ed.). *Democracy and Mass Media*. Cambridge: Cambridge University Press, 1990, pp. 102–36.

Lieberthal, Kenneth, and Michel Oksenberg. *Policy Making in China: Leaders, Structures, Processes*. Princeton, NJ: Princeton University Press, 1988.

Lijphart, Arend. "Democratic Political Systems". In Anton Bebler and Jim Seroka (eds). *Contemporary Political Systems: Classifications and Typologies*. Boulder, CO: Lynne Rienner, 1990.

—— (ed.) *Parliamentary versus Presidential Government*. Oxford: Oxford University Press, 1992.

Lijphart, Arend, and Markus M. L. Crepaz. "Corporatism and Consensus Democracy in Eighteen Countries: Conceptual and Empirical Linkages". *British Journal of Political Science*. Vol. 21, (1991), pp. 235–56.

Lindholm, Charles. *Charisma*. London: Basil Blackwell, 1990.

Linz, Juan J., and Alfred Stepan (eds). *The Breakdown of Democratic Regimes*. Baltimore, MD: Johns Hopkins University Press, 1978.

Lipson, Leslie. "The Comparative Method in Political Studies". *Political Science Quarterly*. Vol. 28, No. 4, (October–December 1957), pp. 372–82.

—— *The Democratic Civilization*. Oxford: Oxford University Press, 1964.

Loewenberg, Gerhard, and Samuel Patterson. "Legislatures and Political Systems". In Louis Cantori and Andrew Ziegler (eds). *Comparative Politics in the Post-Behavioral Era*. Boulder, CO: Lynne Rienner, 1988. pp. 263–83.

Lowenstein, Karl. "Autocracy Versus Democracy in Contemporary Europe, I". *American Political Science Review*. Vol. 29, No. 4, (August 1935), pp. 571–93.

—— "Autocracy Versus Democracy in Contemporary Europe, II". *American Political Science Review*. Vol. 29, No. 5, (October 1935), pp. 755–84.

Lowi, Theodore J. "The Return to the State: Critiques". *American Political Science Review*. Vol. 82, No. 3, (September 1988), pp. 885–91.

Luard, Evan. *The Blunted Sword: The Erosion of Military Power in Modern World Politics*. New York, NY: New Amsterdam, 1988.

—— *The Globalization of Politics*. New York, NY: New York University Press, 1990.

Lundestad, Geir. *East, West, North, South: Major Developments in International Politics*. Gail Adams Kvam, trans. Oslo: Norwegian University Press, 1986.

McDaniel, Tim. *Autocracy, Modernization, and Revolution in Russia and Iran*. Princeton, NJ: Princeton University Press, 1991.

McDonough, Peter. "Repression and Representation in Brazil". *Comparative Politics*. Vol. 15, No. 1, (October 1982), pp. 73–99.

MacIver, R. M. "Society and the State". *Philosophical Review*. Vol. 20, No. 1, (January 1911), pp. 30–45.

McLennan, G. D. Held, and S. Hall. *The Idea of the Modern State*. London: Open University Press, 1984.

Macklin, David. "A Social-Psychological Perspective on Modernization". In Chandler Morse, et al. *Modernization by Design: Social Change in the Twentieth Century*. London: Cornell, 1969, pp. 85–146.

Macridis, Roy. *Modern Political Regimes: Patterns and Institutions*. Boston, MA: Little, Brown, 1986.

Macridis, Roy, and B. E. Brown (eds). *Comparative Politics: Notes and Readings*. 6th edition, Chicago, IL: Dorsey, 1986.

Macridis, Roy, and Steven Burg. *Introduction to Comparative Government: Regimes and Change.* New York, NY: HarperCollins, 1991.

Madsen, Douglas, and Peter G. Snow. "Recruitment Contrasts in a Divided Charismatic Movement". *American Political Science Review.* Vol. 81, No. 1, (March 1987), pp. 233–38.

Maier, Charles S. (ed.). *Changing Boundaries of Political Activity.* Cambridge: Cambridge University Press, 1987.

Manor, James (ed.). *Rethinking Third World Politics.* London: Longman, 1991.

Maravall, J. M. "Subjective Conditions and Revolutionary Conflicts: Some Remarks". *British Journal of Sociology.* vol. 27, no. 1, (March 1976). pp. 21–34.

Martindale, Don. *Institutions, Organizations and Mass Society.* Atlanta: Houghton Mifflin, 1966.

Marx, Karl. *Selected Writings in Sociology and Philosophy.* New York, NY: McGraw-Hill, 1964.

Marx, Karl, and Friedrich Engels. *The Communist Manifesto.* Paul Sweezey, trans. New York, NY: Monthly Review Press, 1964.

Mason, T. David. "Indigenous Factors". In Barry Schutz and Robert Slater (eds). *Revolution and Political Change in the Third World.* Boulder, CO: Lynne Rienner, 1990, pp. 30–53.

Mastnak, Tomaz. "The Powerless in Power: Political identity in the Post-Communist Eastern Europe". *Media, Culture, and Society.* Vol. 13, No. 3. (July 1991), pp. 399–405.

Matheson, Craig. "Weber and the Classification of Forms of Legitimacy". *British Journal of Sociology.* Vol. 38, No. 2, (June 1987), pp. 199–215.

Mayer, Adrian C. "Rulership and Divinity: The Case of the Modern Hindu Prince and Beyond". *Modern Asian Studies.* Vol. 25, No. 4, (October, 1991), pp. 765–90.

Mayer, Lawrence C. *Redefining Comparative Politics: Promise versus Performance.* Boulder, CO: Westview, 1989.

Maynes, Charles William. "America Without the Cold War". *Foreign Policy.* No. 78, (Spring 1990), pp. 3–25.

—— "The New Decade". *Foreign Policy.* No. 80, (Fall 1990) pp. 3–13.

Meadwell, Hudson. "A Rational Choice Approach to Political Regionalism". *Comparative Politics.* Vol. 23, No. 4, (July 1991), pp. 401–21.

Mecham, J. Lloyd. "Latin American Constitutions: Nominal and Real". In Harvey Kebschull (ed.). *Politics in Transitional Societies.* New York: Appleton-Century-Crofts, 1973, pp. 219–27.

Merton, Robert K. *Social Theory and Social Structure.* New York, NY: Free Press, 1968.

Michta, Andrew A. *East Central Europe After the Warsaw Pact: Security Dilemmas in the 1990s.* New York, NY: Greenwood, 1992.

Midlarsky, Manus. "Scarcity and Inequality: Prologue to the Onset of Mass Revolution". *Journal of Conflict Resolution.* Vol. 26, No. 1, (March 1982), pp. 3–38.

—— "Rules and the Ruled: Patterned Inequality and the Onset of Mass Political Violence". *American Political Science Review.* Vol. 82, No. 2, (June 1988), pp. 491–509.

Migdal, Joel S. *Strong Societies and Weak States: State-Society Relations and State Capabilities in the Third World.* Princeton, NJ: Princeton University Press, 1988.

Mills, C. Wright. *The Power Elite.* Oxford: Oxford University Press, 1956.

—— *Peasants, Politics, and Revolution: Pressures Toward Political and Social Change in the Third World.* Princeton, NJ: Princeton University Press, 1974.

Mitchell, Timothy. "The Limits of the State: Beyond Statist Approaches and Their Critics". *American Political Science Review.* Vol. 85, No. 1, (March 1991), pp. 77–95.

Moghadam, Val. "Industrial Development, Culture and Working Class Politics: A Case Study of Tabriz Industrial Workers in the Iranian Revolution". *International Sociology.* Vol. 2, No. 2, (June 1987), pp. 151–75.

Montias, John M. "A Classification of Communist Economic Systems". In Carmelo Mesa-Lago and Carl Beck (eds). *Comparative Socialist Systems: Essays on Politics and Economics.* Pittsburgh, PA: University of Pittsburgh Center for International Studies, 1975, pp. 39–52.

Moore, Barrington. *Social Origins of Dictatorship and Democracy.* New York, NY: Penguin, 1966.

Moore, Clement. "The Single Party as Source of Legitimacy". In Samuel Huntington and Clement Moore (eds). *Authoritarian Politics in Modern Society.* London: Basic Books, 1970, pp. 48–72.

Moshiri, Farrokh. "Revolutionary Conflict Theory in an Evolutionary Perspective". In Jack Goldstone, Ted Robert Gurr, and Farrokh Moshiri (eds). *Revolutions of the Late Twentieth Century.* Boulder, CO: Westview, 1991, pp. 4–36.

Mouritzen, Hans. "Tensions Between the Strong, and the Strategies of the Weak". *Journal of Peace Research.* Vol. 28, No. 2, (1991), pp. 217–30.

Neumann, Sigmund. "Comparative Politics: A Half-Century Appraisal". *Journal of Politics.* Vol. 19, (August 1957), pp. 365–90.

Nordlinger, Eric. "Soldiers in Mufti: The Impact of Military Rule Upon Economic and Social Change in the Non-Western States". In Harvey Kebschull (ed.). *Politics in Transitional Societies.* New York, NY: Appleton-Century-Crofts, 1973, pp. 250–61.

—— *Soldiers in Politics: Military Coups and Governments.* Englewood Cliffs, NJ: Prentice-Hall, 1977.

—— *On the Autonomy of the Democratic State.* Cambridge, MA: Harvard University Press, 1981.

—— "The Return to the State: Critiques". *American Political Science Review.* Vol. 82, No. 3, (September 1988), pp. 876–85.

Nye, Joseph. "Soft Power". *Foreign Policy.* No. 80, (Fall 1990), pp. 153–71.

—— *Bound to Lead.* New York, NY: Basic Books, 1990.

—— "What New World Order?". *Foreign Affairs.* Vol. 71, No. 1, (Spring 1992), pp. 83–96.

O'Donnell, Guillermo. "Corporatism and the Question of the State". In James Malloy (ed.). *Authoritarianism and Corporatism in Latin America.* Pittsburgh, PA: University of Pittsburgh Press, 1977, pp. 47–87.

—— *Modernization and Bureaucratic-Authoritarianism: Studies in South American Politics.* Berkeley, CA: Institute of International Studies, 1979.

O'Donnell, Guillermo, and Philippe Schmitler. *Transitions from Authoritarian Rule: Tentative Conclusions About Uncertain Democracies.* Baltimore, MD: Johns Hopkins University Press, 1986.

O'Donnell, Guillermo, Philippe Schmitter, and Laurence Whitehead (eds). *Transitions from Authoritarian Rule: Comparative Perspectives.* Baltimore, MD: Johns Hopkins University Press, 1986.

—— (eds) *Transitions from Authoritarian Rule: Latin America.* Baltimore, MD: Johns Hopkins University Press, 1986.

—— *Transitions from Authoritarian Rule: Prospects for Democracy*. Baltimore, MD: Johns Hopkins University Press, 1986.

—— *Transitions from Authoritarian Rule: Southern Europe*. Baltimore, MD: Johns Hopkins University Press, 1986.

O'Kane, Rosemary. "A Probabilistic Approach to the Causes of Coups d'Etat". *British Journal of Political Science*. Vol. 11, (1981), pp. 287–398.

Ortega, Marvin. "The State, the Peasantry and the Sandanista Revolution". *Journal of Development Studies*. Vol. 26, No. 4, (1990), pp. 122–42.

Owen, Roger. *State, Power, and Politics in the Making of the Modern Middle East*. London: Routledge, 1992.

Packer, George. "Class Interest, Liberal Style". *Dissent*. Vol. 39, No. 1, (Winter 1992), pp. 51–56.

Paige, Jeffrey. *Agrarian Revolution: Social Movements and Export Agriculture in the Underdeveloped World*. New York, NY: Free Press, 1975.

Pakulski, Jan. "Legitimacy and Mass Compliance: Reflections on Max Weber and Soviet-Type Societies". *British Journal of Political Science*. Vol. 16, (January 1986), pp. 35–56.

Panitch, Leo. "Corporatism: A Growth Industry Reaches the Monopoly Stage". *Canadian Journal of Political Science*. Vol. 21, No. 4, (December 1988), pp. 813–18.

Parsons, Stephens. "On the Logic of Corporatism". *Political Studies*. Vol. 36, (1988), pp. 515–23.

Parsons, Talcott. *The Social System*. New York, NY: The Free Press, 1951.

Pastor, Robert A. *Democracy in the Americas*. New York, NY: Holmes and Meier, 1989.

Pateman, Carole. "The Civic Culture: A Philosophical Critique". In Gabriel Almond and Sydney Verba (eds). *The Civic Culture Revisited*. Boston, MA: Little, Brown, 1980.

Peabody, Robert L. "Authority". In David L. Sills (ed.). *International Encyclopedia of the Social Sciences*. Vol. 1, New York, NY: Crowell Collier & Macmillan, 1968. pp. 473–77.

Peeler, John A. *Latin American Democracies: Colombia, Costa Rica, Venezuela*. Chapel Hill, NC: University of North Carolina Press, 1985.

Pelczynski, Z. A., "Solidarity and 'The Rebirth of Civil Society.' " In John Keane et al. *Civil Society and the State: New European Perspectives*. New York, NY: Verso, 1988, pp. 361–80.

Pempel, T. J. "Prerequisites for Democracy: Political and Social Institutions". In Takeshi Ishida and Ellis Krauss (eds). *Democracy in Japan*. Pittsburgh, PA: University of Pittsburgh Press, 1989, pp. 17–37.

Peters, B. Guy. *European Politics Reconsidered*. New York, NY: Holmes & Meier, 1991.

Pinkney, Robert. *Democracy in the Third World*. Boulder, CO: Lynne Rienner, 1993.

Pion-Berlin, David, "Military Autonomy and Emerging Democracies in South America". *Comparative Politics*. Vol. 25, No. 1, (Oct. 1992), pp. 83–102.

Plano, Jack, and Robert Riggs. *Dictionary of Political Analysis*. Hinsdale, IL: Dryden, 1973.

Plano, Jack, Robert Riggs, and Helenan Robin. *Dictionary of Political Analysis*, 2nd edition, Santa Barbara, CA: Clio, 1982.

Poggi, Gianfranco. "Max Weber's Conceptual Portrait of Feudalism". *British Journal of Sociology*. Vol. 39, No. 2, (1988), pp. 211–27.

Poneman, Daniel. *Argentina: Democracy on Trial.* New York, NY: Paragon House, 1987.

Pontusson, Jonas. "Labor Corporatism, and Industrial Policy: The Swedish Case in Comparative Perspective". *Comparative Politics.* Vol. 23, No. 2, (January 1991), pp. 163–79.

Portis, E.B. "Charismatic Leadership and Cultural Democracy". *Review of Politics.* Vol. 41, No. 2, (Spring 1987), pp. 231–50.

Power, Timothy. "Political Landscapes, Political Parties, and Authoritarianism in Brazil and Chile". *International Journal of Comparative Sociology.* Vols 29–30, (1988), pp. 250–63.

Powell, G. Bingham. *Contemporary Democracies: Participation, Stability and Violence.* Cambridge, MA: Harvard University Press, 1982.

Pye, Lucian (ed.). *Communications and Political Development.* Princeton, NJ: Princeton University Press, 1963.

—— "Political Culture." In David L. Sills (ed.). *International Encyclopedia of the Social Sciences.* Vol. 12. New York, NY: Crowell Collier & Macmillan, 1968, pp. 218–25.

—— "Identity and the Political Culture". In Leonard Binder et al. (eds). *Crisis and Sequences in Political Development.* Princeton, NJ: Princeton University Press, 1971, pp. 101–34.

—— "The Legitimacy Crisis". In Lucian Pye et al. *Crisis and Sequence in Political Development.* Princeton, NJ: Princeton University Press, 1971, pp. 135–58.

—— "The Concept of Political Development". In Harvey Kebschull (ed.). *Politics in Transitional Societies.* New York, NY: Appleton-Century-Crofts, 1973, pp. 49–52.

—— "The Non-Western Political Process". In Harvey Kebschull (ed.). *Politics in Transitional Societies: The Challenge of Change in Asia, Africa, and Latin America.* New York, NY: Appleton-Century-Crofts, 1973, pp. 21–31.

—— "Political Science and the Crisis of Authoritarianism". *American Political Science Review.* Vol. 84, No. 1 (March, 1990), pp. 3–19.

—— "Tiananmen and Chinese Political Culture". *Asian Survey.* Vol. 30, No. 4, (April 1990), pp. 331–47.

Pye, Lucian and Sydney Verba (eds). *Political Culture and Political Development.* Princeton, NJ: Princeton University Press, 1965.

Rajaee, Farhang. *Islamic Values and World Views.* New York, NY: University Press of America, 1983.

Ramet, Sabrina P. *Social Currents in Eastern Europe: The Sources and Meaning of the Great Transformation.* Durham, NC: Duke University Press, 1991.

Rauche-Elnekave, Helen. "Advocacy and Ombudswork for Children: Implications of the Israeli Experience". *Child Welfare.* Vol. 68, No. 2, (April/May 1989), pp. 101–12.

Redner, Harry. "Beyond Marx–Weber: A Diversified and International Approach to the State". *Political Studies.* Vol. 38, (1990), pp. 638–53.

Reeves, Jesse S. "Perspectives in Political Science, 1903–28". *American Political Science Review.* Vol. 23, No. 1, (February 1929), pp. 1–16.

Reich, Walter. *Origins of Terrorism: Psychologies, Ideologies, Theologies, States of Mind.* Cambridge: Cambridge University Press, 1990.

Rejai, M. *Democracy: The Contemporary Theories.* New York, NY: Atherton Press, 1967.

Remmer, Karen. *Military Rule in Latin America.* Winchester, MA: Unwin Hyman, 1989.

—— "Neopatrimonialism: The Politics of Military Rule in Chile, 1973–87". *Comparative Politics.* Vol. 21, No. 2, (January 1989), pp. 149–70.

Resnick, Stephen A. and Richard D. Wolff. *Knowledge and Class: A Marxian Critique of Political Economy.* Chicago, IL: University of Chicago Press, 1987.

Reynolds, Lloyd G. *The Three Worlds of Economics.* New Haven, CT: Yale University Press, 1971.

Rice, Edward. *Wars of the Third World Kind: Conflict in Underdeveloped Countries.* Berkeley, CA: University of California Press, 1988.

Roberts, Adam. "A New Age in International Relations?". *International Affairs.* Vol. 67, No. 3, (1991), pp. 509–25.

Robinson, Pearl T. "Niger: Anatomy of a Neo-Traditional Corporatist State". *Comparative Politics.* Vol. 24, No. 1, (October 1991), pp. 1–20.

Rose, Jerry D. *Introduction to Sociology.* Chicago, IL: Rand McNally, 1974.

Rose, Richard. "Comparing Forms of Comparative Analysis". *Political Studies.* Vol. 39, (1991), pp. 446–62.

Rosenbaum, Walter. *Political Culture.* New York, NY: Praeger, 1975.

Rostow, W. W. *Politics and the Stages of Growth.* Cambridge: Cambridge University Press, 1971.

Rothgeb, John, Jr. *Defining Power: Influence and Force in the Contemporary International System.* New York, NY: St. Martin's Press, 1993.

Rouquie, Alain. *The Military and the State in Latin America.* Paul Sigmund, trans. Berkeley, CA: University of California Press, 1987.

Rourke, John T. *Making Foreign Policy: United States, Soviet Union, China.* Pacific Grove, CA: Brooks/Cole, 1990.

Rourke, John T., Richard P. Hiskes and Cyrus Ernesto Zirakzadeh. *Direct Democracy and International Politics.* Boulder, CO: Lynne Rienner, 1992.

Rubenstein, Richard. *Alchemists of Revolution: Terrorism in the Modern World.* London: I.B. Tauris, 1989.

Rubin, Barry. *Modern Dictators: Third World Coup Makers, Strongmen, and Populist Tyrants.* New York, NY: McGraw Hill, 1987.

Rueschemeyer, Dietrich, and Peter Evans. "The State and Economic Transformation: Toward an Analysis of the Conditions Underlying Effective Intervention". In Peter Evans, Dietrich Rueschemeyer, and Theda Skocpol (eds). *Bringing the State Back In.* Cambridge: Cambridge University Press, 1985.

Rule, James. *Theories of Civil Violence.* Berkeley, CA: University of California Press, 1988.

Rupnik, Jaques, "Totalitarianism Revisited," In John Keane et al. *Civil Society and the State: New European Perspectives.* New York, NY: Verso, 1988, pp. 263–89.

Russell, Bertrand. *Power: A New Social Analysis.* New York, NY: W. W. Norton, 1938.

Rustow, Dankwart. "Ataturk's Political Leadership". In R. Bayly Winder (ed.). *Near Eastern Round Table, 1967–1968.* New York, NY: New York University Press, 1969, pp. 143–55.

Ruttan, Vernon W. "What Happened to Political Development". *Economic Development and Cultural Change.* Vol. 39, No. 2, (January 1991), pp. 265–92.

Ryan, Michael. *Politics and Culture: Working Hypotheses for a Post-Revolutionary Society.* Baltimore, MD: Johns Hopkins University Press, 1989.

Sabine, George H. "Pluralism: A Point of View". *American Journal of Political Science.* Vol. 17, No. 1, (February 1923), pp. 34–50.

Samudavanija, Chai-Anan. "Political Institutionalization in Thailand: Continuity and Change". In Robert Scalapino, Seizaburo Sato, and Jusuf Wanandi (eds). *Asian Political Institutionalization.* Berkeley, CA: Institute of East Asian Studies, 1986, pp. 241–60.

Sandbrook, Richard. "The State and Economic Stagnation in Tropical Africa." *World Development.* Vol. 14, No. 3, (1986), pp. 319–32.

Sangmpam, S. N. "The Overpoliticized State and Democratization," *Comparative Politics.* Vol. 24, No. 4 (July 1992), pp. 401–17.

—— "The State-Society Relationship in Peripheral Countries: Critical Notes on the Dominant Paradigms". *Review of Politics.* Vol. 48, No. 4, (Fall 1986), pp. 596–620.

Sarduy, Pedro Perez. "Culture and the Cuban Revolution". *The Black Scholar.* Vol. 20, Nos. 5–6, (Winter 1989), pp. 17–23.

Sargent, Lyman Tower. *Contemporary Political Ideologies: A Comparative Analysis.* 8th edition, Pacific Grove, CA: Brooks/Cole, 1990.

Sartori, Giovanni. *The Theory of Democracy Revisited.* Chatham, NJ: Chatham House, 1987.

—— "The Party as Part". In Louis Cantori and Andrew Ziegler (eds). *Comparative Politics in the Post-Behavioral Era.* Boulder, CO: Lynne Rienner, 1988, pp. 231–63.

Savells, Jerry. "Who are the Yuppies? A Popular View". *International Journal of Comparative Sociology.* Vol. 27, Nos. 3–4 (1989), pp. 234–41.

Scaff, Lawrence A. "Fleeing the Iron Cage: Politics and Culture in the Thought of Max Weber". *American Political Science Review.* Vol. 81, No. 3, (September 1987), pp. 737–55.

Scalapino, Robert. "Legitimacy and Institutionalization in Asian Socialist Societies". In Robert Scalapino, Seizaburo Sato, and Jusuf Wanandi (eds). *Asian Political Institutionaliztion.* Berkeley, CA: Institute of East Asian Studies, 1986, pp. 59–94.

Scale, Patrick. *Asad of Syria: The Struggle for the Middle East.* Berkeley, CA: University of California Press, 1989.

Scheye, Eric. "Psychological Notes on Central Europe: 1989 and Beyond". *Political Psychology.* Vol. 12, No. 2, (1991), pp. 331–34.

Schiffer, Irvine. *Charisma: A Psychoanalytical Look at Mass Society.* Toronto: University of Toronto Press, 1973.

Schiller, Herbert I. *Culture, Inc.: The Corporate Takeover of Public Expression.* Oxford: Oxford University Press, 1989.

Schlesinger, James. "New Instabilities, New Priorities." *Foreign Policy.* No. 85, (Winter 1991/1992), pp. 3–24.

Schmidt, Elizabeth. "Patriarchy, Capitalism, and the Colonial State in Zimbabwe". *Journal of Women in Culture and Society.* Vol. 16, No. 4, (Summer 1991), pp. 732–56.

Schmitter, Philippe C. (ed.). *Military Rule in Latin America: Functions, Consequences and Perspectives.* London: Sage, 1973.

—— "Corporatism is Dead! Long Live Corporatism!". *Government and Opposition.* Vol. 24, No. 1, (Winter 1989), pp. 55–73.

Schopflin, George. "Hungary: An Uneasy Stability". *Political Culture and Political Change.* New York, NY: Holmes and Meier, 1979, pp. 131–58.

Schubert, James N. "Age and Active-Passive Leadership Style". *American Political Science Review.* Vol. 82, No. 3, (September 1988), pp. 763–72.

Schutz, Barry, and Robert Slater. "Patterns of Legitimacy and Future Revolutions in the Third World". In Barry Schutz and Robert Slater (eds). *Revolution and Political Change in the Third World.* Boulder, CO: Lynne Rienner, 1990, pp. 247–50.

Scott, Alan. *Ideology and the New Social Movements*. London: Unwin Hyman, 1990.

Scott, James C. "Hegemony and the Peasantry". *Politics and Society*. Vol. 7, No. 3, (1977), pp. 267–96.

—— *Weapons of the Weak*. New Haven, CT: Yale University Press, 1985.

—— *Domination and the Art of Resistance: Hidden Transcripts*. New Haven, CT: Yale University Press, 1990.

Scott, W. Richard. *Social Processes and Social Structures: An Introduction to Sociology*. New York, NY: Holt, Rinehart, & Winston, 1970.

Scruton, Roger. *A Dictionary of Political Thought*. London: Pan, 1982.

Seton-Watson, Hugh. *The Russian Empire, 1801–1917*. Oxford: Oxford University Press, 1967, pp. 29–35.

Shapiro, H. J. "Anti-Americanism in Western Europe". *American Academy of Political and Social Sciences*. No. 497, (May 1988), pp. 120–32.

Sharabi, Hisham. *Neopatriarchy: A Theory of Distorted Change in Arab Society*. New York, NY: Oxford University Press, 1988.

Shils, Edward. "Charisma". In David L. Sills (ed.). *International Encyclopedia of the Social Sciences,* Vol. 2, New York, NY: Crowell Collier & Macmillan. 1968.

Shingles, Richard D. "Class, Status, and Support for Government Aid to Disadvantaged Groups". *Journal of Politics*. Vol. 51, No. 4, (Nov. 1989), pp. 933–62.

Shoup, Paul S. "Indicators of Socio-Politico-Economic Development". In Carmelo Mesa-Lago and Carl Beck (eds). *Comparative Socialist Systems: Essays on Politics and Economics*. Pittsburgh, PA: University of Pittsburgh Center for International Studies, 1975, pp. 3–39.

Singer, D. "The Resistible Rise of Jean-Marie Le Pen". *Ethnic and Racial Studies*. Vol. 14, (July 1991), pp. 368–81.

Sioussat, George L. "Notes on Works in Political Science". *The Sewanee Review Quarterly*. Vol. 15, No. 3, (July 1907), pp. 370–76.

Skocpol, Theda. *States and Social Revolutions*. Cambridge: Cambridge University Press, 1979.

—— "What Makes Peasants Revolutionary?". *Comparative Politics*. Vol. 14, No. 3, (April 1982), pp. 351–75.

—— "Rentier State and Shi'a Islam in the Iranian Revolution". *Theory and Society*. Vol. 11, No. 3, (May 1982), pp. 265–83.

—— "Bringing the State Back In: Strategies of Analysis in Current Research". In Peter Evans, Dietrich Rueschemeyer, and Theda Skocpol (eds). *Bringing the State Back In*. Cambridge: Cambridge University Press, 1985, pp. 3–37.

—— "Social Revolutions and Mass Military Mobilization". *World Politics*. Vol. 40, No. 2, (January 1988), pp. 147–68.

Slater, Robert O., Barry M. Schutz, and Steven R. Dorr. *Global Transformation and the Third World*. Boulder, CO: Lynne Rienner, 1992.

Smith, Anthony D. "The Suspension of Nationalism". *International Journal of Comparative Sociology*. Vol. 31, Nos. 1–2, (1990), pp. 1–32.

Smith, Munroe. "The Consent of the Governed". *Proceedings of the Academy of Political Science*. Vol. 5, No. 1, (October 1914), pp. 82–88.

Sniderman, Paul M., Joseph F. Fletcher, Peter H. Russell, Philip E. Tetlock, and Brian J. Gaines. "The Fallacy of Democratic Elitism: Elite Competition and Commitment to Civil Liberties". *British Journal of Political Science*. Vol. 21, (1991), pp. 349–70.

So, Alvin Y. *Social Change and Development: Modernization, Dependency, and World-System Theories.* Newbury Park, CA: Sage, 1990.

Somjee, A. H. *Political Society in Developing Countries.* New York, NY: St. Martin's Press, 1984.

Sorensen, Georg. *Democracy and Democratization.* Boulder, CO: Westview, 1993.

Sowell, Thomas. *Knowledge and Decisions.* New York, NY: Basic Books, 1980.

Spalding, Rose. "State Power and its Limits: Corporatism in Mexico". *Comparative Political Studies.* Vol. 14, No. 2, (July 1981), pp. 139–61.

Spinrad, William. "Charisma: A Blighted Concept and an Alternative Formula". *Public Science Quarterly.* Vol. 106, No. 2, (1991), pp. 295–311.

Stanley, John L. "Is Totalitarianism a New Phenomenon? Reflections on Hannah Arendt's Origins of Totalitarianism". *Review of Politics.* Vol. 49, (Spring 1987), pp. 177–207.

Stark, Frank M. "Theories of Contemporary State Formation in Africa: A Reassessment". *Journal of Modern African Studies.* Vol. 24, No. 2, (1986), pp. 335–47.

Steinberger, Peter J. "Ruling: Guardians and Philosopher-Kings". *American Political Science Review.* Vol. 83, No. 4, (December 1989), pp. 1207–26.

Steiner, Jurg. *European Democracies.* 2nd edition, New York, NY: Longman, 1991.

Stepan, Alfred. *State and Society: Peru in Comparative Perspective.* Princeton, NJ: Princeton University Press, 1978.

Stevens, Evelyn. "Mexican *Machismo:* Politics and Value Orientations". In Paul Kramer and Robert McNicoll (eds). *Latin American Panorama.* New York, NY: G. P. Putnam's Sons, 1968, pp. 388–402.

Stimson, Henry L. "The Principle of Responsibility in Government". *Proceedings of the Academy of Political Science.* Vol. 5, No. 1, (October 1914), pp. 20–26.

Stockwin, J. A. A. "Political Parties and Political Opposition". In Takeshi Ishida and Ellis Krauss (eds). *Democracy in Japan.* Pittsburgh. PA: University of Pittsburgh Press, 1989, pp. 89–111.

Stoessinger, John G. *The Might of Nations: World Politics in our Time.* New York, NY: Random House, 1982.

Stokes, Randall, and David Jaffee. "Another Look at the Export of Raw Materials and Economic Growth". *American Sociological Review.* Vol. 47, No. 3, (June 1982), pp. 402–7.

Stoll, Richard J. "State Power, World Views, and the Major Powers". In Richard J. Stoll and Michael D. Ward (eds). *Power and World Politics.* Boulder, CO: Lynne Rienner, 1989, pp. 135–57.

Strayer, Joseph R., and Hans W. Gatzke. *The Mainstream of Civilization Since 1500.* New York, NY: Harcourt, Brace, Jovanovich, 1979.

Stultz, Newell. "Parliaments in Former British Black Africa". In Harvey Kebschull (ed.). *Politics in Transitional Societies.* New York, NY: Appleton-Century-Crofts, 1973, pp. 262–77.

Swenson, Peter. "Labor and the Limits of the Welfare State: The Politics of Inter-class Conflict and Cross-Class Alliances in Sweden and West Germany". *Comparative Politics.* Vol. 23, No. 4, (July 1991), pp. 379–99.

Szabo, Stephen S. "The New Europeans: Beyond the Balance of Power". *Proceedings of the Academy of Political Science.* Vol. 38, No. 2, (1991), pp. 26–34.

Tachau, Frank, and Metin Heper. "The State, Politics, and the Military in Turkey". *Comparative Politics.* Vol. 16, No. 1, (October 1983), pp. 17–34.

Teiwes, Fredrick. *Politics at Mao's Court: Gao Gang and Party Factionalism in the Early 1950s.* Armonk, NY: M. E. Sharp, 1990.

Tismaneau, Vladimir. "Nascent Civil Society in the German Democratic Republic". *Problems of Communism*. Vol. 38, No. 2, (March-June 1989), pp. 90–111.

Tordoff, William. *Government and Politics in Africa.* Bloomington, IN: Indiana University Press, 1984.

Tucker, Robert W., and David C. Hendrickson. *The Imperial Temptation: The New World Order and America's Purpose.* New York, NY: Council on Foreign Relations, 1992.

Turner, Bryan S. *Theories of Modernity and Postmodernity.* Newbury Park, CA: Sage, 1990.

Ungar, Sanford J. "The Role of a Free Press in Strengthening Democracy". In Judith Lichtenberg (ed.). *Democracy and Mass Media.* Cambridge: Cambridge University Press, 1990, pp. 369–92.

Utiz, S. "Economic Policy Challenges in the United Germany". *World Today.* Vol. 47, (December 1991), pp. 207–11.

Vatikiotis, Michael, Salamat Ali, and Hamish McDonald. "Pax Americana". *Far Eastern Economic Review.* No. 10, (7 March 1991), pp. 10–11.

Vilas, Carlos. "Popular Insurgency and Social Revolution in Central America". *Latin American Perspectives.* Issue 56, Vol. 15, No. 1, (Winter 1988), pp. 55–77.

Villa-Vicencio, Charles. "Piety and Politics". *Africa Report.* Vol. 36, No. 1, (January-February 1991), pp. 47–49.

Wald, Kenneth D., and Michael B. Lupfer. "'Human Nature' in Mass Political Thought: What People Think about People and What People Think about Politics". *Social Science Quarterly.* Vol. 68, No. 1, (March 1987), pp. 19–29.

Walker, W., and M. Sharp. "Thatcherism and Technical Advance: Reform Without Progress (Part I)". *Political Quarterly.* Vol. 62, (April/June 1991), pp. 262–72.

—— "Thatcherism and Technical Advance: Reform Without Progress (Part II)". *Political Quarterly.* Vol. 62, (July/September 1991), pp. 318–38.

Wallach, H. G. Peter. "Political Leadership". *Journal of Politics.* Vol. 50, No. 4, (November 1988), pp. 1090–95.

Wallerstein, Immanuel. *The Modern World-System: Capitalist Agriculture and the Origins of the European World-Economy in the Sixteenth Century.* New York, NY: Academic Press, 1974.

—— *The Modern World-System: Mercantilism and the Consolidation of the European World-Economy, 1600–1750.* New York, NY: Academic Press, 1980.

—— *The Politics of the World Economy: The States, the Movements, and the Civilizations.* Cambridge: Cambridge University Press, 1984.

—— *Social Change: The Colonial Situation.* New York, NY: John Wiley and Sons, 1966.

Ward, Michael D. "Power in the International System: Behavioral Salience and Material Capabilities". In Richard J. Stoll and Michael D. Ward (eds). *Power in World Politics.* Boulder, CO: Lynne Rienner, 1989, pp. 121–34.

Warren, Mark. "Max Weber's Liberalism for a Nietzschean World". *American Political Science Review.* Vol. 82, No. 1 (March 1988), pp. 31–50.

Weigle, Marcia A., and Jim Butterfield. "Civil Society in Reforming Communist Regimes: The Logic of Emergence." *Comparative Politics.* Vol. 25, No. 1, (October 1992), pp. 1–23.

Weiner, Myron. "Political Participation: Crisis of the Political Process". In Lucian Pye et al. *Crisis and Sequence in Political Development.* Princeton, NJ: Princeton University Press, 1971, pp. 159–204.

—— "The Goals of Development." In Myron Weiner and Samuel P. Huntington (eds). *Understanding Political Development*. New York, NY: HarperCollins, 1987, pp. 3–32

—— "Political Change: Asia, Africa, and the Middle East." In Myron Weiner and Samuel P. Huntington (eds). *Understanding Political Development*. New York, NY: HarperCollins, 1987, pp. 33–64.

Westley, Frances. "Bob Geldof and Live Aid: The Affective Side of Global Social Innovation". *Human Relations*. Vol. 44, No. 10, (1991), pp. 1011–36.

White, Stephen, John Gardner, and George Schopflin. *Communist Political Systems: An Introduction*. New York, NY: St. Martin's Press, 1987.

Wiarda, Howard. *New Directions in Comparative Politics*. Boulder, CO: Westview, 1985.

—— "Political Culture and the Attraction of Marxism-Leninism: National Inferiority Complexes as an Explanatory Factor." *World Affairs*. Vol. 151, No. 3, (Winter 1988–89), pp. 143–50.

Williame, Jean-Claude. "Political Success in Zaire, or Back to Machiavelli". *Journal of African Studies*. Vol. 26, No. 1, (1988), pp. 37–49.

Willner, Ann Ruth, and Dorothy Willner. "The Rise and Role of Charismatic Leaders". In Harvy Kebschull (ed.). *Politics in Transitional Societies*. New York: Appleton-Century-Crofts, 1973, pp. 227–36.

Willoughby, W. W. *An Examination of the Nature of the State*. London: Macmillan, 1922.

Wilson, Richard W. "Political Pathology and Moral Orientations". *Comparative Political Studies*. Vol. 24, No. 2, (July 1991), pp. 211–30.

Wolf, Eric. *Peasant Wars of the Twentieth Century*. New York, NY: Harper & Row, 1969.

Wolf-Phillips, Leslie. "Why the 'Third World'?". *Third World Quarterly*. Vol. 9, No. 4, (October 1987), pp. 1311–27.

Wolpin, Miles. *Militarism and Social Revolution in the Third World*. Savage, MD: Rowman and Littlefield, 1981.

—— "Sociopolitical Radicalism and Military Professionalism in the Third World". *Comparative Politics*. Vol. 15, No. 2, (January 1983), pp. 203–21.

Worsely, Peter. *The Three Worlds: Culture and World Development*. Chicago, IL: University of Chicago Press, 1984.

Zagorin, Perez. "Theories of Revolution in Contemporary Historiography". *Political Science Quarterly*. vol. LXXXVIII, no. 1, (March 1973), pp. 23–52.

Index